Neal Gross is Dean of the Graduate School of Education, University of Pennsylvania.

Joseph B. Giacquinta is Assistant Professor of Educational Sociology at New York University.

Marilyn Bernstein is a research associate at Harvard University.

IMPLEMENTING
ORGANIZATIONAL
INNOVATIONS

IMPLEMENTING ORGANIZATIONAL INNOVATIONS

A Sociological Analysis of Planned Educational Change

Neal Gross
Joseph B. Giacquinta
Marilyn Bernstein

Basic Books Inc., Publishers ● New York ● London

Preface

This book reports the findings that emerged from an intensive study of the fate of a promising educational innovation that was introduced into an elementary school. Its primary objective was to isolate factors that inhibit and facilitate the implementation phase of the process of planned organizational change, a problem that has received little attention in the social science and educational literature. We hoped to shed light on issues of central importance to both students of organizational change and to individuals concerned with the practical problems of introducing and incorporating change into educational and other kinds of organizations.

The inquiry focused on a case study of a school that required eight months of field work and related data collection activities. It would not have been possible to conduct our inquiry without the cooperation of many individuals. First, we wish to acknowledge our indebtedness to the entire staff of the school, the Director's staff, and the Superintendent's Office. Their cooperation was essential to the successful completion of our work. We are especially grateful to the Director for his invitation to study the change process taking place in a school under his jurisdiction and for his excellent support, including permission to remain at the school as long as we felt necessary to obtain the kinds of data we believed were needed to complete our investigation.

We have benefited greatly from discussions with many students

v

of organizational change about the problem area examined in this inquiry. We found of special value the views of Robert H. Anderson, Louis B. Barnes, Robert Dreeben, and Elmer Van Egmond.

For their critical appraisal of earlier drafts of the manuscript, we are indebted to John Coulson, Robert Dreeben, Charles F. Haughey, Robert E. Herriott, Benjamin J. Hodgkins, Lawrence M. Lengel, Ray Taylor, and Russell G. Thornton.

We also wish to express our appreciation to James A. Stinchcomb and Ralph G. Lewis who provided valuable assistance in the phase of our study that focused on the review of literature.

Theresa Kovich served as the secretary of the Project. We are indebted to her for her many contributions to the completion of the study in addition to assuming the typing of most of the final manuscript. We are also grateful to Marion L. Crowley who provided us with timely and extremely important assistance of many kinds and to Carol Weiss for her fine editorial aid.

We also wish to express our appreciation to the Harvard Graduate School of Education and its Center for Research and Development on Educational Differences for providing the financial resources needed to conduct the inquiry.

Finally, for their everlasting patience and fortitude Pan Gross and Norman Bernstein deserve special thanks.

The research inquiry described in this book was carried out under the auspices of the Center for Research and Development on Educational Differences and was performed pursuant to Contract OE 5-10-239 with the Office of Education, U.S. Department of Health, Education, and Welfare.

Despite the help and advice received from others, we alone, of course, are responsible for the contents of this book and for whatever shortcomings it may contain.

NEAL GROSS
JOSEPH B. GIACQUINTA
MARILYN BERNSTEIN

Contents

1 Introduction   1

2 The Literature on Planned Organizational Change: A Critical Appraisal   19

3 Research Procedures   41

4 The Climate for Educational Change at Cambire in November 1966   64

5 The Degree of Implementation of the Innovation   90

6 Barriers to the Implementation of the Innovation: Obstacles Encountered by the Teachers   122

7 Obstacles Encountered by the Teachers: Roots of the Difficulties   149

8 Conclusions and Implications   195

Appendix A: Specimen Research Instruments   217

Appendix B: Documents   245

Appendix C: Summary Tables of Selected Background and Personality Characteristics of the Teaching Staff   285

Appendix D: Classroom Schemata   291

References   293

Index   303

IMPLEMENTING
ORGANIZATIONAL
INNOVATIONS

1

Introduction

The fate of innovations introduced into organizations is a fascinating subject, one that is of great practical concern to men responsible for the management of complex social systems and also of considerable scientific interest to students of planned organizational change. An examination of the sociological and social psychological literature on planned or deliberately instituted organizational change reveals that the most common explanation of why innovations introduced into organizations do or do not have their intended effects places primary emphasis on the ability of a change agent to overcome the initial resistance of organizational members to change.

This explanation oversimplifies the problem of accounting for the success or failure of planned organizational change. The problem is much more complicated, because before an innovation can achieve its intentions, it must be implemented by organizational members. We shall contend that the degree to which an innovation is implemented in an organization will be a function of a number of variables, in addition to its members' initial resistance or receptivity to change. Through an intensive case study of the fate of a promising educational innovation that was introduced into an elementary school located in the lowest socio-economic area of a large American city, we hoped to enhance our understanding of conditions that serve to block and to facilitate the implementation of organizational innova-

1

tions. We also hoped to shed light on largely ignored complexities of carrying out organizational change. Since the major questions of the study involve issues of central concern both to educational practitioners and to social scientists, we shall introduce the study by presenting both an educational and a social science perspective on the issues to be discussed in this book.

The Study in Educational Perspective

A salient characteristic of many American public school systems in recent years has been their preoccupation with educational innovations. "When one talks or writes about education these days, the temptation to use such phrases as innovation, educational ferment, technological revolution, or explosive growth is irresistible. One cannot avoid them, for explosive and revolutionary changes are occurring in education" (Chauncey, 1967, p. 9). This concern with change has been attributed to a number of factors: criticisms of progressive education that arose after World War II, the efforts of schools to meet the demands of a rapidly changing society, Sputnik, the knowledge explosion, new theoretical insights into the learning process, and most recently, the civil rights movement, the pressures of community action groups, and expanded federal aid to education (Atkin, 1966; Cronbach, 1966; Hand, 1965; Jennings, 1967).

A large number of innovations were introduced into public schools during the 1950's and 1960's. Fallon (1966) described 628 school practices adopted by 323 school systems between 1957-1964 in all regions of the United States. Stufflebeam (1966) examined 150 innovations introduced into a sample of school systems in the state of Ohio during 1965; Brickell (1961) reported on a large variety of educational innovations in New York State. These educational innovations, instituted primarily to upgrade the academic performance of pupils, have involved changes in the curricula, in the performance of teachers, and in school organization. For example, Detroit's Great Cities

Project and New York's More Effective Schools Program introduced team-teaching and nongrading in schools. Team-teaching requires greater teacher cooperation and specialization and more flexibility in classroom size and scheduling than exists in traditional schools; nongrading requires the teachers' constant awareness of individual needs of their pupils and of differences in their learning rates. These innovations also necessitate important alterations in the roles of the teacher and principal and in the traditional authority structure of the school (Goodlad and Anderson, 1963; Shaplin, 1965). Proposals to decentralize school systems and plans to increase community control of schools represent innovations that focus on changes in decision-making processes. Each of these innovations attempts to upgrade the performance of schools through modification of their basic organizational arrangements.

During the past decade, top officials of school systems in large cities such as New York, Chicago, Detroit, Philadelphia, and San Francisco have been exposed to increasing demands from school boards, parents, neighborhood leaders, teacher organizations, universities, and governmental agencies for educational reforms that will maximize the potentialities and capabilities of educationally disadvantaged students. Partly in response to these pressures, and also because of their own serious concern about the problem, these administrators have attempted to diagnose the educational ills of their inner-city schools and have introduced many major educational innovations, supported in considerable measure by funds from the federal government. However, there has been little to show for their efforts. In the words of a former official of the Urban Coalition, "To put it bluntly, many urban schools simply aren't working; the students know it; the teachers know it; the consultants know it; and the researchers know it!" (Kelly, 1969).

Consider, for example, the results that have emerged from the evaluation of compensatory education programs. Gordon and Wilkerson (1966, p. 156) reviewed over 300 compensatory education programs adopted by school systems since 1960 to remedy the educational handicaps of urban children from low socio-economic backgrounds. Despite the large expenditures of money, time, and energy devoted to these efforts, they concluded that the programs had little impact on upgrading the academic achievement of students. A similar conclusion emerged from the assessment of a number of compensatory programs by the U.S. Commission on Civil Rights (1967, p. 138). As the decade of the 1970's unfolds, therefore, it is not surprising to find that educational administrators in big-city school systems are sorely troubled by the negligible educational effects resulting from the numerous innovations that have been introduced into their schools.

Sensitive to the need and growing demand for improvements in the performance of their school systems and aware of the failure of most innovations to achieve their intended effects, these school administrators have followed closely the educational literature that diagnoses their failures and that proposes solutions to their problems. Five major themes can be distilled from this large body of advice.

The first is that increased funding alone will not solve the problems of big-city school systems. Although there is general recognition that urban schools need, and have a right to claim, considerably greater fiscal support to bring their per-pupil expenditures up to that of their more affluent suburbs, superintendents who hold the belief that a rich educational harvest will result from simply pouring greater amounts of money into ghetto schools have been advised to abandon it. In the words of the section of the 1968 Report of the Rockefeller Foundation concerning ghetto schools:

> Partly, the answer may be found in increased funding. Yet funds for New York City schools, for example, have more than doubled in the past ten years, with an enrollment increase of only one-fifth in school population. Despite this additional money, one out of every three children is still behind the national norms in math and reading. Some of our most thoughtful leaders have raised their voices against the belief that larger expenditures are enough, that more funding in itself is the answer. [P. 127]

A second theme is that most major educational innovations introduced into city schools have not been based on a realistic assessment of the needs and problems of their students. This point of view was stressed by Harold Howe just prior to his resignation as U. S. Commissioner of Education in 1969. He stated:

> Somehow we have got to find a way to make . . . schools in the central city pertinent to the needs of . . . people, to make them schools which . . . address themselves to where these people are in their learning attitudes, feelings about themselves, and readjust the school to picking up the youngster where he is and carrying him forward to a better employment opportunity. [Rockefeller, 1968, p. 127]

A third view, one emerging from an assessment of compensatory education programs, is that the central thrust of most innovative programs has been directed at the wrong targets. Gordon and Wilkerson (1966) assert:

> It is not at all clear that the concept of compensatory education is the one which will most appropriately meet the problems of the disadvantaged. . . . What kind of educational experience is most appropriate to what these children are and to what our society is becoming? Once this question has been posed, it brings into focus the really crucial issue, that is, the matter of whom we are trying to change. We have tended until now to concentrate our efforts on the children. [Pp. 158-159]

A fourth idea stresses the necessity of racially and socially integrated learning environments to improve learning outcomes in urban schools. Thus, in appraising compensatory programs, the Civil Rights Commission maintains:

> One possible explanation is that compensatory programs do not wholly compensate for the depressing effect which racial and social class isolation have upon the aspirations and self-esteem of Negro students. . . . The compensatory programs reviewed here appear to suffer from the defect inherent in attempting to solve

problems stemming in part from racial and social class isolation in schools which themselves are isolated by race and social class. . . . The evidence reviewed here strongly suggests that compensatory programs are not likely to succeed (have the desired effects) in racially and socially isolated school environments. [Pp. 138-140]

A fifth notion, the importance of parent and community participation in decisions affecting their schools has been emphasized by Fantini (1968) as a possible key to the solution of the crisis in urban education. In his view, the compensatory education approach has failed and desegregation does not constitute a meaningful or realistic short-run solution; he also has serious reservations about strategies directed at establishing model subsystems or parallel school programs (1968, p. 10). He views total school reform as the most promising intervention strategy and strongly endorses the proposals of the Bundy Report.

The Bundy Report was significantly titled *Reconnection for Learning*. The plan calls for more than a redistribution of power; it also provides new means of energizing school reform. Reform requires fuel. Sustained school reform needs not only ideas, but human resources and dynamic support from the public and the professional. All too often, the energy for educational reform consists only of a few professionals, practitioners or veterans who have shifted their struggle from the front lines to universities or the author's desk. The Bundy plan expands the base of energy to include the most numerous, and possibly the most powerful, energy source; parents and the community-at-large. It offers the professional who is working for improvement within the system a powerful ally who is also highly motivated to reform the system. Ghetto parents especially have come to the same verdict as the most astute students and practitioners of education: that urban education is failing and desperately in need of reform. [Pp. 11-12]

We acknowledge the relevance of these ideas in efforts to answer the question, "Why have so many promising innovations introduced into inner-city schools had such little effect on pupil learning?" We submit, however, that another possible response to this question that deserves consideration and has been generally ignored or dismissed too lightly is that most of these promising innovations may not in fact have been implemented. Innovations introduced into schools are only *proposals* for change; to achieve their intended effects, they must be implemented. As Hymen, Wright, and Hopkins (1962) have observed:

> The answer to why a program was ineffective may even reduce to the simple fact that it was not in reality operative; it existed only on paper. . . . When the stimulus is not there, there is no process that it can generate. [Pp. 74-75]

No matter how promising an organizational innovation appears on paper or how well its effects are demonstrated in other settings where it has been implemented, the extent to which the innovation is in fact in operation in the adopting organization must be determined before judgments are made about its effectiveness. However, Gordon and Wilkerson and the Civil Rights Commission never considered the possibility that most compensatory educational programs may have been ineffectual simply because they were never effectively implemented. Moreover, most original evaluations of these programs overlooked this possibility; when considered, actual implementation was inadequately measured.[1]

The Study in Social Science Perspective

If one major reason that innovations introduced into educational and other kinds of organizations do not yield their intended effects is inadequate implementation, then it is important to examine and understand the circumstances and conditions facilitating and blocking implementation. However, as a number of students of organiza-

---

[1] See, for example, Higher Horizons Program (Wrightstone et al., 1964); Special Enrichment Program of Quality Integrated Education for Schools in Transitional Areas (Kravetz, 1967); Prevention of School Problems Program (Liddle et al., 1967); The Impact of Head Start (Westinghouse, 1969).

tional change (Bennis, 1966; Guba, 1966; Heathers, 1965; Stufflebeam, 1966) have noted, our knowledge about this aspect of planned
organizational change is limited. The director of the National Institute
for the Study of Educational Change has commented that "several factors exist which militate against success for any venture in planned
educational improvement. Undoubtedly the chief among these is the
rampant conceptual poverty about the change process in general"
(Guba, 1966). More specifically, Bennis (1966) has argued:

> What we know least about — and what continually vexes those of
> us who are vitally concerned with the effective utilization of
> knowledge — is *implementation*. As I use the term, "implementa-
> tion" encompasses a process which includes the creation in a
> client-system of understanding of, and commitment to, a particu-
> lar change which can solve problems and devices whereby it can
> become integral to the client-system's operation. [P. 175]

Our review of the literature in Chapter 2 yields similar conclusions
about the paucity of knowledge about the implementation phase of
the process of planned organizational change. It also raises serious
reservations about the adequacy of the explanation that social scientists have most frequently used to account for the success or failure
of planned organizational change, namely, the ability of management
or a change agent to overcome members' *initial* resistance to change.

We appraised formulations that view the problem in this manner
to be too simplistic because they fail to take into account other conditions that may exist or that can arise when organizational members,
even those not initially resistant to change, attempt to implement an
innovation. They disregard three general and interrelated conditions
of this kind that we reasoned could have a major impact on the fate
of organizational innovations. (1) Organizational members who are
not resistant to change or whose initial resistance to it has been overcome may encounter obstacles in their efforts to implement an innovation which, if not removed, may make it impossible for them to
carry it out. (2) Individuals in organizations are in large part depend-

ent upon their formal leaders to overcome these obstacles and they may not remove, or even be aware of, these constraints. (3) Members who are *initially* favorable toward organizational change may later *develop* a negative orientation to an innovation, and, therefore, be unwilling to implement it as a consequence of the barriers and frustrations they have encountered in attempting to carry it out.

We thought that a strategic way to determine whether there was any empirical support for our own reasoning about circumstances that could influence the degree of implementation would be to conduct an intensive case study of an organization planning to introduce a major innovation whose members did not appear resistant to change. We reasoned that if our reservations about the "initial resistance to change" explanation were groundless, then the implementation effort would be successful. The failure of the implementation effort, on the other hand, would support our contention that a more complex theoretical formulation was needed to account for the success or failure of efforts to implement organizational innovations. This new formulation would have to take into account organizational variables that could influence the implementation phase of the process. In addition, the failure of the implementation effort would provide evidence about whether the types of obstacles that we reasoned would readily confront organizational members attempting to implement innovations do in fact, exist; it also would test our ideas about the dependency of successful planned change on the performance of management. Furthermore, we hoped that the results of the inquiry might lead to the development of a theory that takes into account the complex, dynamic nature of the process involved in successfully implementing organizational innovations. An opportunity to conduct such a case study arose in an inner-city elementary school in the fall of 1966. Our findings (see Chapter 5) revealed that the educational innovation was not being implemented in May 1967. Therefore, the extensive body of data collected during the study was used to determine whether there was any empirical justification for our ideas about circumstances and conditions that may block the implementation of organizational innovations.

We now turn to a description of the innovation we examined.

The Educational Innovation: The Catalytic Role Model

The educational innovation to be implemented was a new definition of the teacher's role; we shall call it the catalytic role model. The innovation was conceived of as a solution to the problems of motivating lower-class children and of improving their academic achievement. Before describing the innovation, it is relevant to consider its objectives, and the assumptions upon which it was based.

During a private talk the innovator disclosed his conception of the aims of this organizational innovation:

> Basically we wanted to create a place that . . . any sensible, red-blooded American kid would want to go to, maybe even if we were terribly successful, a place that would be difficult for them to stay away from. . . . Mainly most of our kids are sort of normal kids who would rather be anywhere but school; so the first thing that we wanted to do is create a kind of atmosphere, a kind of free and easy approach where the teachers weren't lording it over the kids all the time and telling them what to do; we then wanted to create an environment or an atmosphere where kids could make choices, where they had choices to make and where they made them, where they were able to make them and were able to make relatively sensible, interesting choices and do something with them; after that, we wanted to get across to the kids that it was legitimate to use their minds and not only legitimate but that partly it was fun, it would be fun and that there was satisfaction, intrinsic satisfaction, in using your mind. . . . One of the things that we've said is that we don't give a damn about achievement tests, that's not what we're after . . . we say school isn't reading scores . . . we've told teachers, if you want to prepare children for Classical High School, don't come here to teach . . .

The major objectives of the catalytic role model were more formally spelled out in a document prepared by the innovator and dis-

tributed to the teachers in January 1967 (Appendix B-3). He specified them as follows: (1) to allow children to discover the intrinsic
satisfaction and delight of successful employment of their own intellectual and aesthetic energies at whatever level those energies are or
can become capable of operating; (2) to encourage children to
become increasingly self-motivated and increasingly *responsible* for
their own learning and education — to make their education as *self-
directed* as possible; (3) to ensure that children emerge from school
convinced that they are, to some large extent, able to cope with the
world, that they possess the necessary intellectual and aesthetic
skills, and are therefore *competent* to manage themselves and their
lives in such a fashion that they might have some positive effect on
that world if they so choose; (4) to help children acquire the following mental skills or operational competencies: observation, comparison, classification and categorization, perception of problems,
intuition and hunching, hypothesis building and testing, extrapolation, interpretation, building of models, and appreciation; (5) to
make the job of teaching more productive; (6) to make schools
instruments that better reflect and better serve their community.

According to the innovator, the basic assumptions underlying the
innovation may be specified as follows: (1) "American society now
requires its schools to assist children to become independent, responsible, thinking adults." (2) "Human beings can no longer, in the middle of the twentieth century, comprehend in any meaningful fashion
more than a small fraction of the immense body of knowledge and
the intellectual and technical skills available." (3) "Human beings can
no longer construct a series of 'correct' answers or interpretations of
observed facts to which all thinking people can agree." (4) "It is not
how much we know that is important but what we are able to do
with what we know." (5) "Human beings tend to 'learn' best those
things which they feel to be relevant to their lives and interests, and
which they feel they themselves have in some measure chosen to
learn." (6) "It is possible as well as desirable to devise an educational
process that will encourage children to become increasingly respon-

sible for their own learning." (7) "The profession of the teacher — as it is presently conceived and practiced — is neither a sensible nor a possible one to expect large numbers of people to practice success-fully." (8) "The institution called 'school' as we know it today is rightly and of necessity undergoing vast changes not only in the instructional process that occurs inside its walls but in its relation-ship to the world outside those walls — to parents, the local commu-nity, to other civic and social agencies and forces, and to the community at large." (January Document, Appendix B-3).

With this understanding of the objectives and assumptions of the innovation, we now turn to the expectations for the role perform-ance of teachers attempting to conform to the catalytic role model. This new definition of the teacher's role viewed the teacher as assist-ing children to learn according to *their* interests throughout the day in self-contained classrooms.[2] She was expected to emphasize the *process*, not the content, of learning. She was expected to allow pupils maximum freedom in choosing their own activities.

This role definition was based on the assumption that the basic purpose of the "new school" is to maximize the potential talents and interests of each child, to help children to develop their interests and capacities, to help them learn how to learn, and not to teach them a set of standard concepts or facts. Children are seen as different types of candles to be lit; the task of the teacher is to light each candle. Given this conception of schooling and children, the teacher's task is to create the type of classroom atmosphere in which children feel free to pursue their own interests, to learn what they, not the teacher, view as important. To do this, the teacher is expected to flood the classroom with a variety of educational materials, primarily self-

---

[2] The notions that children should be allowed to move freely from classroom to classroom and work outside and in the hallways were not built into the innovation. Moreover, although this new role has implications for other systemic properties such as "authority structure," none were clearly specified by the innovator as part of the innovation; therefore, they were not considered part of the proposed organizational change and were omitted as sources of criteria for assessing the degree of implementation found in May 1967.

instructional, that are based on "pedagogically sound" ideas so that whatever materials a child decides to work with will make a contribution to his education. This rich classroom environment would be arranged according to basic areas (see Appendix D, p. 291 for a schematic plan of the room arrangement). The teacher is expected to facilitate contact between children and the self-instructional materials; she is also expected to encourage children to teach each other. Within the limits imposed by availability of materials and the necessity to cope with problems of "disruptive" children, the teacher is expected to allow students to decide which materials they wish to work with, how long they will work with them, and with whom they wish to relate. Teachers are not expected to keep pupils at their desks in order to listen to or carry out their directives. The teachers are expected to allow children to select the part of the room in which they wish to work, to explore their own interests, and to choose from among a wide variety of materials — for example, a gerbil, a balance game, mystery powders, an Eskimo film cartridge, a math game, an electric typewriter, an ant colony, or a set of interesting and relevant books. The teacher does *not* impart a set body of knowledge and skills to all pupils in the class simultaneously. The pupil is given primary responsibility for directing his own education, and the teacher is expected to assist him when she perceives that her help is needed.

In short, the new role model for a teacher is one that stresses her primary function as a catalyst or guide. The innovator does note, however, that at times it may be necessary for a teacher to apply subtle coercion to get some children who are not spending enough time on basic skills like reading to do so. It is assumed, however, that children will need basic skills in order to pursue their interests, and therefore, they will be learned in the normal course of the child's efforts to fulfill his interests and basic curiosity to learn. In Chapter 5 we shall present the dimensions of teachers' performance that we used as indices of their conformity to this definition of their role.

This conception of the teacher's role contrasts sharply with the traditional conception that prevailed at Cambire Elementary School[3] in November 1966. Traditionally, an elementary school has been a place where children are offered a specific body of information and a number of skills. Children are seen as bottles to be filled depending on capacity and, given this basic conception, the primary task of the teacher is to fill these bottles. The teacher is expected to impart or cover a specified body of information and to drill children so that they learn skills such as reading and writing. The teacher is expected to direct the children's energies so that they will learn a standard set of subjects, usually in concert with all or sections of their class and usually in chunks of time during the day. The teacher, therefore, is expected to limit interaction among students and to assign materials to be read or work to be completed in order to achieve curricular objectives of the school. The teacher is expected to be a director of pupil learning. She takes the initiative in teacher-pupil interaction and their communication is primarily in the form of questions and answers. Teachers are expected to assess, reward, and punish children on the basis of how thoroughly they have covered the curriculum content and how correctly they have retained it. In short, this role definition for the teacher is one that stresses her function as the director of the child's achievement on academic standards established by the school or the larger system.

Two further points deserve emphasis in this discussion of the innovation. The first is that whereas some innovations in organizations specify slight or moderate alterations in the role expectations of their members, in this case, as noted, the innovation consisted of a radical redefinition of the role of the teacher and a fundamental change in her primary functions.[4] The second is that although we have described the innovation in considerable detail, our primary

---

[3] This is a fictitious name employed to protect the anonymity of the school.
[4] For an excellent study that focused on the implementation of a new definition of the role of a nurse in a mental hospital ward, see Schwartz, 1957.

interest in it was not in appraising its intrinsic value or the philosophy of child-centered instruction on which it is based. Rather, our primary interest was to use it as a vehicle to study the *process* that unfolded after the innovation was presented to the teachers and to determine the degree to which it was implemented by them.

Key Concepts

In designing the study we used a number of key concepts. Since social scientists vary in the use of these terms, it is necessary to make explicit our definitions of them.

We conceive of *formal organizations* as rationally contrived, deliberately designed, and goal-oriented social systems that organize individuals in a formalized authority structure and in a division of labor that links members to one another as occupants of interrelated positions. We use the concept of *role* to refer to a set of expectations or standards applied to the behavior of incumbents of positions (Gross et al., 1958, p. 6).

We view *organizational change* as behavioral change with reference to role performance, the authority structure, the division of labor, or the goals of an organization. Katz and Kahn (1966) have a similar conception of organizational change. They state:

> The major error in dealing with problems of organizational change both at the practical and theoretical level is to disregard the systemic properties of the organization and to confuse individual change with modifications in organizational variables, behavior related to such things as role relationships. . . . The confusion between individual and organizational change is due in part to the lack of precise terminology for distinguishing between behavior determined largely by structured roles within a system and behavior determined more directly by personality needs and values. The behavior of people in organizations is still the behavior of individuals, but it has a different set of determinants. . . . Scientists and practitioners have assumed too often that an individual change will produce a corresponding organizational change. This assumption seems to us indefensible. [Pp. 390-391, 450-451]

In short, organizational change, as we shall use the term, refers to changing the behavior of individuals as members of an organization.

The term *organizational innovation* shall be used to refer to any proposed idea, or set of ideas, about how the organizational behavior of members should be changed in order to resolve problems of the organization or to improve its performance. The term *proposed organizational change* will be used interchangeably with organizational innovation. In this investigation, the catalytic role model is viewed as a set of ideas about how elementary school teachers should behave in their classrooms in order to improve the education of their pupils.

The term *degree of implementation* will be used to refer to the extent to which, at a given point in time, the organizational behavior of members conforms to an organizational innovation. Put another way, degree of implementation refers to the extent to which organizational members have changed their behavior so that it is congruent with the behavior patterns required by the innovation. In this investigation, the operational definition of implementation of the organizational innovation will be the extent to which teacher role performance at the end of a six-month period of attempted implementation conformed to the specifications of the catalytic role model. These specifications are presented in Chapter 5.

Two different uses of the term *planned organizational change* are found in the literature. Some writers use the term to refer to deliberate efforts to instigate a process of change in an organization without reference to any specific innovation. The emphasis is on "getting change going," that is, identifying organizational problems and setting forces in motion to cope with them. Others view planned organizational change as deliberate efforts to introduce changes into the organization, that is, modifying specific patterns of organizational behavior; in this case the change has reference to concrete organizational innovations. We shall use the term *planned organizational change* to refer to the total process that follows after an effort has

been made to alter organizational behavior through the introduction
of an innovation.

We distinguish three basic stages or time period in this process:
(1) the period of the initiation of an organizational innovation;
(2) the period of its attempted implementation; and (3) the period
during which an innovation is incorporated into the organization. A
somewhat similar way of viewing changes in the behavior of individuals is Lewin's (1958, pp. 197-211) notions of unfreezing, changing, and refreezing. *Initiation* covers the period of time in which a
particular innovation is selected and introduced into an organization.
More specifically, it is the stage in which an organization defines a
problem, decides on an innovation to resolve it, and presents the innovation to organizational members. The period of *attempted implementation* begins after the announcement that an innovation will be
adopted and focuses on efforts to make the changes in the behavior
of organizational members specified by the innovation. If during this
period organizational members do not make the required changes in
their organizational behavior, the process breaks down. *Incorporation*
is the period when a change that is implemented becomes an enduring
part of the operation of the organization. In the literature, this stage
in the process is usually not separated for examination from implementation.[5]

Overview

In Chapter 2 we present the major conclusions that emerged from
our appraisal of the literature on planned organizational change, the
evidence on which they were based, and consider their implications
for our study. In Chapter 3 we describe the major methodological
problems encountered in the investigation and the procedures
employed to secure data for the examination of the basic questions

---

[5]One study which did make this distinction is an inquiry conducted by Miner
(1960). It deals with the maintenance of superstitious practices within an
African tribe in spite of the implementation of an innovation contrary to them.

of the study. In Chapter 4 we examine data about external and internal conditions in the school just prior to the announcement of the innovation to the teachers, with special reference to the extent to which these conditions would be conducive to the successful implementation of the innovation. We also present data which reflect the nature of teacher performance in their classrooms at that time. In Chapter 5 we present our assessment of the degree of implementation of the innovation in May 1967. We also discuss the rationale underlying the evaluation and the assessment procedures that were employed. In Chapter 6 we present data that shed light on the factors that account for the degree of implementation of the innovation that prevailed in May 1967, at the time of our assessment, and at points earlier in time, beginning with its announcement in November 1966. In Chapter 7 we attempt to isolate the conditions prevailing during the period between announcement and assessment that could account for the existence of these factors. In Chapter 8 we consider theoretical and research implications of our study as well as practical implications emerging from our findings.

2

The Literature on Planned Organizational Change: A Critical Appraisal

To place our study in proper perspective it is necessary to examine the literature on planned organizational change with special reference to its treatment of the implementation of organizational innovations. This chapter presents the major conclusions that emerged from our review of this literature, the evidence upon which they were based, and their implications for our inquiry.

Some people have attempted to apply a model arising from studies of the diffusion and adoption of innovations among aggregates or collectivities of people such as farmers, doctors, and housewives to explain successful planned change in organizational settings. We will first consider the work done in this tradition and present our reservations about it. Then, in more detail we shall discuss planned organizational change studies and speculative papers[1] that focus on the antecedents, the initiation, and the implementa-

---

[1] In contrast to the study of *planned* change, that is change resulting from conscious, deliberate efforts to improve the operations of a system, there is also the study of *unplanned* change, that is change that is not a consequence of conscious, deliberate efforts to improve the functioning of a system. Included in this area is what Washburne (1954) calls "sociocultural drift," and what

19

tion of organizational innovations with special reference to their use-fulness in understanding why schools vary in their success in carry-ing them out.

The Diffusion and Adoption Studies

There have been a number of major reviews of diffusion and adop-tion studies in the past few years (Katz et al., 1963; Lionberger, 1964; Rogers, 1962). Rogers reviewed 506 studies in anthropology, rural sociology, educational and medical sociology. He classified them under the following problem areas: stages individuals go through in the adoption process, characteristics of innovations and their rate of adoption, attributes of early and late adopters, influ-ence of opinion leaders on the flow of ideas, and the role of change agents.

Several general observations may be made about these studies: (1) they generally deal with the spread or adoption of rather simple technical innovations such as hybrid seed, tranquilizers, or audio-visual aids; (2) the agricultural studies have focused on the spread or adoption of innovations among individual farmers residing in a par-ticular county, state, or region; (3) the studies of medical innova-tions have primarily dealt with their diffusion and adoption by doctors in a single community; (4) the anthropological studies have focused on the spread of such practices as the use of new tools, wells, and modern farming techniques within nonindustrial socie-ties; and (5) the education studies have primarily dealt with adop-tion rates of innovations in school systems.

Moore (1963) calls "evolutionary change"; Ogburn (1938) and Sorokin (1937) have dealt with this general kind of change at length. This review will not include work related to the latter area, since it is concerned with change resulting from efforts specifically directed at obtaining the particular change being studied—i.e., planned change. Moreover, because our concern is with the problem of implementation, which precedes the questions of incorporation and effects, our discussion omits studies related to these aspects of the planned organizational change process.

After his extensive review of adoption and diffusion studies Rogers proposes a model to explain why individuals do or do not adopt innovations. He identifies five critical stages in the adoption process: awareness, interest, trial, evaluation, and adoption. He also suggests a sixth stage, discontinuance. This model has frequently been cited in the educational literature (Carlson, 1965; Eicholz and Rogers, 1964; Miles, 1964; Owens, 1970) as a useful formulation for analyzing the successful introduction of innovations in schools.[2]

We believe, however, that this model has little use in explaining the success or failure of the implementation of innovations in schools or other types of organizations. Its lack of utility is due to certain of its assumptions which are not applicable to the implementation of *organizational* innovations. One of its basic assumptions is that during any of the intermediate stages between awareness and use, the individual is free to decide himself whether the innovation shall be tried, and if tried, whether it should be continued. If the innovation does not interest him, he is free to reject it. If he is not pleased with his evaluation of it, he can discontinue his use of the innovation. This assumption does not apply to major educational innovations in most school situations, for example, those in which teachers are asked to redefine their roles by their superordinates, or in cases where compensatory programs for lower-class urban schools have been designed by top administrators and teachers must carry them out. Moreover, the adoption of a particular program by administrators does not necessarily mean that it will be instituted or implemented at the school level. A study conducted by Carlson (1965a, pp. 74-84) revealed that the mere adoption of programmed instruction by school superintendents did not necessarily lead to the desired change at the school level.

---

[2] The approach to change in education proposed by Clark and Guba (1965) parallels the Rogers model in certain important respects. It emphasizes several processes including the development, adoption, and diffusion of educational practices.

The Rogers model is concerned with the adoption of simple technological innovations by individuals, and it assumes that they can try out innovations on a small scale without the help or support of other persons. It also assumes that persons can undertake trials in an either/or fashion and that short trials are sufficient to render an effective evaluation. Many educational innovations, however, cannot be tried on a small scale and cannot be implemented by teachers unless they have the cooperation and support of their colleagues. Furthermore, many educational innovations are so complex that they cannot be tried in an either/or fashion, and some require several years of full implementation before an adequate evaluation of their effectiveness can be made.

Not surprisingly, the studies concerned with the adoption of innovations by individuals support the generalizations that before any innovation has a high adoption rate among a collectivity of individuals it must be of proven quality and value, easily demonstrable in its effects, and information about it must be readily available; in addition, its cost must be reasonable, and it must be accessible to the adopter (Miles, 1964a, pp. 634-639).

In short, while Rogers' model may be useful in understanding the adoption of simple innovations among aggregates of individuals, it appears to be of little value for explaining the implementation of organizational innovations.

Antecedents of Organizational Innovations

Most studies of large-scale organizational change ignore historical conditions that may influence the success of a planned change effort. Several studies, however, do suggest the importance of such conditions, which may be internal or external to the organization.

Greiner, in a paper entitled "Antecedents of Planned Organizational Change," examined data from a study of a large, petro-chemical plant in which Managerial Grid training was introduced in an effort to improve decision-making behavior of 800 managers

(Greiner, 1967). His analysis suggests that historical and unplanned forces played an important part in setting the stage and giving impetus to the planned change program. The author states that the major implication to be drawn from his study ". . . is that future researchers and change agents need to give greater weight to historical determinants of change, with special emphasis being attached to the developing relationship between an organization and its environment. It is within this historical and developmental context, I think, that we may be able to explain better why a particular 'planned' change program may succeed in one organization but not in another" (p. 52). Greiner concludes that "historical events established important pre-conditions which enhanced the ultimate effect of Grid training. Without these prior conditions, external pressure, internal tension, outside expertise, it is entirely possible that Grid training might have been a 'flop' at Sigma" (pp. 52-53).

In a survey of a number of studies of organizational change Greiner (1967a) found that four of the eight cases he classified as "successful" were preceded by a build-up of outside pressure and internal tension. He suggests that outside pressure may raise a system's level of anxiety, increase its search for relief, and hence, make it susceptible to influence.

Earlier studies (Burns and Stalker, 1961; Mann and Neff, 1961; and Gellerman 1963) support the notion that organizational members who have been asked to make frequent changes in their work patterns in the past are more likely to carry out an innovation than members who have been infrequently requested to alter their performance. A past history or prevailing atmosphere of change, in short, may contribute to future successful change.

Moreover, Greiner has noted that successful change in some organizations appears to be a consequence of the introduction of an outside change agent at the managerial level. He also observed that some studies advance the notion that a change agent with perceived high prestige and expertise is more likely to be successful in obtaining change than one without these characteristics (Hovland and Weiss, 1951; Tannenbaum, 1956).

In summary, antecedent conditions that have been reported to
be associated with successful implementation of organizational innovations include external pressure, internal tension, a previous atmosphere of change, and an outside expert with a positive image.

The Initiation of Organizational Innovations

A great deal of the literature on planned organizational change is
concerned with the question, "How are organizational innovations
most effectively initiated?" A number of studies and essays emphasize the importance of change agents and participation of subordinates as important determinants of successful initiation.[3]

In his review of strategies of change employed in six different
organizations, Buchanan (1967) found that most of them placed
stress on change agents who conducted group discussions and
T-groups. Leavitt (1965) has noted that a great deal of the literature on planned change assumes that a change agent will be used to
facilitate initiation (Bennis, 1966; Bennis et al., 1961, pp. 617-689;
and Lippitt et al., 1958). The importance attributed to change
agents during the initiation phase of planned organizational change
seems to be based on the following reasoning: in general, members
of an organization are unable, or find it difficult, to diagnose their
problems in a realistic or competent manner. Outside change agents
with expert knowledge are assumed to possess the ability to
approach situations in a more objective and a more sophisticated
manner; consequently, their analyses are usually more realistic and
penetrating than those of organizational members. It is also assumed
that outside change agents can more readily set forces in motion

----

[3] The notions of "change agent" and "participation" have varying definitions.
Some, for example Lippitt, use "change agent" to mean simply outside helpers,
while others require that the person(s), labeled change agents, actually direct
planned change efforts. Like some, Coch-French, use "participation" to mean
extent of influence in decision-making, others mean simply involvement, while
for others physical presence is enough.

that will increase the amount and flow of communication among members of the organization, which in turn will result in their greater awareness of the need for change and their greater commitment to proposed innovations.

The importance of subordinate participation in initiating innovations is also given great emphasis in the literature. Advocates of participation vary as to the amount of participation by subordinates which they believe important. In the educational literature some writers have argued that participation is necessary throughout the total planned change process (Benne and Birnbaum, 1960; Dufay, 1966; Oliver, 1965; Trump, 1967). Others maintain that participation of subordinates is necessary for only certain decisions, for example, defining the need for change (*National Elementary Principal*, 1961); selecting or developing alternative change possibilities (Dentler, 1964); adopting a specific change (Byerly and Rankin, 1967); determining the strategy of implementation (Rocky Mountain, 1964). However, some educators maintain that critical decisions about planned organizational change must be made by the administration (Bishop, 1961; Brickell, 1961; Heathers, 1963, 1965, 1967*b*).

Not only is participation assumed to be necessary for successful initiation, but in addition, it is argued that a strategy of collaborative initiation, one which involves participation of subordinates with superordinates, usually with the involvement of an outside change agent, will have the greatest impact on the degree to which an innovation is successfully implemented.

Those writers who have stressed the importance of participation of subordinates in planned organizational change have used one or more of the following arguments in support of their views: (1) participation leads to higher staff morale, and high staff morale is necessary for successful implementation (Bennis, 1966); (2) participation leads to greater commitment, and a high degree of commitment is required for affecting change (Goodlad and Anderson, 1963; Mann and Hoffman, 1960; Oliver, 1965); (3) participation leads to greater clarity about an innovation, and clarity is necessary for implementation (Anderson, 1964; Gale, 1967); (4) beginning with the postulate of basic resistance to change, the argument is that participation will reduce initial resistance and thereby facilitate successful implementation (Argyle, 1967; Oliver, 1965; Peterson, 1966); and (5) subordinates will tend to resist any innovation that they are expected to implement if it is initiated solely by their superordinates (Agnew and Hsu, 1960; Wigren, 1967).[4]

While all these lines of reasoning may be plausible, evidence to test the relative effectiveness of strategies of initiation that stress participation in comparison with other methods, for example, imposition from the top, is not available. Most proponents of subordinate participation use as the basis for their advocacy of this approach personal experience, logical argument, or the findings of a few empirical studies. For example, Argyris offers the following arguments for participation:

... participation is desired (from those affected by the change) in order to (1) decrease resistance to change, (2) develop the most

[4] With respect to the concept of participation, it should be noted that the great majority of planned change proposals, especially those in education, are based on the assumption that successful change can take place within the context of the present organization by changes in the organizational behavior of the members presently there. However, it is also important to stress that not all serious proposals for change make such assumptions. Some, while still proposing that change can be made within the present organizational structure, believe that successful change can only occur when present members are replaced with people who are either more malleable or who already perform according to the innovation and who, therefore, do not need to change their present behavior. An example of this kind of proposal would be one which specified the hiring of teachers who perform according to a progressive role model to replace traditional teachers in a school where a progressive approach is to be introduced. Some proposals involve both the retraining of some present members and the replacement of others. Still other proposals begin with the assumption that successful change cannot take place in the present organizational context; for an example in education see Fantini and Weinstein (1968). Such proposals usually offer alternate organizational structures that either go around the existing structure or completely replace the original structure once it has been abandoned.

effective processes for a lasting change within the organization, and (3) represent more adequately the needs of the participants involved in the change. The Coch and French studies and the Morse and Reimer studies are excellent examples of this approach. In the case of the former it was found that the experience of being allowed to participate in decisions usually reserved for management (the design of a new job, setting of the price rate, etc.) increased the workers' effectiveness. In the latter, it was found that high control from above tended to reduce the effectiveness of work groups. [Argyris et al., 1962*a*, pp. 91-93]

Yet, close scrutiny of the Morse-Reimer (1955) study of the effects of various degrees of subordinate participation in decision-making in a large business firm reveals that both the high and low groups on the independent variable, participation, showed significant increases in productivity, the dependent variable; therefore, this investigation does not offer support for the varying effectiveness of different strategies. Moreover, the Coch-French study (1948), which French (et al., 1960) tried to repeat in a Norwegian factory without success, is rife with methodological deficiencies: lack of control of third variables, improper use of statistical techniques given the size of the sample, and failure to test a number of critical assumptions made in their argument which were testable. For example, it was assumed but not demonstrated that members of the experimental group, because of their participation, saw the need for change and therefore had a more positive attitude toward changing than members of the control group.

The kind of evidence required can only come from carefully conducted longitudinal studies of large numbers of organizations in which the major independent variable would be type of initiation strategy used and the dependent variable would be degree of implementation, and in which the presumed intervening variables, such as morale and clarity of the innovation, were systematically studied. Investigations of this kind are, unfortunately, not available.

When both conditions, the presence of a change agent and participation of subordinates, are proposed in combination as necessary for an effective strategy of initiation, the result is the notion of power equalization. The proven effects of participation in connection with the use of an outside change agent are doubtful, as Leavitt (1965) notes:

> Bennis, Benne, and Chin in their reader, *The Planning of Change* (1961), are so enamored of it that they have quite specifically set out power equalization as one of the distinguishing features of the deliberate collaborative process they define as "planned change" in organizations. A power distribution in which the client and change agent have equal, or almost equal, opportunities to influence is a part of their definition of "planned change." . . . The issue of validity remains a critical and difficult issue. When empirical studies have been undertaken to evaluate outcomes, the results have been equivocal at best. . . . Even several of the individual case analyses . . . have led to equivocal or negative results. PE practices have been carried much more by their transferable operational techniques and by their impact on persons than by their demonstrated results. [Pp. 1158-1159, 1167]

Herzberg, Mausner, and Snyderman (1959) indicate similar doubts about the participation of subordinates in decision-making, especially with reference to goal determination:

> The idea, first, that the participation of subordinates in decision-making was possible, and second, that it was desirable has been the subject of a great deal of controversy. . . . There is no question that a genuine attempt to extend the scope of participants has been made in some places. The interpretation of these attempts and of their purported success is far from clear. . . . Within certain limits, it is likely that more latitude than is currently available to most people in industry can be given to individuals to develop their own ways of achieving the ends that are presented to them by a centralized authority. This is a reasonable solution to the problem of motivation, more reasonable than the usual formulation of participation. To expect individuals at lower levels in an organization to exercise control over the establishment of over-all goals is unrealistic. Thus, when participation is suggested in these terms, it is usually a sham. [Pp. 127-128, 137]

As they note, even if participation were shown to be effective, it is problematic whether subordinates have the knowledge, competence, or the desire to make major decisions about important organizational changes.

In summary, our review of the literature reveals that the use of change agents and participation are generally believed to be strategic variables with respect to the successful initiation of change proposals, and that it is assumed that a strategy of initiation involving a change agent and subordinate participation typically leads to the successful implementation of innovations. However, there is a paucity of research evidence to support either of these propositions. There is even less evidence to support the propositions that participation is positively related to variables such as the clarity of an innovation, the morale of the staff, and its commitment to an innovation and that these variables are positively associated with implementation. Also, it deserves note that the widely held assumption that most organizational members are resistant to change is, to date, far more rhetorical than demonstrable. Moreover, the assertion that a major change initiated by management creates or exacerbates resistance to change among its subordinates has been buttressed with little evidence.

The Implementation of Organizational Innovations

The greater attention given to initiation than to implementation in the literature is illustrated by the treatment given these topics by Lippitt, Watson, and Westley in their book, *The Dynamics of Planned Change* (1958). They view planned change as a deliberate and collaborative process involving a change agent and a client system, and discuss in detail studies concerned with the training and role of the change agent related to problems of initiation: helping organizations clarify and diagnose both internal and external problems, establishing a firm change-relationship, and helping organizations examine and select alternate solutions and goals. The only attention they give directly to what we are calling implementation and which

they label "Phase 5" is in the section of their book on "The Trans-
formation of Intentions Into Actual Change Efforts" (pp. 139-140)
and "Change Methods Used in Phase 5: The Initiation of Change
Efforts" (pp. 221-226). In fact, they end their brief discussion by
saying,

> In our sample of change projects many agents do not speak of
> their efforts to provide either direct or indirect support for
> change efforts in the client system's sphere of existence. As a
> result, we can report here only a limited variety of methods
> appropriate to Phase 5. Much creative work remains to be done
> in developing methods for use in this crucial part of the helping
> process. [P. 226]

In the literature on planned organizational change that deals with
the period of implementation, many "facilitators" of implementation are mentioned. Those most often considered are: (1) external
and internal support for the change (Brickell, 1961; Fantini and
Weinstein, 1963; Wigren, 1967); (2) adequate funding (New York
State Education Department, 1965; Miller, 1967; (3) adequacy of
plan for meeting organizational members' needs and the organizational problem under consideration (Fowler, 1956; Lippitt, Benne,
and Havelock, 1966; Parloff, 1960); (4) member acceptance of the
need for the change (Abbott, 1965; Fantini and Weinstein, 1963);
(5) retraining of members for new tasks (Heathers, 1967b; Jung,
1967; York, 1955-II); and (6) the presence of a change agent to give
needed support and advice (Brown, 1966; Fantini and Weinstein,
1963; Lippitt, Benne, and Havelock, 1966; Radcliffe, 1967). While
some authors stress the importance of one or two conditions, others
place emphasis on several. Unfortunately, however, most of these reports are open to criticism on conceptual and methodological grounds.
    They are weak conceptually because they generally treat the
implementation of organizational innovations as an event rather
than as a process (Ginzberg and Reilley, 1957) that involves an interrelated set of conditions that can shift over time — for example, the

acceptance or the clarity of a change proposal. Nearly all reports presently in the literature treat conditions as unchanging and implementation as the result of an accumulation of isolated conditions rather than as a result of an interrelated and complex set of forces.

Many criticisms can be made of the literature on methodological grounds. Conditions isolated as barriers or facilitators to implementation are generally not "uncovered" through rigorous and systematic analyses of organizations undergoing change. Rather, written largely from the perspective of practitioners and/or active change agents, most explanations are based on highly subjective accounts of their experiences during an effort to introduce an educational change. Typically, no supporting evidence is offered about conditions that are presumed to serve as important factors influencing organizational change. With few exceptions (Greiner, 1965) the intent is not to test or generate either hypotheses or theories about implementation but to report change experiences or to advocate the importance of certain factors.

A great deal of the literature turns out to be speculative or hortative in nature. For example, Bennis (1966) in *Changing Organizations*, after noting (p. 175) that the problem of implementation is a "continually vexing one," nevertheless proceeds to note without supporting evidence a number of facilitators or "shoulds" during implementation efforts:

> The *client-system* should have as much understanding of the change . . . as possible. . . . The *change effort* should be perceived as being as self-motivated and voluntary as possible. . . . The *change program* must include emotional and value as well as cognitive (*informational*) elements for successful implementation. . . . The *change-agent* can be crucial in reducing the resistance to change. [P. 176]

In his article "Barriers to Change in Public Schools" Carlson (1965*b*) specifies three often mentioned major barriers to change without evidence to support his contentions. The obstacles he cites

are lack of a change agent, lack of awareness about new educational
practices (knowledge utilization, and the like), and insufficient pressure on, or need for, schools to change:

> Part of the explanation of the slow rate of change in public schools
> according to many students of organizational change, lies with
> the absence of an institutionalized change agent position in pub-
> lic education. A *change agent* . . . can be defined as a person who
> attempts to influence the adoption decisions in a direction he
> feels is desirable. He is a professional who has as his major func-
> tion the advocacy and introduction of innovations into prac-
> tice. . . . In addition to the lack of a change agent, schools are
> also handicapped in change activities by the weakness of the
> knowledge base about new educational practices. . . . There is no
> struggle for survival for this type of organization service in orga-
> nizations like schools – existence is guaranteed. Though this
> type of organization does compete in a restricted area for funds,
> funds are not closely tied to quality of performance. These orga-
> nizations are domesticated in the sense that they are protected
> by the society they serve . . . it seems reasonable to suggest that
> the domestication of public schools is a hindrance to change
> along with the lack of a change agent and a weak knowledge base
> about educational innovation. [Pp. 4-7]

In a typical school report C. L. Byerly and Stuart C. Rankin
(1967), officials of the Detroit School District, make a series of
recommendations based on their impression of factors related to
successful implementation, the timing of introduction, the line-staff
relationships, the instructional leadership of the principal, and the
need to provide help to teachers. They assert:

> One of the difficulties which accrue to a city-wide change is the
> development of some feeling of "Do we have to do this?" rather
> than "Can't we do it, too?" Other school systems should con-
> sider the alternative of expanding similar programs more
> slowly. . . . The line-staff relation may be a critical factor in the
> expansion of new programs in other school systems, as it is in
> ours. We strongly recommend that guidelines, purposes, calen-

dars, and bulletins be developed jointly by those with line and staff responsibilities. This combination was most effective in Detroit. . . . Two items which have received some emphasis in Detroit . . . but which we believe should receive a great deal more attention are (1) instructional leadership by the principals and (2) more attention to helping teachers with the management of flexible grouping in the classroom. Willingness to delegate authority and share decision-making on instructional matters with the staff is an essential ingredient in sound leadership by the principal. [Pp. 44-45]

An appraisal of this document and many others of a similar nature reveals that they usually include a set of assertions about factors associated with the successful implementation of innovations which are supported by dubious evidence. The factors isolated usually derive from the testimony of practitioners involved in change efforts, and the reliability of their observations is open to serious question. Barnes (1967) indicates the problems that arise when participants in change efforts also attempt to observe them:

This problem need not concern us if we are interested only in organizational change, but it becomes crucial as soon as we turn our thoughts to the *study* of change. Some behavioral scientists (e.g., Blake and Mouton, Argyris, Shepard, Bennis, Sofer, Rice, Jacques, Trist, F. Mann) seek and apparently achieve proficiency in both areas. But behavioral scientist critics decry these dual attempts to change organizations and also do research on the changes. The possible bias of social scientist involvement is of major concern. . . . In essence, the critics of observer "involvement" want a science built upon the observation of human behavior rather than a science which involves attempts to practice as well as observe. Observers, so the reasoning goes, remain detached and relatively objective. Participants become involved and overly subjective; they begin to overvalue and push their own beliefs and "normative" theories. [Pp. 74-75]

Although there are exceptions, most reports about innovations in schools that require changes in teachers' behavior ignore the teachers'

perspectives and typically present only the administrators' or outside change agents' perceptions of the attitudes or performance of
the faculty. An inquiry conducted by Peterson on the implementation of team-teaching in a high school (Peterson, 1966) and a case
study of an effort to implement nongradedness in an elementary
school (Glogau and Fessel, 1967) serve as good illustrations of this.
Both studies are written from the perspectives of the educators who
administered the programs. They do not offer objective reports of
what teachers said, felt, or how they behaved. Instead, Peterson
gives a very general account of *his* perceptions of what went on;
Glogau and Fessel, on the other hand, present page after page of
their interpretations of what transpired at staff meetings. Teachers'
comments, when presented, are restricted to their perceptions
about their pupils' reactions.

In both of these studies the actions and reactions of teachers are
filtered and interpreted by people with "vested" interests. The validity of their perceptions is open to challenge and such procedures
lend support to the criticism offered by Barnes. One may legitimately hold serious reservations about the findings presented in
such reports.

A number of studies use inappropriate methods to assess the
degree of implementation. Some assert that successful implementation occurred, but the evidence is based on very subjective personal
assessments (Childs, 1966; Dufay, 1966; Marland, 1963; Wigren,
1967). Others offer no evidence at all. For example, an administrator (Gale, 1967) presented a description of factors related to the
implementation of nongradedness in a local school system, but no
data are presented to buttress the alleged successful implementation
of the innovation.

The methods used in many studies to determine behavioral
changes are highly questionable. For example, in a study that
focused on the relationship between types of leadership behavior
and the degree of implementation of comprehensive classroom curriculum plans, the extent of classroom change was measured by

interviews with the teachers (Kline, 1966). In a hospital study in which the author was attempting to measure the impact of four conditions on the extent to which ward nurses changed their role behavior according to different therapeutic-milieu-schemes, the extent of change in their performance was measured by self-administered questionnaires (Parloff, 1960). However, in this instance the author recognizes that his procedures may have led to an overestimate of actual change. Wilkie (1967) examined the degree to which a model school implemented team-teaching, nongrading, and other innovations. His analysis was based completely on teacher interviews.

The use of interview responses or subjective appraisals in investigations to determine the extent of organizational change has important implications for their conclusions. Having once "determined" the degree of organizational change from such data, investigators search for conditions they take to be explanatory. However, if the operational definitions of the degree of organizational change are highly questionable, then the conditions isolated can hardly be viewed as explanatory. The importance of obtaining an accurate measure of the dependent variable in any study cannot be overstressed. Work based on systematic observations of the behavior in question is clearly a necessity. Our awareness of the importance of obtaining an objective and unbiased measure of the degree of implementation led us, in this investigation, to obtain direct classroom observation of teacher behavior and to use formal assessment procedures and observation schedules (Chapter 5).

Our review indicated that the literature is deficient in several important respects. First, there has been little concern for testing theories or generating testable hypotheses about factors influencing degree of implementation. Second, data used to isolate conditions having an impact on implementation are typically obtained only from the perspective of those who initiate them; they generally ignore the point of view of organizational members who must make the behavioral changes specified by the innovation. Third, the method used to assess the degree of implementation of an innovation in many studies is open to serious question; careful measurement would require collecting and analyzing data based on systematic observations and not using data about "effects" as indices of successful implementation.

The Implementation of Organizational Innovations: The Major Explanation Found in the Literature

In their attempts to account for the success or failure of deliberate or planned organizational change, social scientists have generally tended to conceive of the problem as one of overcoming the initial resistance to change of organizational members. Argyle's (1967) consideration of change in organizations provides a good illustration of this type of formulation. He states:

> In the first place, there is usually resistance to change of any sort. . . . In social organization, patterns of behavior become established and are of great stability because individuals work out drive-reducing ways of adapting, and fear that any change will be to their disadvantage in some way. Changes in industry are resisted by workers because they are afraid that they will be paid less or will have to work harder to earn the same amount. Wage-incentive schemes have often foundered for this reason. Changes are resisted by managers because they are afraid that their position will be weakened somehow or that they will be further from the center of power. Current changes in prisons are resisted by prison officers and prisoners alike because they have no desire to associate with each other. . . . There is anxiety either about possible material loss or about the disruption of a well-established and satisfying social system. [P. 95]

As a consequence of this definition of the problem, many explanations of the success or failure of attempts to implement organizational change focus on the ability of management or a change agent to overcome members' initial resistance to change.[5]

---

[5] For examples see Argyle, 1967; Bennis, 1966; Coch and French, 1948; Lawrence, 1954; Zander, 1961.

Thus Argyle (1967), after his enumeration of a number of reasons why organizational members will resist change, states, "It may be impossible to bring about change in the teeth of such resistance, and it is usually possible only if the new scheme can be shown to be advantageous. This may be achieved by means of financial incentives, honorific ranks, training courses, or by sheer persuasive skill" (p. 95).

The premise of initial resistance to change of organizational members appears to be linked to the power-equalization concept (Leavitt, 1965) which has been frequently invoked to account for the differential success of organizations in implementing innovations. This explanation assumes that members of an organization who must implement an innovation will offer resistance to it unless they have been involved in formulating the innovation in the first place. It is further assumed that this resistance constitutes the major obstacle to the implementation of an innovation. To overcome this resistance, management must therefore share its power with those who must implement the innovation by allowing them to participate in decisions about the change to be made. It is further assumed that the individuals who must implement the innovation will then perceive the innovation as self-imposed and thereby become committed to it.

Thus, in discussing styles of administration as they bear on organizational change, Argyle (1967) maintains:

> The main principle here is that subordinates should be persuaded and motivated rather than ordered — so that they actually want to behave in the new way. This persuasive and democratic style means allowing people to take part in discussion and decisions. [P. 94]

And Leavitt (1965), in his review of power-equalization approaches to organizational change, notes:

> Power equalization has thus become a key concept in several of the prevalent people theories, a first step in the theoretical causal chain leading toward organizational change. It has been constructed as an initial subgoal, a necessary predecessor to creative change in structure, technology, task-solving, and task implemen-

tation. Although the distances are unmarked, there is no obscurity about direction: a more egalitarian distribution is better. [P. 1159]

The theme of resistance to change is also stressed in the group dynamics literature that deals with the problem of organizational change. It is asserted that through human relations training in sensitivity or T-groups, organizational members' resistance to change can be "unfrozen" and a positive orientation to change can be instilled.[6] This type of training is also proposed for efforts to improve communication and problem-solving skills. Resistance to change, however, never becomes a minor factor.

Formulations that tend to view the problem of implementing organizational innovations as simply one of overcoming members' *initial* resistance to change ignore three interrelated conditions that seem to us to be of critical importance. The first is that organizational members who are *not* resistant to change may encounter a number of obstacles in their efforts to implement an innovation. The second is that members of an organization are in part dependent upon their formal leaders to overcome these obstacles, and the required aid may or may not be provided. The third is that members who are *initially* favorable to organizational change may later *develop* a negative orientation to an innovation as a consequence of the frustrations they have encountered in attempting to carry it out.

When we review the findings of our case study in the final chapter, we shall consider whether they offer support for the reservations we have expressed about the way the problem of the implementation of organizational innovations has generally been formulated.

---

[6] For specific examples see Argyris, 1962; Bradford, Gibb, and Benne, 1964; Jacques, 1951; Miles, 1959; Lewin, 1947; Schein and Bennis, 1965. For reviews of the work related to this area see Greiner, 1967; Katz and Kahn, 1966; Leavitt, 1965; R. E. Miles, 1965.

Summary

This chapter reviewed and appraised studies and essays on planned organizational change with special reference to the problem of implementing organizational innovations. We arrived at the following conclusions. The model growing out of diffusion and adoption studies has little use for understanding what transpires during an organizational implementation effort. The planned organizational change literature suggested internal and external organizational conditions existing prior to a planned change effort that could have an impact on the degree of implementation of an innovation. Some writers noted that the particular strategy of initiation used might also influence the degree of implementation. Only a small part of the literature considered the period during which the implementation effort occurred. Many studies had serious methodological or conceptual shortcomings.

Our review of implementation studies corroborated the observations of Bennis, Guba, Heathers, and Stufflebeam about the paucity of knowledge concerning the conditions influencing the implementation of organizational innovations. It revealed that the major explanation offered for the success or failure of organizations to implement innovations assumes that members of an organization are initially resistant to change and that it is the ability of management or a change agent to overcome their resistance that accounts for the success or failure of efforts to implement innovations. We argued that this explanation ignores important considerations about obstacles to which members who are not resistant to change may be exposed when they make efforts to implement innovations, about the possible importance that management, as part of the role set of subordinates, may play in creating or overcoming these obstacles, and about the possibility that members who are not initially resistant to an organizational change may later develop a negative orientation to it.

We concluded that most social scientists have not recognized the need to conceptualize the success or failure of the implementation of organizational innovations as the result of a complex set of inter-related forces that occur over an extended period of time after the innovation has been introduced. Our review indicated that there was a great need for in-depth studies of organizations, such as schools, trying to implement organizational innovations in order to isolate factors that inhibit and facilitate their implementation. Such studies, we contended, were also needed if heuristic models and hypotheses about the implementation of organizational innovations were to be developed.

3

Research Procedures [1]

The rationale for the selection of the basic research strategy and the specific techniques we used in our inquiry was based on a point of view similar to that expressed by Homans: "People who write about methodology often forget that it is a matter of strategy, not of morals. There are neither good nor bad methods, but only methods that are more or less effective under particular circumstances in reaching objectives on the way to a distant goal" (Homans, 1949, p. 330).

This chapter presents the major methodological problems encountered in designing and carrying out the study and the reasons for the decisions made about them. We shall consider first why we decided to employ the case study method. Then we shall discuss the following matters: selecting the school in which the study was to be conducted, securing formal administrative approval for the inquiry, gaining entry into the school, defining the role of the fieldworker, and establishing rapport with the school staff. Finally, we shall describe the procedures followed and the major problems encountered during the field-work phase of the investigation.

---

[1] Readers with little interest in methodological issues may wish to skim this chapter.

Rationale for the Use of the Case Study Method

During the early fall of 1966 we specified the essential objectives of the study as follows: (1) to increase our knowledge of conditions, in addition to members' resistance to change, that may serve to block or facilitate the implementation of organizational innovations; (2) to ascertain whether there was any empirical support for our contention that most previous explanations of the differential effectiveness of planned change had been based on a truncated version of the process; and (3) to examine the consequences of the role performance of management for the implemention phase of the process of change. In our deliberations about the most efficacious means to pursue these objectives, we decided, largely because of budgetary constraints, to undertake an intensive field study of one elementary school whose faculty could be anticipated to hold positive attitudes toward educational change. We also concluded that the research design should include five additional specifications.

First, data would need to be obtained from staff members of a school involved in an effort to institute planned change that indicated their attitudes, performance, and social relationships at different points in time. More specifically, data would be required that covered a span of time that began with the period just prior to the introduction of an innovation into the school, included the periods of time when it was introduced and when efforts were first made to implement the innovation, and that ended at the point in time when a "fair" assessment could be made of the extent to which the innovation had been implemented. This methodological specification was viewed as a prerequisite because we wanted to obtain a detailed description of the organizational dynamics that occurred after the introduction of a major innovation into an educational organization.

Second, the study should be so designed that we could examine the research issues in a natural, rather than an artificial or contrived, setting. Third, procedures should be used that would permit us to observe the performance and reactions of members to a proposed organizational change as unobtrusively as possible. Fourth, the field procedures used should permit the development of rapport between the observer and the observed that could be maintained over a relatively lengthy time period. Fifth, the research strategy should make provision for the use of a variety of techniques for obtaining data. We anticipated that, in addition to observing the performance of individuals and of groups, we also would need to conduct formal and informal interviews, to request teachers to complete a set of questionnaires, and to analyze public and private documents. We believed that a variety of techniques would be required not only to gather different types of relevant information, but also to obtain information to check the reliability of data.

These specifications resulted in our use of the case study (Goode and Hatt, 1952) or field study method. This method is designed: "to utilize to the full the advantages of seeing the situation as a whole and of attempting to grasp fundamental relationships. From this . . . can come the insights which can furnish the hypotheses for later, more detailed, quantitative study" (Katz et al., 1953, p. 75). The case study method[2] was selected becauss it provided a strategic way to explore the complex organizational problem we proposed to study; it permitted us to carry out in-depth observations of the several aspects of the dynamics of an effort to institute planned change into an organization; it also made provision for the use of a variety of data-gathering methods, a desideratum for our inquiry.

Selection of the School

In September 1966 members of the project staff were engaged in exploratory talks with leading educational administrators in large cities in New England about the possibility of conducting intensive

---

[2] For detailed discussions of the case study method, see Lipset et al. 1956; Scott, 1965.

case studies of elementary schools in slum areas characterized by
high and low "academic productivity." During one of these meetings the director of a Bureau of Educational Change in a big-city
school system informed us that to his knowledge there were no
elementary schools in the ghetto in his community that were characterized by high academic performance. However, he mentioned
that large-scale organizational innovations were under consideration
for schools under the control of his office and expressed considerable interest in understanding more about the process of educational
change.

We indicated our strong interest in this problem and noted that
intensive and sustained examinations of the way school personnel
respond to major educational innovations would be of value both
to educators and social scientists interested in the process of
planned organizational change. The director assured us of his full
support and the likely cooperation of his staff if we wanted to
carry out such a case study in the elementary school under his
jurisdiction. He also stated his belief that the approval of the superintendent of schools for such a research project could be obtained.
In addition, from the director's description of the Cambire Elementary School it appeared to be small enough to conduct an intensive
and sustained study. The final decision to conduct the study was
made in the middle of October, 1966.

Securing Formal Administrative Permission for the Study

Social scientists who wish to conduct studies in school settings
often meet initial resistance from educational administrators. We
did not encounter this problem since, as noted, the director of the
Bureau of Educational Change had a strong interest in and positive
orientation to the proposed study from the outset. Several informal
meetings were held with him and his top-level assistants prior to the
initiation of field work activities. In these sessions we discussed the
general strategy we proposed to use in carrying out the inquiry and

the kinds of information that we needed to obtain. These meetings also provided an opportunity for the administrators and our staff to explore issues such as the amount of time required to carry out data-collection procedures, the type of cooperation that we would need from them, and the value of the study for the school system. In addition, they allowed us to obtain a great deal of preliminary information about the characteristics of the pupils and of the staff at Cambire, the nature of the current educational program, and the salient features of the neighborhood in which the school was located.

The following set of tentative agreements were arrived at during these meetings: (1) in order to minimize disruption of school activities, only one member of the project staff would be used as the fieldworker in the school; (2) he would be permitted to remain at the school for as long as we felt it necessary to obtain the data required to complete the study; (3) we could use whatever data-collection methods we felt appropriate to study the process of organizational change — provided that they would not interfere with the operation of the school; (4) the role of the fieldworker would be that of an observer and not that of an advisor or evaluator; (5) we would share the results of our inquiry with the director of the bureau; and (6) the final report would be written in such a manner that it would assure the anonymity of the school and its personnel.

Letters formalizing these agreements were sent to the associate superintendent of the school system and to the director of the Bureau of Educational Change (see Appendix B-1) on October 21, 1966. Shortly thereafter, we received notice that the central administration and the director of the bureau had officially approved the project.

Gaining Entry into the School

We were concerned with two major problems in our consideration of the strategy to employ in introducing the study and fieldworker to the teachers at Cambire. The first was how to minimize the possibility that they would perceive the fieldworker as an agent of the administration. The second was how to overcome obstacles to which he might be exposed as a consequence of the strong negative feelings of the teachers to an inquiry conducted at the school during the preceding summer.

In view of our limited knowledge at this time about Cambire, we decided that the best course of action would be to explore probable consequences of several alternatives for entry into the school with its administrators. One option considered was to call a special meeting of the teachers at which time the project staff would be introduced and the objectives of the study would be explained. Another was to have the director of the bureau send a memorandum to each staff member about the study. It was decided that it would be wise to discuss the problem of entry with the three subject specialists in the school prior to making a final decision about the procedure to be followed.

The three specialists held the view that the most efficacious procedure would be for the fieldworker to enter the school with as little fanfare as possible, but with "inside" support. They volunteered to tell the teachers informally that a social scientist would be spending time at the school to study educational change and to identify problems facing teachers and administrators during this process. We accepted their recommendation since it had the merit of not only minimizing the possibility of initial teacher resistance to the inquiry, but also of maximizing the chances that the teachers would perceive the study as a sincere effort to shed light on a problem of importance to them and to their school system.

These tactics proved to be sound. The specialists did an excellent job of preparing the teachers for the entry of the fieldworker into Cambire; they accepted him from the outset as a student of educational change and displayed considerable interest in the study throughout his stay at the school. As data presented in Chapters 6 and 7 will indicate, the teachers exhibited little reluctance in expressing openly their views to him.

Defining the Role of the Fieldworker

Fieldworkers in schools or other organizational settings may
define their role in different ways, for example, as a participant or a
nonparticipant observer. In view of the nature and the amount of the
data required, we decided that the fieldworker should adopt the role
of a nonparticipant observer for two reasons; first, because it would
minimize the effects of the fieldworker's behavior on what transpired in the school during his field-work activities;[3] and, second,
because it would place minimum constraints on his activities in the
school.

A sustained effort was made to minimize, as much as possible, the
effects of the fieldworker on the operation of the school. For example, since the assistant director of Cambire who was responsible for
the day-to-day management of the school was in a strategic position
to influence teacher attitudes and behavior, we decided not to interview him formally during the field-work stage of the study, but to
wait until afterward, in order to avoid the possibility that our questions might lead him to do things differently than he intended. This
decision was made because we did not wish to influence the organization's "natural processes." In spite of all of our precautions, however,
we were not completely successful in eliminating the fieldworker's
effect on events that occurred at Cambire as is evidenced by the two
following examples. During an informal conversation between the
fieldworker and three teachers shortly after his arrival at Cambire,
one teacher complained that the director of the Bureau of Educational Change infrequently visited the school. The two other teachers
agreed with this complaint, but none of them volunteered information about why the director seldom came to the school. To explore
this matter the fieldworker inquired, "Has anyone ever asked him
why he does not visit the school more frequently?" His question

---

[3] For a brief review of effects of investigators on organizations, especially
under laboratory conditions, see Barnes (1967, pp. 82-90).

resulted in one of the teachers' raising the matter with the director and requesting him to visit the school more often. The second example occurred at the close of a formal interview with a teacher. She informed the fieldworker that as a consequence of the questions he had asked she was now aware for the first time that she and the director had fundamental disagreements about some of the basic assumptions of the innovation that had been introduced into the school.

Although a nonparticipant observer should be expected to attempt to minimize his influence upon the individuals he is observing, he cannot avoid interacting to some degree with them. If he restricts his interaction with organizational members too greatly, they may well perceive him as odd, snobbish, or uninterested in them and, hence, be unwilling to provide him with the information that he wishes to obtain from them. The observer needs to establish rapport with those individuals who possess data he requires, but the line is a fine one between maintaining a "pleasant" relationship and one that is "too cordial." The problem is, as Scott (1965, p. 272) put it, "The observer's relationships with subjects may influence what it is he observes or the report of his observations." We tried to cope with this matter at our staff meetings in which the fieldworker's reports were continuously examined. These discussions were useful in articulating the feelings and the perceptions of the fieldworker and resulted in challenging his interpretation of events he reported as taking place at Cambire. These discussions frequently resulted in efforts to obtain additional evidence bearing on the questions that had been raised.

Establishing Rapport at the School

The fieldworker engaged in a variety of activities designed to establish and maintain rapport with faculty members of the school. As noted, we rejected the idea of the fieldworker's being formally introduced by the assistant director to the teachers because of our concern that they might identify the study as a project initiated by the central administration. Instead, we decided that as appropriate occasions presented themselves, he should introduce himself to teachers, individually or in groups, during his first few days at the school and explain the purpose of his presence by saying: "I'm here as an observer interested in understanding what happens to schools when they attempt to change, and to learn about the kinds of problems teachers face during this process." He emphasized that the inquiry was a university, not a school system, project by saying:"I'm a member of a university team engaged in studies of schools interested in educational innovations."

We assumed that the fieldworker would enhance his rapport with the teachers if he informed them that he was an impartial onlooker and one who would treat the information they gave him in an anonymous and confidential manner. His promise of confidentiality and anonymity was tested a number of times during the initial phase of field-work activities. During the first few weeks several teachers attempted to ascertain the views their colleagues had expressed to him. His response was that since this information was told in confidence, he did not feel free to disclose what had been said. Individual or small groups of faculty members also attempted to find out his opinions about many kinds of educational issues, for example, his orientation to teacher discipline and his assessment of new types of curriculum. The fieldworker always responded in a pleasant way that he did not want to evade their questions, but that he either had no firm convictions on the matter or that the issue was so complex that he did not feel it could be answered simply. He tried to give the teachers the feeling that he had no qualms about their statements or their behavior; he scrupulously avoided doing anything that could be interpreted as criticism of their performance.

These tactics seemed to work. After several weeks, efforts to find out his views about educational issues and about what other teachers had said were abandoned; moreover, most teachers displayed no hesitation in expressing to the fieldworker their candid feelings about their superiors at Cambire and their evaluation of the school. Many frank discussions about these matters were held among teachers in his presence.

The staff of the Bureau of Educational Change and the administrators of the school gave excellent cooperation to the fieldworker during the entire data-collection period. They granted every request we made, including such matters as arranging for interviews, attending staff conferences of the bureau, examining private documents in their files, and being permitted to conduct classroom observations.

In an effort to maintain good relations with the staff and to express appreciation for their cooperation, we permitted the fieldworker to be of service to them in ways that would not affect the study. For example, he obtained information about the anthropology curriculum at a local university for one teacher's daughter who was doing a report on this subject. He also volunteered to find out what accounted for the delay in the processing of the application of a relative of the assistant director for admission to a school of education in the area. Although he received several social invitations from the teachers during the months of field work, each was declined with the explanation that other staff members might obtain the wrong impression if he accepted; he noted, however, that he would be happy to get together after the field work was completed.

In view of the high degree of cooperation from the faculty and administrators at the school, these procedures seemed to be efficacious. However, as Blau and Scott (1962, p. 24) note, obtaining a favorable balance of obligations may have unanticipated consequences:

> . . . the observer can produce a favorable balance of obligations which motivates the members of the organization to cooperate with the research. But it should be mentioned that there is the opposite danger of having respondents too eager to cooperate, since this situation may also bias their verbal statements as well as their overt behavior.

Another danger is that the observer may accept uncritically the assessment of events of organizational members who are most cooperative. We attempted to minimize these possible pitfalls by being continuously alert to them and by obtaining maximum data from diverse sources to check our interpretation of critical issues involved in the inquiry.

Data Collection: Procedures and Problems

The design of the study necessitated three phases of field-work activities, each with a primary focus on obtaining different types of data. The first phase was concerned with a description of the culture of the school, its social structure and the role performance of the teachers prior to the introduction of the innovation (November 15, 1966) and up to the time (January 13, 1967) when efforts were begun to implement it; the second phase was designed to obtain as detailed a description as possible of the circumstances and conditions that had a bearing on the degree to which the innovation was being implemented by April 23, 1967, five months after it was first presented to the teachers; and the third phase focused on an assessment of the degree to which the innovation had been implemented by the teachers in late April and May 1967.

A number of techniques were used to obtain the data. They included: informal observations of the behavior of teachers and pupils in classrooms and of interactions between and among these groups, systematic observations of role performance, informal and formal interviews, self-administered questionnaires, and the analysis of private and public school records and documents. We now turn to a description of the data-collection techniques used, and the major methodological problems encountered, during each of the three phases of field-work activities.

Phase I: During the first month of field-work activities, a great deal of time was devoted to becoming acquainted with both the

teachers and their administrators and in developing rapport with
them. We decided not to observe classrooms in a sustained and
systematic manner during the early phase of the study because of
our concern that some of the teachers might seriously resent having
an uninvited outside observer in their classrooms for lengthy periods
of time. The development of rapport with the teachers was still in
its initial stage at this time and we were concerned that in-depth
classroom observations might result in the fieldworker's being perceived as a "snooper" from the central administration. Instead, we
decided to rely on the use of a more unobtrusive strategy during the
initial phase of field-work activities to obtain data about the culture
and social structure of the school and the teachers' role performance.

One aspect of our tactics focused on conducting two informal
and unstructured interviews with each of the three subject-matter
specialists to obtain their over-all perceptions of the school and of
the way teachers performed in their classrooms. A second was to
conduct informal interviews with each teacher in an effort to determine how they perceived their roles and to obtain data about the
normative climate and the social structure at Cambire. A third element of the strategy included engaging the teachers, specialists, and
administrators in informal conversations whenever possible about
matters pertaining to the division of labor among the staff, unique
features of the school, the sociometric patterns that existed, and the
norms of the school. A fourth aspect was for the fieldworker to ask
teachers nonthreatening questions about their performance that
encouraged them to invite him to visit their classrooms as an interested observer. All classrooms were informally observed at least
once during this period, and several of the teachers invited the fieldworker to visit their classrooms several times.

During this phase of the study the fieldworker usually spent
three days each week, randomly selected to guard against bias, at
Cambire. Most of his time was devoted to informal observations and
interviews. He also occasionally went to the offices of the Bureau of
Educational Change for meetings or informal conversations with the

director or his assistants. He usually arrived at the school by 8:30
A.M. and seldom left before 2:30 P.M.; he also frequently attended
faculty meetings at Cambire, held from 2:30 to 4:00 P.M. two days
each week.

Before describing the problems encountered by the fieldworker in
conducting informal observations and interviews, it is relevant to
present a brief description of physical characteristics of the school
that had a bearing on the way he carried out his tasks.

In 1962 when a local university assessed all school buildings in
the city they recommended that the Cambire School "should be
abandoned for school purposes in the next few years." Of red brick
exterior, the two-and-a-half story building had a total of eight classrooms, including one on the first floor that was allocated to the early
childhood program of the school system. Each room contained about
800 square feet of floor space. The rows of formerly bolted down
desks and seats had been replaced with new furniture, including movable desks, chairs, and work tables. In addition, each room contained
storage cabinets, movable bookcases, new equipment and a variety
of curriculum materials. Some rooms contained microscopes, type-
writers, and telephones. Although each room had four or five large
windows, the lighting for reading purposes was not adequate. The
school contained no gym or auditorium. The building's interior walls,
inside and outside the classrooms, were cracked, water damaged, and
discolored. Dark varnished woodwork and half dark walls against
light cream ceilings and half cream walls created "an uncomfortable"
contrast. The hard wooden floors were dark with age as was the dark
composition floor of the basement. The basement contained the
boys' and girls' bathrooms and an area, once used for "exercise
classes," had been converted into a part-time classroom. The custodian's office was also in the basement. The physical building presented a curious blend of the new and the old.

The small size of the school and its limited facilities made it
impossible for the fieldworker to establish a "home base" at Cambire — that is, a place where he could go to write notes, to maintain

records, or to hold informal conversations. The old building had a large 5' × 20' closet between each of the rooms and each had a window at one end; most of the closets had been converted into tiny rooms. One was used by the teacher aides and contained a telephone, a coffee pot, a mimeograph machine, work tables, and cabinets. The teachers took their coffee breaks here and, although the fieldworker found that discussions in the teacher aides' room were extremely revealing, he also discovered that it could not be used as a place where he could write up his notes or conduct private conversations. Another closet was used as the nurse's office. Still another was converted into a toilet for the children in the early childhood program that was partially housed at Cambire. After being in the school for a week, the fieldworker located a closet that was used as a storeroom by the art teacher. She offered it to him as an office, but shortly thereafter it was converted into a reading room for pupils.

Our inability to secure an office for the study at Cambire had both positive and negative effects on field-work activities, as is indicated by these observations in an early field-work report:

> Since there is no place I can call my own, I am forced to move around from a closet to the administrative offices, then to the aides' room and again to a closet or the hall. This circumstance brings me into frequent contact with staff members and results in many interactions that would not have occurred if I had a permanent place to stay. In short, I am forced to make "rounds" in the school and, therefore, come into frequent contact with the members of the staff.

> The lack of an office, however, is having negative as well as positive consequences for my field observations, especially with respect to recording them. Note-taking constitutes a difficult problem. I feel very uncomfortable in bringing out a notebook and writing in process-style what is happening during a conversation. This is because I feel that while writing I will be blocked from "hearing" certain things and also I may inhibit what might

be said. I, am therefore, making it a practice not to write down things during these informal episodes but to record them later. But then I find that I sometimes fail to record information of importance because there is no place to go immediately afterward and write down what has happened. I even tried going out to my car; but since the door to the school is locked I cannot get back in without ringing the bell each time.

The procedures adopted by the fieldworker to collect and record data after two weeks of these frustrating experiences, and used consistently throughout the remaining field-work phase of the research, were as follows: first, to spend as much time as possible at the school observing and listening; second, to make mental notes of events that seemed important for the study; third, to jot down as soon as possible after these selected episodes key phrases and statements in a small notebook; four, to use these notes each night as the basis for the recollections of observations and conversations. The expanded notes were later typed and filed according to date. Although these procedures probably resulted in missing some details, they appeared to be a reasonably effective way to capture most of what the fieldworker had observed or heard, and to record activities and happenings of relevance for the investigation.

During the first phase of field-work activities, the research team also examined a number of reports prepared by the educational staff at Cambire. One set of documents consisted of reports for the months of September, October, and November 1966 that the Office of Evaluation of the Bureau of Educational Change requested each teacher to prepare. The teachers were asked to specify the objectives of their classroom activities, the teaching methods they used, the types of instructional materials available in their classrooms, an estimate of their success in achieving their objectives, and the implications of their report for needed changes in the existing educational program.[4] A second type of report we examined was school newslet-

---

[4] Copies of reports prepared by the teachers were made available by the bureau.

ters that were distributed to parents. They averaged three pages in length and reported such things as planned field trips or those that had already taken place, the types of instructional programs used in certain classes, new supplies and equipment available to teachers, dates for parent meetings and the organizational structure of the school. A third type of document was reports prepared by the director of the bureau indicating his assessment of, and plans for, Cambire. A fourth source of written material that was of special value was the teaching schedules posted inside the main office at Cambire. The fieldworker used them as a point of departure in some of his conversations with the administrators, the specialists, and the teachers in his efforts to obtain a description, prior to efforts to implement the educational innovation, of the formal and informal culture and social structure of the school, the attitudes of teachers toward educational change, and their role performance. The information that resulted from these various data-collection procedures was analyzed to ascertain its consistency with respect to the issues under examination. The conclusions that emerged with reference to the internal and external climate for change at Cambire and the role performance of teachers in early January 1967, will be presented in Chapter 4.

Phase II: Although the catalytic role model had first been mentioned to the teachers in November 1967, efforts to implement it did not begin until the middle of January 1967. At that time the administrators instituted major shifts in the organization of the school day designed to encourage teachers' efforts to perform in accordance with the catalytic role model.

The fieldworker now began to focus his informal observations and informal interviews on "the attempt to implement the innovation" phase of the study. Although data collected earlier revealed that all of the teachers at Cambire were very receptive to major educational change, his observations and informal conversations with the teachers suggested that they varied in their initial response patterns to the innovation because of their feelings about the way it had been announced, the nature of the innovation itself, or both circumstances. His observations also suggested that the teachers did not have a clear understanding of the innovation and that during their initial efforts to implement it, they were being exposed to a number of additional barriers that were creating great difficulties for them. Moreover, they appeared to be receiving little help in coping with these problems from their administrators who had asked them to change their role performance. Our reasoning led us to anticipate that unless such obstacles to carrying out the innovations were recognized and effectively dealt with by the school administration, they would serve to preclude its implementation.

During the middle of February, we began work on developing a schedule to be used in conducting formal interviews with teachers that were scheduled to be initiated in the latter part of April. The schedule (see Appendix A-1) was designed to ascertain teachers' perceptions about the innovation, barriers and facilitators to their efforts to implement it, and to ascertain if shifts in their perceptions had occurred over time: when they first heard about the innovation, just before their first efforts to implement it, when they first tried to implement the proposed change, when they made subsequent efforts, and at the time that they were to be interviewed. In short, the formal interview schedule, which contained fixed-choice and open-ended questions, was developed to secure from the teachers their perceptions about the events that transpired over a five-month period in connection with the innovation, whether their feelings and perceptions about it had changed during this period, and, if they had, why they had changed.

We were aware of three major drawbacks in asking people to be retrospective about their experiences: first, they may be so far removed that poor recall about specifics may lead to faulty reporting; second, intervening experiences may modify original perceptions; third, the desire to be consistent may lead subjects consciously to distort their feelings. We believed, however, that the time lag was not

sufficiently long to distort in any appreciable way the teachers'
memories about the matters that we proposed to raise with them.
In addition, we felt that by asking teachers to be retrospective about
shifts in perceptions toward the innovation, such a task might serve
to sharpen the clarity of their reactions to their experiences. We
tried to allay any fears about inconsistency or failures of memory by
acknowledging these as natural and by guaranteeing anonymity and
confidentiality. Finally, we anticipated that the rapport that was
now clearly apparent between the fieldworker and most teachers
would also help to encourage honesty; while there were a few
instances of intentional distortion, the kinds of responses most
teachers gave reflected considerable candor and the recognition of
the importance they attributed to the research inquiry in which
they were participants.

Drafts of sections of the schedule were revised for content and
style during the latter part of February and pretests of the total
interview schedule were conducted during the first two weeks of
March with colleagues and several teachers who had been involved in
change situations at one time or another. Revisions in style and content were made on the basis of the results of the pretests and incorporated into the schedule. The final draft of the schedule used as
completed on March 15. It contained seventy-three basic questions,
some having as many as ten parts.

The pretests had made several things quite clear. First, data
obtained from responses to the schedule could provide a systematic,
comprehensive picture of an individual's perception of the "change
process" at different points in time and of circumstances that inhibited or facilitated their efforts to implement an organizational innovation. Second, if teachers' responses were recorded by the interviewer rather than taped, the interview would usually last between
three and four hours. Approximately a half-hour could be saved by
taping the interview. However, we decided that the interviewer
would record the subject's responses, rather than tape them, because

the pretests revealed that teachers tended to be less inhibited when the former procedure was used. Further, reliance on taping interviews could result in "losing the interview" because of poor reproduction or transcription problems. Third, the interview would have to be broken into at least two or more parts because subject interest began to wane and interviewer writing fatigue set in after an hour or so.

The administration of the teacher interview schedule was initiated on March 20 and was completed on April 13, 1967. All of the full-time teachers at Cambire were administered the full schedule; the early childhood teachers, the subject specialists, and most of the interns and student teachers were administered a modified form, since many of the questions pertained only to the regular elementary teachers. Data from the modified interviews were to be used to obtain other perspectives on events that occurred at Cambire.

During the week of March 13 the interviewer explained to each person to be interviewed why it was important to have a detailed, formal interview with them and also indicated that it would be necessary to hold two or more sessions with them. Two teachers joked about "being used as a CIA agent," and "what do you want, a life history?" Everyone, however, willingly consented to be interviewed.

While we recognized the importance of attempting to standardize the interviews, we found it impossible to do so with respect to the place of the interview, its length, and number of sessions. As noted, the school had no free room that could be used as a regular place for interviewing. In addition, teachers had only small chunks of free time available for interviewing; furthermore, not only did their free time overlap, but often when teachers were available, space was not. Scheduling the interviews was the *major* problem. After considering and dismissing a number of alternatives including using the nearby YMCA and employing additional interviewers, the decision was made to arrange interviews with the teachers when they had a block of free time in their schedules and when there was an available room that could be used for an interview.

The converted closet-reading room and the closet-nurse's room were favorite places. Occasionally the aides' room was used before school. When interviews were held after school, either the aides' room or an empty classroom was used. The student teachers were all interviewed at university offices in the late afternoons. Interruptions during the interviews conducted at school were minimal.

The interview sessions were scheduled during periods when teachers said they had free time that was long enough to allow us to administer complete sections of the schedule. Most of the regular teachers completed the interview schedule in four sessions of about forty-five minutes apiece. Some teachers required five sessions; others only three. No regular teacher completed the interview in less than three sittings. Because the schedule for the student teachers was shorter than the one used in interviewing the regular teachers, three sessions were usually sufficient for the former group. No session was scheduled for less than half an hour while some lasted nearly an hour and a half.

To develop and maintain rapport with the respondents and to make the interviews as objective as possible, the following procedures were used. During the first meeting with each subject the interviewer opened the session with a set of standard introductory remarks designed to indicate the importance and purpose of the interview, to give assurance of anonymity and confidentiality to the respondent and to establish rapport (see Appendix A-1, Introduction to the Interview Schedule). A time chart was placed in front of the respondent, explained, and referred to often during the session to specify the period of time under discussion. In later sessions the investigator opened the interview with remarks about the guarantee of anonymity and of confidentiality; he then presented a brief review of the previous session, and, using the time chart, identified the time period on which the questions that would be asked would focus. The questions were asked in a straightforward, neutral manner and each subject's answers were recorded in near entirety to minimize possible interviewer bias created by response selectivity.

Most teachers apparently felt at ease during the interviews. They responded to many "touchy" questions in a manner that indicated they were convinced of the confidentiality of the interview. There was little resistance to additional interview sessions. Theses experiences suggest that this aspect of the data collection was well received by the teachers. This conclusion is buttressed by the fact that a number of them voluntarily remarked that the interview served as a "soul searcher" or "a way of getting things off our chests," or "I enjoyed talking with you." No teachers were overheard discussing the contents of the interview. Some joked about its length.

Phase III: The final phase of data collection placed stress on systematic classroom observations; it began on April 24 and ended on May 12 (see Appendix A-2 for the Observation Schedule). During this period the fieldworker spent every day at the school full time except for the afternoons of May 2 and May 3. The description of the procedures used to determine the degree of implementation of the innovation during this time period will be presented in Chapter 5.

The teaching staff was also asked during the third phase to complete a personality inventory (Edwards Personal Preference Schedule[5]) and a questionnaire designed to obtain data on background characteristics, aspects of career aspiration, and job satisfaction (see Appendix A-3). In order to standardize the conditions under which teachers would answer the questionnaires, they were invited to lunch on May 3, 1967, and in the afternoon completed the questionnaires in a group session. After lunch we thanked them for coming, for their cooperation, and explained the relevance of this kind of information for the study.

Most staff members took about an hour and a half to complete the questionnaires. After they had completed them, some teachers expressed mild resistance to the Edwards Schedule which consists of 225 pairs of forced-choice statements about personal preferences. We

---

[5] See Buros (1965) for a discussion of the validity and reliability of the Edward Personal Preference Schedule.

were aware that this might happen because similar complaints were raised by two of the five people who were used in a pretest of the questionnaires the week before.

As in the case of those pretested, the teachers who objected felt that the Edwards forced them to make often "difficult," "unrealistic," and sometimes "ridiculous" choices. The pairs they felt to be especially ridiculous involved items designed to measure heterosexuality, one of the fifteen personality variables the Schedule purports to measure in addition to achievement, deference, order, exhibition, autonomy, affiliation, intraception, succorance, dominance, abasement, nurturance, change, endurance, and aggression. One teacher was so disturbed about this instrument that he refused to talk to the fieldworker at school for several days. Another failed to complete the job satisfaction part of the questionnaire, perhaps because of negative feelings about the Edwards Schedule. However, most of the staff did not complain and several even voiced feelings of pleasure about the challenge of the Schedule.

Collecting information from documents, daily observations, and informal talks at the school continued during this phase of the study, in addition to the systematic observations of the classrooms and the self-administered questionnairs. The final day of fieldwork activities was May 12, 1967.

On May 18, 1967 the members of the project held a private afternoon conference with the director of the Bureau of Educational Change to present him with some of the preliminary findings of the study, and to offer him a series of tentative recommendations based on them. The director welcomed this opportunity to discuss the outcome of our study and appeared to be interested in our recommendations.

In order to comply with the original agreements about anonymity and confidentiality to the respondents, several precautions have been taken in the preparation of this study. All names including those of the school system, the school, the change, and the participants have been masked. Responses of teachers that might readily be identified have been masked to further obscure their sources. Also, when references in magazines and newspapers which reveal true identities are used as evidence, they are referred to in general terms; specific references are not cited.

Summary

This chapter described the research methods used in our inquiry and the major methodological problems encountered in carrying it out. We first presented the rationale for our use of the case study method. We then described the circumstances that led to the selection of the school that was the *locus* of our investigation. We then reported the procedures that were used to obtain formal administrative approval for the study and to gain entry into the school. We also discussed the definition of the role of the fieldworker and the strategies he employed to establish rapport with the faculty of the school. We then presented a description of the various data-collection techniques that were used during each of the three phases of field-work activities and the way we attempted to resolve the major methodological issues that arose during each period.

4

The Climate for Educational Change at Cambire in November 1966

We reported in Chapter 1 that the strategy we decided to follow in order to ascertain whether there was any basis in fact for our reservations about the "overcoming-initial-resistance-to-change" explanation of the success or failure of the implementation of organizational innovations was as follows: we would conduct an intensive case study of an effort to implement an innovation in an organization whose members were not initially resistant to change. We reasoned that if our criticisms were groundless, then we should find that the implementation effort would be successful. However, its failure would offer support for our contention that a more complex formulation is needed to explain the success or failure of the implementation of organizational innovations. We selected the Cambire Elementary School as the locus of our investigation because it was a laboratory school and we assumed that teachers in this type of school would be likely to accept educational change. Since this was an assumption that could be empirically tested, we felt it important to obtain data bearing on it. In this chapter we shall inquire whether our empirical findings offer support for this assumption.

We noted in Chapter 2 that students of planned organizational change have suggested that conditions in the external environment of organizations may have an important influence on the extent to which innovations will be successfully implemented. We therefore also shall present data on conditions external to the school that could affect the implementation of the catalytic role model.

In addition to reporting data about conditions within and outside of the school at the time the catalytic role model was first presented to the teachers, we also shall present some historical information about the school that had a bearing on the establishment of Cambire as a laboratory school.

In the final part of the chapter, we shall present our findings about the type of role performance exhibited by teachers in November 1966, prior to the introduction of the innovation. These data were obtained through the use of the essentially unobtrusive techniques described in Chapter. 3.

Conditions External to the School

Community Attitudes toward Educational Change

The Cambire School was located in the central city of an eastern metropolitan area of the United States that contained a number of affluent suburbs. Like other urban complexes, this region had been confronted with serious financial, housing, and transportation problems. Moreover, a number of its major social and economic ills were in part attributable to ethnic and racial antagonisms and the flight of the white middle class from, and the migration of predominantly lower-class southern Negroes to its central city.

The Cambire School was embedded in a district of the central city where the rates of in- and out-migration were extremely high. Prior to World War II nearly all of its residents were white; in 1967,

60 percent of its 60,000 inhabitants were Negroes. In that same year the district had the highest incidence of welfare and aid-to-dependent-children cases of all areas in the city; it was also characterized by extremely high rates of criminal arrest, of unemployment, and of school dropouts compared to other sections of the city.[1]

Since the early 1960's, politically active Negro citizens in this part of the community had been centrally involved in the civil rights movement and had pressured city officials for improved conditions in housing, jobs, and social welfare. They also had expended great effort in attempts to obtain new schools for black children and to improve the quality of education in ghetto schools. They criticized the board of education and its administrators on many grounds: their failure to take steps to improve the average achievement test scores of students in the system which were below national norms, their lack of concern about the small percentage of students who went on to college, and the slow pace of the school building program. They also had been upset by the failure of their school system to introduce educational innovations found in surrounding suburbs and in other cities. A number of Negro leaders had chastised the school board for its unwillingness to deal with, or even recognize, de facto segregation in its schools, and some had contended that arguments about school integration and busing only served to direct attention away from the severe educational shortcomings of the system as a whole. Through activities such as picketing and public confrontations with school officials, they had been persistent in their demand for school reform.

The Response of the School System: Commitment to Educational Change

In 1965, the school board and superintendent publicly recognized and expressed a willingness to attempt to deal more effectively with

---

[1] Taken from official city statistics.

the problem of educating lower-class children as well as of improving the learning of all students. In a joint statement they outlined plans to use the Title I and III funds available to them through the Elementary and Secondary Educational Act for these ends:

> The basic problem and the basic challenge of education is the continued revitalization of the entire educational process — not only new school buildings and new sources of funds but a whole new look at what goes on in our schools and a full-scale attempt to produce new and better ways for teachers to teach and children to learn. . . . For the first time in many years sufficient funds are available to begin a major attack on the problems of education in a large urban center . . . we intend to take full advantage of this unparalleled opportunity. We feel that the immediate problem divides itself into two quite complementary parts. The first of these is a concentrated assault on the problems of education for the most disadvantaged children of the city, both Negro and white. This is largely a matter of doing the very best job that funds and the state of our present knowledge permit. The second part of the problem is the task of learning how to do the job better. For this part of the problem nothing less than a major commitment to innovation will do. We intend that the primary emphasis of our innovative efforts will again be on the educational problems of disadvantaged children, for it is here that the problems are most pressing and our knowledge the least secure. We feel also, however, that our answers to the problems of the disadvantaged will lead us quite rapidly to many educational innovations that are applicable to all . . . children. We thus intend that the commitment to innovation be a general commitment to the improvement of education for all.[2]

The commitment of the top school officials to change is underscored in the same document which reported that the large grant of federal money which the school system was awarded would be used to establish and develop two new departments, one of which was designed to promote innovation in the system:

---

[2] Taken from a school system memorandum.

We have established within the school system two new agencies
which will be directly responsible for enriched education and
innovation. These are the Department of Compensatory Education, which has the operational responsibility for the enriched
programs for disadvantaged children, and the Bureau of Educational Change, which holds the primary responsibility for overall planning and for the operation of innovative programs in the
system. . . . We feel that these two departments will together be
able to mount a concentrated and innovative attack on the problems of education of disadvantaged children and thus take a large
first step in the continuing process of revitalizing [our] schools.

The Bureau and the Cambire School

The bureau was charged with the responsibility of developing and
administering laboratory schools that would focus on improved
means of educating children, primarily "disadvantaged" students,
from preschool through high school. These schools were assigned
the task of developing and testing new programs and materials that
could then be diffused to other schools in the system. They were
also expected to serve as training centers for both teachers and
administrators:

> In order to begin and carry on a large-scale program of educa-
> tional innovation in the education of disadvantaged children, we
> are in the process of establishing a number of laboratory schools
> in which promising existing programs can be explored and in
> which new programs can be developed . . . [they] will also serve
> as a training ground for teachers and administrators so that suc-
> cessfully tested programs can be spread to other schools when
> adapted for use in differing educational situations. . . . Located
> in an area representing the most pressing social, economic, and
> educational problems . . . , an integral part of the school system.
> . . . [they] will be designed and administered by the Bureau of
> Educational Change in cooperation with community agencies
> and people in the disadvantaged areas.[3]

---

[3] Taken from a school system document.

The personnel of the laboratory schools included a central staff and field staffs of varying size for early childhood, elementary, junior high, and senior high levels. The central staff was headed by the director of the bureau, Mark Williams, who was directly responsible to the superintendent's office. The director's central office staff included a coordinator of innovative programs, a program analyst, a research specialist for both measurement and evaluation, an office manager, and several secretaries. The central staff, physically separated from the field staffs, was located in an old building in the district, and the junior high and high school staff were both located in the same school. Cambire housed the elementary staff and a small part of the early childhood staff. The remainder of the early childhood staff was located in another elementary school building. Each field staff was directed by an assistant directly responsible to the director of the bureau. At the time the study was initiated, Cambire School was the only laboratory school operating on a full-time basis.

The part the director played in creating the bureau and the laboratory schools and the rationale for their development were described in his own words as follows:

> I . . . talked in early 1965 to the superintendent. . . . He had been elected on what to a lot of people in the city looked like a reform platform; he had a lot of ideas about recruiting teachers outside the area and opening up the school system to outside influences. . . . He proceeded to describe his difficulties in getting change going in the school system. . . . It became clear to me and subsequently to him that one reason he was in such difficulty was, as he said, because he simply had no mechanism in his system for coping with change; he knew that there were changes coming, he knew that the system had to change but he was uncertain about how to go about it; and he was on top of a system that simply had no way to change, and certainly no way of coping with any kind of radical change . . . but he did want to introduce some changes and he was having a deuce of a time figuring out how to do it. . . . I said to him that he needed to create a mechanism, an office for research and development and particularly to set up a

subsystem for experimentation. . . . The order finally was generated to plan for a grant, so I left my position and came in to work
full time on it, and getting this office set up. . . . What we [I] did
was to determine what a subsystem, an office of research and
development might be . . . the Bureau of Educational Change was
created. . . . We developed a proposal which said that about 20
percent or about $800,000.00 of Title I should be put into R and
D, and into the support of the bureau and laboratory schools. . . .
The general plan was that the office would work directly under
the superintendent. . . . Now the purpose of this laboratory
school part was to come up with new ways of doing things, to
experiment with new curriculum materials, new ways of organizing classrooms, new ways of organizing teachers, we had a
pretty broad mandate . . . the lines of authority run from the
school to the bureau and on up, so that we're in charge of the
school.

The Director of the Bureau: An Outside Change Agent

The director of the bureau had been described as an "outsider in
a system administered by civil servants who came up through the
ranks" and a "former journalist who has been associated with an
independent, curriculum development firm, and a well-known foundation working on school architecture and equipment."[4] Many educators believed that he had been instrumental in helping the school
system obtain federal funds and in introducing new ideas and curriculum materials into the schools. However, some black parents
viewed him and the bureau as deterrents to fundamental educational
change because they wanted an immediate major overhaul of the
system; furthermore, a group of militant liberal whites considered
Mark Williams as "a patsy" for the system because of his willingness
to work with officials whom they believed had shown little interest
in educational innovations in the past.[5]

---

[4] Taken from a magazine article.

[5] Taken from a newspaper article.

Mark Williams' views about the need for major change and many of the problems of educational reform are reflected in an excerpt from an article he wrote about new curricula prior to his appointment as bureau chief:

> Evaluation, teacher recruitment and training, the continuing development of new programs, further research into how people learn, all of these enormously important tasks depend upon the creation of a viable and permanent system of educational research and development that is an integral part of the larger American educational system. The current wave of reform is not the first that has hit American education. The deplorable history seems to be a burst of reform followed by twenty-five years of stagnation followed by another go at bringing things up-to-date. This is an exceedingly wasteful process. . . . Whatever particular solutions are eventually arrived at, they will in the final analysis be largely a matter of American education facing up to what may be the distinguishing characteristic of our age.

In summary, a number of external conditions which, it could be argued, would tend to facilitate rather than block the acceptance of organizational change, were present at Cambire at the time the catalytic role model was first presented to the teachers. These included a positive orientation to change on the part of both parents and top school officials, their recognition of the need for upgrading the performance of the school, and the employment by the higher administration of an outside change agent whose responsibilities included the establishment of innovative laboratory schools, one of which was Cambire.

Conditions Internal to the School

In the middle of November, the time at which the catalytic role model was first mentioned to the teachers, our data indicated that the normative climate of the school placed great emphasis on the need for educational change and that the teaching staff was receptive to educational innovations. Prior to presenting the findings that led us to these conclusions, it is relevant to report what we discovered about the orientation to change at Cambire in earlier years.

The Normative Climate toward Educational Innovation

Cambire Prior to 1962: The school was built at the turn of the century. An elderly teacher in the school system who had been a pupil at Cambire in the 1920's noted that "for nearly forty years it served a Jewish neighborhood almost exclusively." However, by the late 1940's the residents in its school neighborhood were nearly all lower-class Negroes as a result of in- and out- migrations. There was little turnover in the staff that taught its Negro pupils during the 1950's and early 1960's. The school was traditionally organized; that is, Cambire during this period was a tightly controlled graded school with self-contained classrooms. It followed closely a standard curriculum developed for all elementary schools in the system by the higher administration. Sally Jones, the woman who served as principal of Cambire at that time recalled what the school was like:

> Community-school-home relations were excellent, we had a great deal of contact with the home between 1950 and 1962. . . . I've always felt that children need forms of excellence. We have to direct them in their appearance and expectations, how they look, talk, act. We can't allow the children to run the school nor degenerate it. We are judged according to these things.

In further describing the school, she stated:

> Excellent work was being done here during these years, but without all this "bally hoo"! . . . I *also* had strong rapport with the community! . . . We had a newsletter for parents and the Community Council was involved in our activities to a great extent.

After showing the interviewer a folder she had kept on the reading

scores of children at Cambire when she was principal, she stated:
"They were learning how to read very well under the old system!"
The former principal also stressed her belief in the traditional
approach to education and alluded to her own effectiveness in using
it at Cambire:

> Teachers, I am convinced, have a responsibility to teach civic and
> moral virtues. . . . Between 1950 and 1960 we had almost no
> teacher turnover; we had a stable faculty; most had their master's
> degrees and at least five years' experience. . . . I felt that we had
> a team and teachers who knew the parents. It was a real neighbor-
> hood school. We had self-contained classrooms. We used film-
> strips, opaque projectors, went on bus rides to airports, aquari-
> ums, took train rides. We had field trips for all grades [K-4, 200
> children] to the pond and several museums. . . . We used these
> trips as tools for citizenship, put great stress on manners in addi-
> tion to the learning of the academic materials . . . a lot of people
> think that these things aren't important anymore; I don't think
> they are right.

An interview with the custodian who had worked at Cambire for
the previous twelve years also provided data about the school's traditional orientation prior to 1965. When he was asked, "What was
it like around here when Sally Jones was in charge?" he responded
with strong feelings, and at first in a low, hushed tone:

> Oh, when Sally Jones was principal you could hear a pin drop;
> she came in every morning *exactly* at the same time. I could hear
> her footsteps to her room. . . . She knew when a kid was coming
> down or going up those stairs; she knew where every kid was
> going to and coming from . . . she was strict but very fair! She
> really made those kids toe the line, and they learned! Kids never
> talked back; the teachers, all of 'em, were here for a long time
> and knew what they were doing. She saw to it that the shades
> *had* to be drawn exactly so; if they weren't, she'd let you know
> about it; oh she was a wonderful principal . . . classes were quiet,
> orderly; teachers made sure of that. . . . Now [disgustedly] with
> kids running around all over the place, this school is like a pigpen.

They talk back; but this is none of my business, I just do my work. [Then, as if he had not said this, he continued] they run up and down the stairs, I don't know, I don't think this is good, all these new ideas like those Ca . . . Ces, . . . [he tried to say Cuisenaire Rods, the interviewer helped him say it] . . . what can you do, things change . . . since she left everything has been in an uproar.

The custodian also described the complete turnover in staff that had occurred after the previous principal's departure and a much publicized conflict with parents. In his words:

Miss Jones was here for a long time, nearly fourteen years, there wasn't any turnover in staff . . . then when she left, in about [hesitatingly] September of 1963, Mrs. Smith took over as acting vice principal . . . she's at the Fields School now . . . then Mrs. Zingal came in and finally Mr. Jackson took over. That was the year the building was determined unsafe by the parents, when the school was put into another district and the parents fought it. That was when there was so much publicity about the school. By then all of the teachers who had worked for Sally had left.

A Period of Upheaval and Transition (1962-1965): Inspection of the yearly lists of faculty at Cambire during the period between Sally Jones' departure and the takeover by the bureau (1962-1965) supports the custodian's statement that there had been a complete turnover in staff. By 1965 no one remained who had been there in 1962. During the 1965-1966 school year the number of pupils attending Cambire had dwindled to less than a third of its previous enrollment, largely because of a conflict between parents and the school board over the changing of school district lines and the parents' belief that the building was unsafe. The director of the bureau summarized the conditions he found at the school when his office took it over:

It was a very small school, obviously, and very old. It was, I think, built in 1875; it's a typical sort of Quincy graded school, not in very good shape. We got it because nobody else wanted it! And nobody else wanted it for some very good reasons. . . . The new YMCA was being built next door, the parents of the kids in the school got very disturbed not only because they were disturbed in general about the city's schools but in particular because they thought it was very unsafe to send children to school through all the bulldozers and construction work; so they sued the city to have Cambire declared an unsafe school; they lost in the courts, so a large number of them took their kids out and voluntarily bused them out to another school. . . . When we arrived on the scene, Cambire which has a normal capacity for about 200 had about somewhere between seventy and ninety kids in it with a full complement of teachers. . . . Every time it got back in the newspapers one district would drop it and send it over to somebody else's district. It was a school really that nobody wanted . . . it was sort of given to us.

Cambire as an Experimental School (September 1965-July 1966): Shortly after the bureau assumed responsibility for the operation of Cambire in 1965, its director instituted a number of changes designed to create an innovative atmosphere in the school. One focused on altering the administrative structure of the school to reflect its concern with educational change. At the beginning of the year the director abolished the positions of principal and assistant principal at Cambire and established three new positions: administrative director, assistant to the administrative director, and instructional director. In the middle of the year Rudy Gault was named instructional director, and he was charged with the responsibility for planning and directing innovative educational programs at Cambire. His position was equal in formal status to that of the administrative director. The former assistant principal, Phil Jackson, was appointed assistant to the administrative director. A second change was the addition of subject specialists to the school on a full-time basis. Their responsibilities included identifying existing promising educational innovations that could be introduced into Cambire, proposing new educational strategies, working with teachers in establishing new programs, and facilitating their use of new materials and procedures. A third change was the enlargement of the existing instructional staff through the addition of teachers selected by the bureau rather than by assignment through the personnel office.

A fourth change, initiated later that school year, involved experimentation with a number of new educational programs and materials. These included learning games; eurythmics; a vocal, instrumental, and choral music program; a museum project on natural history; a reading program based on the integrated linguistics approach taught by a university professor; a teacher-training program for university graduate students; a teacher-aide program that used students from several nearby colleges. In addition, new types of materials such as modular blocks, clay, sand tables, pebbles, shells, sand, sawdust, room dividers, and floor-based blackboards were made available to teachers. The bureau also kept the school open in the afternoons so that a tutoring program sponsored by the local community council could be conducted for Cambire children and for children from other schools. The director also encouraged parents of pupils at Cambire to form their own independent parent-community group. By the end of the year the population of the school had risen to 190, near to its full capacity.

A special one-month summer school opened at Cambire during the latter part of June. Most of the staff who were on the faculty at the close of the school year and a group of educators from a nearby university participated in the program. Its major objective, according to the director of the bureau, was to develop innovative curricula and programs that would be instituted at Cambire in the fall. A decision had been made by the administrators to retain the traditional subjects, but to teach them in new ways. It was hoped that the summer school faculty would show how this might be done. The staff members from the university, however, were primarily interested in conducting projects related to their own basic academic interests; for example, one group wanted to compare the "in-school" and "out-of-school" language used by students to explore certain theoretical ideas in socio-linguistics. Another staff member from the university was concerned with the reactions of pupils to new educational experiences, for example, preparing and submitting recommendations to public agencies and writing one-act plays.

Data obtained from informal interviews and other sources revealed that conflict arose between staff members recruited from the university and the regular staff at Cambire shortly after the summer school opened. The controversy centered on which group was to have the final decision about the activities to be undertaken. For example, the instructional director had spent a great deal of time and energy developing a unit on the airplane that was designed to teach reading, mathematics, and social studies in an interesting way. The school personnel wanted to try out this unit during the summer. Their proposal, however, was rejected by the university personnel who wanted, as noted, to work on projects of special interest to them. In the director's words:

> . . . the summer of 1966 . . . really consisted of a bunch of interested university people coming in and working with the staff at the Cambire . . . working more or less as equals with the staff . . . and that was quite a fascinating summer. It started off very rocky with both sides quite misunderstanding the other much of the time. Although it was supposed to have been spent in developing curriculum materials for the coming year, most of the time was spent bickering. The school people felt imposed upon. Their attitude was "who the hell are these people who don't know anything about urban schools coming in and trying to tell us what do do?" And the university people felt fairly frustrated by these old liners. . . . By the end of the summer there were some very interesting things going on in the classrooms; it took quite a while, however, before any meaningful communications were established.

In discussing relationships between the professors and the teachers at the summer school, a member of the university group noted:

Rudy had begun preliminary work during the spring of 1966 on a set of curricula materials that were built around the theme of flying. He wanted the activities of the entire summer school program to focus on the theme of airplanes: reading, math, science, the whole bit. He had a fully developed plan. When the university people . . . arrived for the summer it was presented to them. Well, there weren't even any negotiations; the university people said flatly, "No!" We all had a lot of different things we wanted to try, and to adopt Rudy's proposal would mean we couldn't do any of them. Mark was so interested in getting outsiders involved in the activities at Cambire that even if he thought Rudy's idea a good one, he didn't support it; since it wasn't acceptable to the outsiders, the upshot of the whole thing was that Rudy lost. His program and all of his planning went into the trash can.

Despite the interpersonal strain that occurred among the faculty of the summer session, the climate of change and experimentation, which was initiated earlier in the year, was maintained; the staff continued to be exposed to many new ideas.

During the middle of the summer, the administrative director and her assistant accepted new assignments that had been offered them in the system. The director of the bureau, Mark Williams, decided to abolish the two vacant positions. He then appointed Rudy Gault, the former instructional director, as an assistant director of the bureau and assigned him responsibility for the day-to-day operations at Cambire and for supervision of its educational programs. He was placed in charge of curriculum development, supervision of personnel, program implementation, and the general administration of the school. Williams reserved for himself the right to make the final policy decisions with respect to the operations of the school. In a progress report submitted to the superintendent's office in July 1966, he stated: "The school will be under the immediate supervision of the assistant director-elementary, who will in turn, be directly responsible to the director of the Bureau of Educational Change." Rudy had been employed by the school system for fifteen years, first, as a science teacher, and later, as an assistant principal. During this period he had earned a master's degree and another professional degree. In 1966 he was working on his doctorate degree as a part-time graduate student.

Cambire in the Fall of 1966: During the first two weeks of November 1966, the period just before the time that the catalytic role model was first presented to the teachers at Cambire, we found that an intense change-oriented atmosphere permeated the school. All the teachers were trying out new curricular materials in their classrooms or were experimenting with new teaching methods. Each was attempting to conform to a normative climate that stressed the need for schools to institute basic changes in their educational programs and practices. The heavy emphasis placed on the need for change at Cambire is indicated by a statement of its educational philosophy in the fall of 1966 to which all staff members subscribed:

> The elementary school must always strive to keep pace with changing times. To meet the unpredictable situations of a rapidly changing society, the modern school must prepare children for the future through process-centered instruction. . . . The child must be the focal point of the education process. Teachers should be expected to collaborate and confer with ample time allotted for planning. New materials, new content, and new techniques should be continuously explored and re-thinking, based upon an evaluation effort, should become the essence of our teaching efforts.

Three subject matter specialists in language arts (John Helman), in math and science (Alex Wiley), and in social studies (Stuart Franklin), were assigned full time to the school. Each of these specialists had spent part of the previous year and all of the summer at Cambire and they had many ideas about ways to improve teaching and learning at Cambire. They were expected to "report to, and confer with, the assistant director in the determination and implementation of educational policy and also conduct classes and function in cooperation with the classroom teachers." All of the specialists were seasoned teachers; in addition, John had considerable previous administrative experience and had been involved in an earlier, minor educational change effort of the school system.

The teacher-pupil ratio was quite low: eleven full-time teachers served the 175 elementary pupils enrolled at Cambire in the fall. Only three of these teachers had taught at the school during the 1965-1966 academic year. The remaining eight were new to the school; they had been selected because they had expressed strong interest in educational change.

In addition to trying out new curricula and experimenting with novel instructional methods, the teachers also were attempting to treat children in a more egalitarian way. A number of the teachers observed that they appreciated the additional $1,500.00 in salary which they received for staying late two afternoons each week for staff meetings, and for the time they had spent during part of the previous summer on developing new curricular materials. they viewed their salary bonus as an indication of the administration's desire and interest in introducing new educational programs into Cambire.

The administration also encouraged informality in relationships among members of the staff. Most teachers interacted with their administrators on a first name basis. Teachers appeared to be at ease in their relaxed and informal relationships with each other, the parents, and the children. Teachers permitted children to talk to each other in the halls between classes, during lunch, and also during classes. Parents were invited to visit school at any time.

The pervasive normative climate for change was reflected in a teacher's remark: "You have to do new things even if they don't amount to anything good, just so long as they are not what you are used to."

Mark Williams estimated that the average per-pupil expenditure at Cambire was $1,500.00 per year, an amount nearly twice as much as the resources allocated to most of the other elementary schools in in the city. He summed up his view of the prevailing atmosphere at the school by saying that Cambire was a place where "change is the rule rather than the exception. . . . Cambire is a kind of a model of this in that the pressure there is for change rather than standing still, and you're criticized if you don't change rather than if you do."

We now turn to additional evidence that supported our assumption that the staff at Cambire was not initially resistant to organizational change. Teachers at Cambire volunteered to work in the school because it was an innovative school. A number of the staff members were recommended by their former principals as teachers who were especially creative or interested in educational innovations. Of the eleven primary and intermediate teachers at Cambire, eight joined the staff in the fall of 1966, two had been appointed during the 1965-1966 year, and one had been there since 1964 with a brief leave during this period. While two of the first-year teachers at Cambire had not been chosen by the bureau but rather had been selected by the central personnel office, the interviews with the teachers revealed that all of them had volunteered to teach at the school knowing that it was going to be experimental and that they would be expected to do new things.

All of the teachers expressed the conviction that there was a great need for educational change in ghetto schools. During our informal talks with them about why they came to Cambire, a theme that ran through their comments was their strong desire to try innovative ways of teaching children because of their dissatisfaction with the effectiveness of their previous efforts. Without exception all indicated that new approaches were required if teachers were to motivate ghetto children. Moreover, when we asked each teacher during our formal interviews whether they believed that there was the need for basic change at Cambire and schools similar to it, all responded, "Yes." The following succinct statements from several of the teacher interviews reflect their positive attitudes toward the need for change:

Changes are needed all over, not just specifically here at Cambire.

Few things which have been tried have worked. . . . Conant just recently said that we haven't found the way yet to educate this type of child.

Yes, there is a great need to try new ways; since the traditional isn't working, new ways are needed to improve learning.

As noted, the staff was in fact trying out new materials. The school was organized along semidepartmental lines with the result that a class could have one teacher for reading and another for math or science. All teachers were experimenting with new curricular materials. In addition, the basic curriculum included programs new to teachers such as the linguistics approach to reading as part of the Merrill Series, the Cuisenaire Rod approach to mathematics, the Senesh Plan in social studies, and the EDC curriculum for science. A more detailed discussion of the types of new materials teachers used will be presented later, when we describe the actual classroom performance of teachers during this period.

Even though teachers felt the subject specialists and administration gave them inadequate help in carrying out new programs, they still expressed satisfaction with their jobs because they were encouraged to try new approaches. When asked, "Would you want to stay next year at Cambire if you were asked?", one teacher replied: "I know it sounds crazy, but yes I would. There is a great deal of freedom to do what one wants, that's great! Most of us think this is great. I like Williams for that reason . . . he trusts us, and thinks we can do good things." Another teacher when asked, "How do you like it here at Cambire?" put it this way: "I think it's great; it's fascinating. But [it is] not for anyone; one must want to change, to learn, to pick up new things."

In short, the findings that emerged from our observations at Cambire prior to the introduction of the catalytic role model strongly support the conclusion that the staff was not resistant to educational change at that time, but indeed was favorable to it.

Before concluding this section of the chapter, it is relevant to examine data gathered about several background and personality characteristics of the staff and to consider the extent to which they might lead teachers to be resistant to educational change. Although there is a paucity of empirical findings on the extent to which social, educational, professional, and personality characteristics of teachers are related to resistance to change, a number of attributes might be assumed to be correlated with it. One could argue, for example, that a middle-aged, poorly educated staff whose members were on tenure and felt little need for achievement would be resistant to the introduction of changes into their school. On the other hand, a relatively young, newly employed, well-educated staff with strong basic needs for achievement might be less resistant to change. Data about the personality and other characteristics of the staff are summarized in Appendix C in Tables C-1, C-2, C-3, and C-4.

The data presented in these tables reveal that the majority of the eleven teachers were under forty years of age, were Caucasian, and came from middle- or working-class urban backgrounds. Over half of the teachers were married and were women. Most staff members had attended public elementary and secondary schools and private undergraduate colleges. All had earned at least a bachelor's degree, and most possessed either a higher degree, were working toward one, or expressed the intention of earning one. The majority of the teachers had taught for less than five years; most had not been employed in the school system for over four years, and had taught in no more than two of its schools.

The teachers' responses to the Edwards Personnel Preference Schedule[6] revealed that the majority of the teachers showed a

---

[6] Because of the general problem of measuring accurately personality characteristics, especially with paper and pencil instruments, these data summarized in Appendix C, Table C-4, must be taken only as suggestive. For a fuller discussion of the definitions of the needs from which these are taken, see Allen Edwards, *The Personal Preference Schedule Manual,* rev. ed. (New York: The Psychological Corporation, 1959), p. 11.

relatively strong need to do one's best (achievement); to follow
instructions and do what is expected (deference); to make plans
before starting on a difficult task (order); to keep at a job until
finished (endurance); and to experience novelty and change in daily
routine (change). The majority of the staff also demonstrated a relatively weak need to say witty and clever things (exhibitionism); to
be loyal to friends (affiliation); to argue for one's point of view
(dominance). The teachers were normally distributed on the need to
be able to come and go as desired (autonomy); to analyze one's
motives (intraception); to have others provide help when in trouble
(succorance); to feel guilty when one does something wrong (abasement); to help friends when they are in trouble (nurturance); and to
attack contrary points of view (aggression). Most teachers fell between
the fortieth and seventieth percentile on consistency of response.

We interpret these data about educational, social, professional,
and personality characteristics of the teaching staff as not reflecting conditions that would interfere with staff receptivity to educational innovations.

The Performance of Teachers Prior to the Introduction of the Innovation

We have just seen that the teachers at Cambire were very receptive
to educational change and were trying new curricular materials just
prior to the introduction of the catalytic role model. However, it is
critical to note that the role performance of these teachers was still
fundamentally traditional in nature. In November 1966 we found
that the school day was programmed and scheduled into clearly
defined periods within which teachers were trying to inculcate a
specific body of knowledge and a number of skills to classes of
children grouped according to age-grade. The teachers were putting
all children through the same sequence of standard subjects. In short,
their role performance conformed to the traditional model discussed
in Chapter 1 on page 14.

As noted in Chapter 3, we used various kinds of observational procedures to obtain information about the teachers' behavior just prior to the announcement of the catalytic role model. The schedules of teaching assignments were posted in the main office and showed that the school day began shortly before nine in the morning and ended just after two in the afternoon with the ringing of the school bell. Our observations indicated that there was seldom any deviation from this five-hour school day; furthermore, no teacher questioned this pattern. Recess lasted from 10:30 to 10:50 each morning. The remainder of the day was divided into forty-five minute periods. Bells marked the beginning and end of each period, recess, and lunch. Common to most teachers' schedules were reading and mathematics periods every morning before recess. Language arts, science, history, geography, and social studies along with various craft subjects made up most of the remaining periods of the week. The children moved from room to room to take different subjects or to participate in various group activities.

The staff was organized along semidepartmental lines. teachers without completely self-contained classrooms were not responsible for teaching all subjects. Rather, there were three teams of three teachers: two primary teams and one intermediate team. For example, the intermediate team consisting of Fred Jackson, Stan Pollard, and Linda Miller all taught reading and math; Stan and Fred taught social studies, while Linda taught science. Stan was responsible for all the fourth and half of the fifth grade children, Fred for the rest of the fifth and all of the sixth graders. Faith Bailey, Louise Hamilton, and Maxine Green split up the first-grade children for various subjects; Ruth Johnson, Paula Keller, and Arthur Bradley split up the second and third graders.

Careful examination of written teacher reports made to the bureau, school newsletters to parents, and informal interviews with teachers and subject specialists reflect the staff's coordinated emphasis on the children's learning both a set of skills and a body of knowledge. In addition to many subject-oriented, innovative materials already mentioned, standard workbooks and approaches were in evidence in classrooms for various subjects. For example, many teachers were using phonetic keys, basal readers, and standard workbooks for reading. In mathematics, data showed that teachers were stressing the learning of the skills of addition, subtraction, multiplication, and division. Teacher reports revealed that some classes were also learning about geometry and algebra. The findings in the areas of science, social studies, and the various arts and crafts were comparable. Even though Cambire had built into its schedule a one-hour, Tuesday afternoon activity period during which children were allowed to select an activity of special interest to them (for example, art, creative writing, poetry reading, swimming, music appreciation, discussion seminar, reading, dramatics, ceramics, community walks, math clinic, reading clinic, science, and public speaking), once a child chose his activity, he was required to spend the following weeks on it.

A teacher-directed classroom clearly emerges from the observation notes of the field worker taken during informal classroom visits. The first abstract is from the notes taken on the classroom performance of an intermediate teacher:

> He was very loud about his direction of the class. They were having a grammar lesson and he was shooting questions at them, calling them to the board, pitting one kid against another; the class was the traditionally oriented, competitive-for-teacher's attention-and-rewards type. He could really stir them up. Children were up and down; lots of hand waving, lots of disappointment, lots of overt competition and disagreement between students. The lesson lasted about thirty-five minutes; he then gave them a workbook exercise to do to complete the hour.

The second excerpt describes a primary teacher's class:

> Her general approach to the children, well documented by my sitting in the art closet next to this room for a number of weeks, is to be extremely directive, authoritarian; she is continually

scolding and structures everything in a high pitched voice. As she
started today she gave me sheet number one for mathematics,
and turning around to the class she commanded: "Let's get out
our Cuisenaire Rods. . . . Billy, shut up! Sit up! Jackie, I want
you to stop doing that!" Three children arrived shortly from
another room, because of departmentalized reading. She began
asking the class to do a number of exercises with the blocks such
as building stairs and making trains. She then asked them to name
the color upon hearing the symbol, e.g., u for blue, k for black,
r for red, which they all did in a dull monotone. These were
morning exercises that were more like drills. This lasted about
fifteen minutes. She then passed out a work sheet. This happens
daily. And, they began working with rods in order to find out the
answers. She went around the room during this period helping
children individually. . . . This lasted about twenty minutes when
a messenger from the office came in with a note informing
teachers of a hastily arranged meeting during recess.

The last abstract is from a visit to another primary teacher's class:

She was a very quiet, methodical person; her class was also conducted in this way. She had three groups of readers; while working with the first group, the other two groups were doing seat
work. As soon as she finished drilling one group, that group
would go back to their seats and another would come to the
front board. The class was what one might term "traditional" in
that the teacher directed the activity, all children did the same
thing, in this case reading. Talking at seats was strongly discour-
aged. What was new was the actual reading approach being used,
i.e., linguistics. However, she is the only one using it. She likes
this approach because it allows the children to begin writing
sentences much earlier than when using Phonetic Keys to Reading
(PKR) and if supplemented by an organic approach to language
arts, she feels this would really get these kids going verbally much
earlier and probably will keep them going.

In short, the data gathered on teachers' performance in November 1966 showed that teachers at Cambire were serving as directors
of pupil learning. They spent most of their time and energy in trying

to impart a particular body of information, or a set of skills, to their pupils grouped according to age-grade within a total-school schedule of classes.

Summary

In this chapter we have presented a body of evidence that revealed that a very positive external and internal climate for change existed at Cambire, as we had anticipated, just prior to the announcement of the catalytic role model.

Externally, the parents and higher administrative officials had expressed a strong interest in obtaining improvements in the educational program of the school. The director was well known as an educational innovator and as a person who had strong beliefs about the necessity of educational change. He was given considerable autonomy in the operation of the Cambire laboratory school and freedom in selecting its faculty. He had attempted to secure a staff which was dissatisfied with the existing educational program offered to children in the ghetto and which had evinced a strong interest in educational change. Because of support by Title III funds, the financial and personnel resources of the school were substantially greater than those of other elementary schools. In addition to the teaching faculty, which had been enlarged, there were three subject specialists, student teachers, and teacher aides. Teachers received an additional payment of about 15 percent of their base salaries to compensate them for the additional time and energy they were required to expend as members of a laboratory school staff.

Internally, a basic norm of the school in the fall of 1966, as a result of various administrative efforts over a two-year period, was that teachers should accept and promote educational change. Moreover, data revealed that the teachers were not resistant to change, and in fact, were very receptive to educational innovation, as evidenced by a number of conditions that prevailed, including the following: they volunteered to teach at Cambire knowing that change was expected of them; they expressed very positive attitudes toward the need for educational change in ghetto schools; they were making efforts to introduce new materials and approaches in their classrooms; they were displeased about the amount of help the subject specialists and the administration were giving them in support of their innovative efforts; and in spite of this dissatisfaction, they expressed satisfaction about the fact that they were in a school where they were free to try new methods. The information we gathered about their social, educational, professional, and personality characteristics did not suggest that these characteristics would interfere with the staff's receptivity to change.

The evidence gathered about teacher performance in November 1966 revealed that the fundamental conception of schooling was basically traditional in nature. Although often done with the aid of new materials and programs, standard subjects were being taught by the staff to children grouped into classes according to age, with smaller groups formed within these classes for purposes such as reading. The staff and the school day were controlled by a master schedule. The basic objective of teacher performance in the classroom was typical of that in most schools classifiable as traditional, that is, the imparting of a particular body of knowledge and a set of skills to groups of children during regular periods each day through lessons organized and directed by the teacher.

Since we found that the conditions external and internal to the school were supportive of educational change, we concluded that Cambire was in fact an elementary school in which initial resistance to change was minimal in November 1966. But, also upon the basis of the evidence gathered and analyzed on teacher performance, we concluded that the teaching staff, while not resistant to change, was performing in accord with the traditional role model in November 1966. Let us now turn to our assessment of their performance in May 1967.

5

The Degree of Implementation
of the Innovation

Evidence presented in Chapter 4 suggested that a climate hospitable
to educational change existed at Cambire at the end of November
1966. Some social scientists have maintained that this circumstance
would tend to "predispose" the teachers to implement the new role
model announced at that time. To what extent was the innovation,
in fact, implemented in May 1967? This is the question we propose
to examine in this chapter. First, however, we shall discuss the rationale underlying the evaluation and the assessment procedures
that were employed.

Evaluation Rationale

Our definition of the degree of implementation of an organizational innovation, as noted earlier, has reference to changes in the
organizational behavior of members. We contend that even for the
most technological of organizational innovations, for example,
closed-circuit television, their introduction and presence in a school
provides no evidence about the degree of their implementation. We
maintain that teachers must exhibit new behavior patterns *before*
it can be said such innovations are actually being implemented.

Moreover, the implementation of the organizational innovation under examination, the catalytic role model, required not only that teachers perform many new tasks but also that they no longer behave as they previously did in their classrooms. Therefore, the assessment of the degree of implementation in May 1967 required gathering data about the extent to which the teachers no longer behaved in accord with the traditional role model and the degree to which they conformed to the catalytic role model.

We examined the degree of implementation of the innovation from two perspectives: (1) the *quantity* of time teachers devoted to trying to implement the new role model and (2) the *quality* of their performance during this period of time. The measurement of the quantity of innovative effort required assessing the proportion of classroom time that teacher behavior conformed to the traditional teaching pattern: teacher-directed, group instruction of single subjects in blocks of time. The measurement of the quality of their innovative effort necessitated assessing the extent to which nontraditional teacher behavior conformed to the new catalytic role model as indicated by a set of twelve behavioral indices that are specified later in this chapter.

In short, two basic questions were asked in the assessment: (1) To what extent did teacher behavior in the classroom in May still conform to the traditional role model that they had followed in November? (2) To what extent did their performance that was non-traditional in nature conform to the requirements of the new role model? Our assessment of the degree to which the innovation was actually being implemented was based on data secured to answer these two questions.

Before we present and interpret the data it is necessary to specify the kind of evidence that we decided would lead us to conclude that there was a maximum or minimum degree of actual implementation. If the evidence revealed that the classroom performance of all the teachers during the assessment period was consistently high on the twelve behavioral indices, we would then assess the degree of actual implementation as maximal; on the other hand, the degree of actual implementation would be assessed as minimal if it were found that most teachers were spending nearly all of their time behaving according to the traditional model. If it were found that the quality of effort that was made to conform to the new role model was high, but little time had been devoted to attempts to carry out the innovation, it would be appropriate, we reasoned, to judge such behavior as minimal implementation. Furthermore, if the quantity of innovative effort of most teachers was high but the quality of their performance was low, this too would represent minimal implementation in most cases, but not in this case. We reasoned that because the innovation involved a major change in role performance that had been proposed only six months prior to the assessment, we could not legitimately expect *all* teachers to be performing in accord with *all* the specifications of the new role model. But we reasoned that it would be possible for all teachers to be making maximal efforts to do so. That is, they could be continually trying to behave in conformity with the new, not the traditional, model.

For our purposes, therefore, we would treat such a finding as a successful implementation effort, although we were aware that it would not constitute an example of maximal implementation unless the quality of performance were also high.

Data-Collection Procedures

Two general ground rules were specified for the classroom observations in order to minimize the possibility that chance fluctuations in the daily classroom behavior of teachers and systematic observer bias would contaminate the implementation assessment: (1) the fieldworker must spend a number of weeks observing classrooms, and (2) he must conduct the observations in a randomized and unannounced order. The first was carried out by setting aside three weeks, from April 24 through May 12, for classroom observations related to the assessment. The second could not be carried out as easily. The observations of the classrooms by the fieldworker prior to the period of assessment and statements made by teachers during the formal interviews revealed that many of them were not devoting large blocks of time each day to efforts to implement the new model. Consequently, observations of classrooms on a completely randomized basis during the three weeks set aside for classroom assessment might not provide the fieldworker with the opportunity to observe adequately the quality of some teachers' performance in connection with the innovation.

To minimize this possibility, the fieldworker asked each teacher for his weekly schedule in order to obtain some indication of when the teacher planned to make efforts to implement the innovation. This information allowed him to rearrange his schedule of classroom visitations so that he would be able to minimize the possibility that he would overlook innovative efforts. He usually prefaced his query with the following remarks:

> I'd like to visit your classroom several times during the next few weeks in order to get a feel for the innovation as you see it and as we have talked about it in our interview. Can you give me your weekly schedule?

He also casually checked with teachers at the beginning of each week to note any changes in their schedules.

These procedures and the observer's presence in classrooms did not appear to have any significant influence on the performance of most teachers. This is not to say that his presence in the school had no influence on teacher behavior. That it did is evidenced by the following situations: (1) one teacher informed the fieldworker that another teacher told his pupils days in advance of the observer's classroom visit, "an important visitor will be coming in, and when he does you should be quiet, do not move around too much, and no fighting!"; (2) a teacher-in-training told him that one teacher gave her pupils explicit instructions to remain at what they were doing when the fieldworker visited the class unless they received permission from her to do other things. Moreover, during his visit to her class, this teacher insisted on talking continually to the fieldworker rather than interacting with her pupils; (3) another teacher revealed to the fieldworker, after he had visited her class several times, that she told the children about his probable visits and asked them to be "extra nice the next time he came." Evidence to be presented later indicates, however, that minimal implementation existed in each of these three classes; therefore, whatever the bias caused by the observer's queries and presence, they did not materially influence the teacher's performance, and, therefore, the findings of the assessment.

The following procedures for collecting data were used during the three-week period of observing classrooms. To assess the *quantity* of innovative effort the observer monitored all classrooms daily to determine whether or not teachers were making any efforts to alter their traditional role performance. This involved making daily rounds throughout the building to observe classrooms. Each round included a "spot check" for each class and usually took two to three minutes. The number of daily spot checks varied for each class; their frequency was determined by the activity the teacher was requiring the class to engage in and the extent to which the fieldworker sensed it would continue before a possible shift might occur. As many as fifteen checks were made on some classes and as few as five for others; overall during the three-week period nearly 500 spot checks were made.

To determine the quantity of innovative efforts made by teachers, we observed whether teachers were making "traditional or innovative efforts" during the spot check; we employed the following ground rules. If the teacher was directing the group as a whole, or requiring the students to sit at their desks and to engage in the same activity, this was interpreted as evidence that the teacher was behaving according to the traditional role, and thus was not trying to implement the catalytic role model.[1] Any time it was

---

[1] Activities like field trips and outside music lessons were interpreted as traditional behavior because they involved the whole group and no student choice.

apparent that the teacher was permitting the children to work individually, or in small groups on different subjects, or allowing them to move freely about the room, this was interpreted as teacher effort to implement the new role model, and thus, as "innovative effort." The fieldworker noted on a daily record (see Appendix A-2, pp. 236-238, which he maintained for each teacher, whether the teacher's behavior at the time of his observation reflected performance in conformity with the traditional or the new role model.

Extended observations in the classrooms were conducted to measure the *quality* of the implementation effort. Since the observer's very presence might have influenced teacher or student behavior, the following steps were taken to minimize this possibility. When entering a room the fieldworker made himself as inconspicuous as possible by finding the most obscure corner from which to observe. In taking notes he jotted down key phrases or events to help him remember afterwards what had happened during the class period. When the observation ended he would go to a quiet place in the building to complete the observation schedule (see Appendix A-2). First, he would write down as much as he could remember about the physical arrangement of the room and the interpersonal activities that had taken place in it; then, after reviewing all of the evidence, he reported his observations on the teacher's behavior on each of the twelve behavioral criteria listed below, using a five-point scale (from "not at all" to "completely"). Did the teacher:

1. Make the materials existing in the room available to students?
2. Arrange the room into work areas?
3. Utilize the room according to these work areas?
4. Permit students to choose their own activities?
5. Permit students to decide whether they want to work individually, in pairs, or in groups?
6. Permit students to move freely about the room?
7. Permit students to interact with each other?
8. Permit students to decide how long they want to remain at

a particular activity — that is, move freely from one activity
to another?

9. Move about the room?

10. Work with (as) many individual(s) or groups (as possible)?

11. Try to act as a guide, catalyst, or resource person between
children?

12. Try to act as a guide, catalyst, or resource person between
children and the materials?

These twelve behavioral indices used in evaluating the
extent to which teachers were making efforts to behave
in accord with the catalytic role model deserve further
comment.

Since teachers could vary on how well they performed different
role requirements, they were assessed on each of them. They, therefore, could vary in the number of the twelve criteria to which their
behavior would or would not conform; for example, a teacher could
"permit students to move freely about the room" and "arrange the
room into work areas" but not meet any of the remaining criteria;
another could conform to five or all of the twelve criteria. Each
teacher's behavioral profile on the quality of his innovative efforts
is presented in Table 5-9, p. 116.

These twelve criteria were selected on the basis of an analysis of
documents describing the new role model and as a consequence of
discussions with Mark Williams, the innovator who introduced it
into the school. It should be noted that behavior in conformity with
these twelve criteria would not provide a complete description of
the performance of a teacher who would fully carry out the innovation. For example, the criteria make no reference to whether a
teacher has a plan to control his movements in the classroom or
whether he "keeps tabs" on the activities of each child, nor do they
take into account whether teachers keep records of each child's
interests, learning, and accomplishments. We did not evaluate teacher's

behavior with respect to other aspects of the new role model restrictions. We believe that observations of teachers' performance employing the twelve criteria that were used would provide a clear picture.

The twelve indices vary considerably in their ease of performance. Allowing students free access to all materials in easier to comply with than arranging the room into work areas, while seeing to it that children use the areas of the room appropriately — for example, the science area for "doing science" — is somewhat more difficult; the most difficult specifications to conform to, we assumed, were to act as a guide or facilitator between children and between children and materials. The assessment was based to a large extent on a set of criteria that were less stringent than others that could have been used. Teachers were judged according to whether they permitted students to pick materials, subjects, workmates, to move around the room, and to interact freely. Actually, a more rigorous assessment would have required that the role performance be judged on whether the teacher as a catalyst not only permitted, but effectively encouraged these kinds of student behavior. Since it requires much less effort and training for a teacher to stand off and allow pupils to engage in a certain type of behavior than to encourage them effectively to perform in a certain way, the teacher ratings on a number of criteria will be higher than they would be if the more stringent encouragement specification had been used. The reason for the use of the less stringent basis of evaluation was a practical one: it would have been difficult or impossible at times to determine whether the teacher was merely permitting or actually encouraging. To guard against the possibility of penalizing teachers through misinterpretation of intent, it was therefore decided that the fieldworker would assess their behavior only on the basis of whether or not they permitted students to engage in different types of behavior. After each individual classroom observation, which ranged from thirty to seventy minutes, he attempted to find out whether the teacher(s) thought it to be a typical session.

Observations were conducted in eight classrooms: four primary classrooms, two regular intermediates, one special intermediate, and the art room. The fieldworker visited one primary, one intermediate, the special, and the art room each three times, spending on the average, two hours of observation time in each class. Observations were carried out four times in another primary room and the second intermediate room; nearly three hours of observations were carried out in each of these rooms. In the remaining two primary rooms, it was possible to schedule visitations that lasted an hour in one case, and one and a half hours in the other. In total, over twenty-one hours were spent observing, in-depth, the *quality* of staff performance with reference to its conformity to the new role model. During the three weeks devoted primarily to this aspect of the assessment, most of the fieldworker's remaining time was spent monitoring classrooms to assess the *quantity* of the staff's performance.

To obtain a measure of the reliability of the fieldworker's data would have required that another observer be present in classrooms during the period of assessment. This was not done for two reasons. First, at the time of the assessment visitors were continually in the building and classes; another observer would have added to the already high degree of resentment that we noted teachers had toward outside visitors. Second, we reasoned that an additional observer would interfere with the high degree of rapport that the fieldworker had established with the teachers during the earlier part of the school year. To check on the accuracy of the fieldworker's observations, we decided to use data from other sources, namely, data that we would obtain during formal and informal interviews with the teachers, teachers-in-training at the school, and subject specialists.

Data-Reduction Procedures

In order to treat qualitative observational data in a quantitative manner, it is necessary to translate, through a coding scheme, the raw data into numerical values. The following reports the procedures that were used.

The quantity of innovative effort made by each teacher was calculated in the following manner: the amount of time recorded in minutes that he spent each day performing according to the traditional model was divided by the total minutes of classroom time that were available to the teacher, and then this percentage from one hundred percent. "Available classroom time" was specified as 250 minutes; this figure was determined as follows. We subtracted a half hour for lunch and a half hour for recess from the total time between 9:00 A.M. (when school officially started) and 2:10 P.M. (when the bell rang for children to get their wraps to go home). Because in some instances the observer was not able to get complete daily pictures for every classroom, the percentages were adjusted by dividing the observed time devoted to the traditional approach by the total monitored time. In most cases "minutes available" and "minutes monitored" were the same. The data are summarized in daily, weekly, and overall percentages in Tables 5-2 through 5-8 for individual teachers and for the total staff.[2]

To demonstrate *how* the qualitative assessment was made for teachers, we will present abstracts of two in-depth observations made by the fieldworker of the Intermediate #1 teachers, who exhibited the greatest quantity of innovative effort in their classroom. Each abstract, following the form of the observation schedule (Appendix A-2), includes the fieldworker's general overview of

---

[2] Neither the art nor the special intermediate teachers were used in this analysis. The art class was scheduled separately for halves of classes at different times during the week. The children had to go to art whether they chose to or not. Moreover, the art teacher would visit some classes but at that time everyone would have to do art. Because of this, art activities contributed to the traditional approach. In the case of the special intermediate class, the teacher never had a schedule from the beginning of the year nor dealt with the children with a traditional approach. The field worker reported that the teacher seemed to consciously omit either kind of effort. The children were primarily watched during the day.

teacher behavior in the classroom during the period of observation and then his specific evaluation of teacher behavior on each of the twelve behavioral indices. Sketches made of the classroom for each observation are not presented here. Each sketch of the physical aspects of the room at the time of observation permitted us to note whether "areas" were apparent, the kinds of equipment that were used and the types of materials that were made available. After the two abstracts are presented, the procedures used to calculate an average rating for each teacher on the twelve criteria will be discussed in some detail.

April 24 Observation (11 A.M. to 12 NOON): The General Overview Two teachers were in the room with twenty-four children. The classroom was quite noisy, and small group and individual activities were in evidence. The two teachers allowed a number of children to work with microscopes on such things as human skin, hair, and saliva, permitting some to remain all period, others to leave early, and others to join later; up to eight children were involved at one time, at other times only two. Stan visited the group four times. Linda, a large part of the period (about twenty-five minutes), coordinated the efforts of four girls drawing a large map in connection with a social studies unit; at other times she "talked" to the two or three children who were either reading independently or working on math problems. Stan also walked among students to some extent, but did not make contact during the period with a large number (ten to thirteen) of the twenty-four children in the room. Along with the use of microscopes, reading, working on math, and map making, teachers allowed a noticeable number of children to engage in "gaming" — for example, playing cards, Peggity, and Clue were several of the activities. Neither teacher approached a hard core of seven or eight children who became involved in this sort of activity, and who did not switch from it while I was there during the observation. There were four boys who did not use any of the materials in the classroom and created a number of disturbances by playing tag, punching and shoving each other, and then running close to either

Stan or Linda to avoid being caught by the others. However, neither teacher tried to encourage them to become interested in doing other things. Stan, losing his temper twice, did send two of the four downstairs to the office the second time. The lunch bell ended the period.

April 24 Observation (11 A.M. to 12 NOON): The Specific Evaluation[3]

1. Neither teacher placed any restrictions on using materials available in the room; both teachers were therefore rated as high on permitting use of available materials.

2. The room was arranged into science, reading, and drawing areas, so both teachers were rated as high on room arrangement.

3. Both were rated as moderate on utilization of room. The science area was being used for science; however, both teachers allowed children who were playing cards there to remain. The teachers also permitted the reading area to be used for playing games and for children to talk about TV programs. The art area was in fact not used as such; the teachers permitted everything to be pushed back to make room for some of the card players.

4. Both were rated as high on permitting student choice of subjects. Neither placed restrictions on the children other than those who were "horsing around" and even then they were not stopped by Stan, except for two students who began a fistfight.

5. Both were rated as high on permitting students to choose with whom they wanted to work. However, Stan was slightly more restrictive than Linda; he talked to a number of students admonishing them to "do your own work," "don't ask him for help, do your own thinking." Linda, more passive, allowed the children to do what they wanted to do without comment. Neither encouraged children to interact in order to learn from each other.

---

[3] It should be noted that the original five point rating scales were collapsed for this analysis: 1 and 2 were set equal to 1; 3 equal to 2; 4 and 5 equal to 3. Therefore, in the discussion and statistics which follow 1=low, 2=moderate, and 3=high.

6. Stan was rated moderate on permitting movement and Linda was rated high, since Stan stopped a number of students from moving about whom he thought "weren't doing much" and were "bothering others," while Linda did not say anything with respect to these matters.

7. Because Linda did nothing to inhibit interaction among the children while Stan actually admonished a number of children who were interacting by demanding that they do their own work, and restricted others who were in his eyes "fooling around," Linda was rated as high on permitting students to interact with each other and Stan, moderate. Neither encouraged children to interact.

8. Again, Linda did nothing along these lines to inhibit the children while Stan wanted quite a few (seven) of the children to start working, especially those of whom he would say "they're flitting about from one thing to another" or "they're doing nothing to settle down to get some work done, this isn't just a play period"; Linda was rated as high and Stan, moderate.

9. Both teachers spent about half the time during the observation moving about the room. But, neither attempted to get to all children. The other half of the time they simply stood and watched unless some child came to them and initiated the interaction with a question or a plea for help. Both were rated "moderate."

10. Of the time spent moving about, Stan interacted more with different groups and individuals. Linda did very little. Stan was, therefore, rated "moderate," Linda as "low."

11. and 12. Stan was very restrictive; for example, at the microscopes he would issue directives such as "That's enough with the hair; put the slide with saliva on," "It doesn't take all day for you to look at the skin." He asked questions, but they were not of a probing nature. Linda was much more passive and didn't ask any questions to which children could react or which led them to ask additional questions. The teacher interaction with children did not indicate efforts to act as catalysts either between children, or between children and materials. Both teachers, therefore, were rated low on their

efforts to act as catalysts between children and materials or between children. The numerical equivalents for these ratings are presented in the first and second columns of Table 5-1. Stan is coded as "A" and Linda as "B."

Table 5-1 also summarizes the performances of Stan and Linda at three other points in time; it reveals that the behavior of each of these teachers was highly consistent at each of these points in time. We have selected the observations made on May 1 to illustrate their performance.

May 1 Observation (12:35 P.M. to 1:20 P.M.): The General Overview There were twenty-six children in the room; both teachers were present. The high noise level which the teachers permitted in class was at times almost deafening. Throughout this period nearly half (twelve out of twenty-six) of the children at one time or another, were pushing, tickling, shoving, feigning fighting, while there were five who engaged in these activities the entire period. This kind of behavior went "unnoticed" by both teachers. Most of the time the majority (seventeen out of twenty-six) of children were engaged in active conversation and game playing – for example, Spill and Spell, Rook, Peggity, without either teacher ever talking to them. Only one girl was observed reading a book during this period; neither teacher approached her. The three girls with the microscopes were talking about several TV programs they had watched the night before. A boy tried to put a plastic model of human anatomy together; neither teacher approached him. Three children seemed to be passing their time individually, but without benefit of materials; they were sitting quietly, alone. Stan was playing Rook with eight children, while at different times others were allowed to watch. The three girls working with Linda consumed most of her time. Most of the children were not approached by the teachers, nor did these children go to them except for nonacademic reasons – for example, "Johnny's pushing me, he took my box." The teachers did not concern themselves with the total classroom membership. Moreover, there was no interaction between the teachers at all. This innovative

Table 5-1. Profiles of Ratings for Intermediate #1 Teachers (A and B) for Each Period of Observation and Their Overall Ratings

Criterion	April 24 60 min.		April 28 60 min.[a]		May 1 45 min.		May 12 60 min.		Overall Rating	
	A	B	A	B	A	B	A	B	A	B
1. Make available all materials	3.00	3.00	3.00	3.00	3.00	3.00	3.00	3.00	3.00	3.00
2. Arrange room into areas	3.00	3.00	3.00	3.00	3.00	3.00	3.00	3.00	3.00	3.00
3. Utilize the areas	2.00	2.00	—	—	1.00	1.00	1.00	1.00	1.36	1.36
4. Permit choice of subjects	3.00	3.00	3.00	3.00	3.00	3.00	3.00	3.00	3.00	3.00
5. Permit choice in number of learning mates	3.00	3.00	3.00	3.00	3.00	3.00	3.00	3.00	3.00	3.00
6. Permit free movement	2.00	3.00	3.00	3.00	3.00	3.00	3.00	3.00	2.73	3.00
7. Permit student interaction	2.00	3.00	3.00	3.00	3.00	3.00	3.00	3.00	2.73	3.00
8. Permit shift in activities	2.00	3.00	3.00	3.00	3.00	3.00	3.00	3.00	2.73	3.00
9. Teacher movement in room	2.00	2.00	1.00	1.00	1.00	1.00	1.00	1.00	1.62	1.62
10. Interact with students	2.00	1.00	1.00	1.00	1.00	1.00	1.00	1.00	1.62	1.00
11. Try to act as a catalyst between children	1.00	1.00	1.00	1.00	1.00	1.00	1.00	1.00	1.00	1.00
12. Try to act as a catalyst between child and materials	1.00	1.00	1.00	1.00	1.00	1.00	1.00	1.00	1.00	1.00

[a] Blanks in April 28th observation due to insufficient data. Code: 1 = low, 2 = moderate, 3 = high.
[b] Average score adjusted for differences in lengths of observations.

effort ended abruptly when Stan (without consulting Linda at the time) yelled out over the humming class: "OK put everything away and get out your social studies books." The observation ended as the groans and moans of the class were subsiding.

Linda and Stan said later in the day separately that what I saw "was fairly typical, perhaps a little noisier than normal."

May 1 Observation (12:35 P.M. to 1:20 P.M.): The Specific Evaluation

1. There did not seem to be any restrictions whatsoever; children were permitted to go into cupboards; teachers allowed them to handle all materials in the room. Neither Stan nor Linda admonished any child for taking any piece of equipment or materials. Both were rated, therefore, as high on permitting use of available materials.

2. Both were also rated high on room arrangement. The room was arranged into corners—those with recognizable subjects associated were science, reading, and social studies.

3. Both, however, were rated low on utilization. During this period the one child who was in the social studies area was trying to put together a plastic model of a human; neither teacher suggested he go to the science cupboard to get a reference book. The girl who was reading could not do so in the reading corner because the teachers allowed three boys to play Peggity and two girls to sit and talk about TV programs in the same area.

4. Other than the children working with Linda and those playing Rook with Stan, the rest were "on their own," and did what they wanted. Moreover, Stan allowed several students playing cards with him to leave with no restrictions. Therefore, both were rated as high on permitting children to choose their own activities.

5. Neither teacher required children to do other than what they wanted unless, as it happened four times during this observation, their choice of learning mates resulted in some interpersonal problem; these groups were promptly dispersed by Stan to different parts of the room. Therefore, both were rated as high.

6. Both teachers permitted the children to move freely about as

they pleased — for example, one child who worked part of the time with some green plants was even permitted to go downstairs to get tubing and a bottle; he filled it with water and set up his plants near the window, leaving the room several times for such materials as paper toweling and sand with no restriction placed on him by either teacher. Neither teacher, however, tried to act as a guide for him. Both teachers were rated as high on permitting freedom to move.

7. The only time Stan concerned himself with interaction was when it resulted in a discipline problem — for example, fighting and arguing. Other than that, children were allowed to interact freely. Linda never put any restrictions on any child. Both teachers were rated as high on permitting student interaction. However, neither teacher *encouraged* interaction.

8. Since there were no observable restrictions placed on students shifting their activities the observer was led to rate both teachers as high on permitting student movement.

9. Stan remained at the card table during the total period of observation playing Rook (as a participant rather than a teacher — for example, "that's my trick," "put the card back," "you're cheating"). Linda worked all the time with three students on a social studies lesson. She would go from a map on the wall to the books they were reading, completely ignoring the rest of the class during the observation. Therefore, both were rated low on movement about the room.

10, 11, and 12. Since Linda spent all her time with three students on a directed geography lesson and Stan spent all of his time playing cards with several boys, both were rated low on trying to work with many students, on trying to act as a catalyst between children, and on trying to act as a catalyst between children and materials.

The numerical equivalents for these ratings are presented in columns five and six of Table 5-1. As noted earlier, the length of the observations of a teacher's behavior varied, for example, Teacher A in intermediate #1 was observed four times: three sixty-minute observations and one forty-five-minute observation. Therefore, we had to weight each separate rating for this teacher on a particular criterion in proportion to the length of the observation before calculating an average for him on that criterion as well as on the other assessment criteria. We did this by multiplying the rating made during the observation by the length of time he had been observed. Then we summed the weighted ratings for each of the Cambire teachers on a particular criterion and then divided this sum by the total number of minutes that the teacher had been observed on this criterion to arrive at his average rating. To illustrate: Teacher A, on permitting freedom of movement, had a sixty-minute rating of 2 on April 24, a sixty-minute rating of 3 on April 28, a forty-five-minute rating of 3 on May 1 and another sixty-minute rating of 3 on May 12; $(60 \times 2) + (60 \times 3) = (45 \times 3) + (60 \times 3) \div 225 = 2.73$. This average rating is recorded in Table 5-1 under the "Overall Rating" column for Intermediate #1, Teacher A. We used this procedure for all teachers on each of the twelve evaluative criteria; the averaged ratings for each teacher along with the overall school ratings are presented in Table 5-9. We obtained the overall school ratings presented in Table 5-9 by adding together all of the averaged teacher ratings on each of the criteria and then dividing by the total number of teachers used.

Findings

To reiterate an important point, this assessment focused on teachers' classroom behavior to determine the degree of implementation of the innovation. The line of reasoning was simply that the central thrust of the innovation, as conceived by Mark, was an entirely new classroom role for teachers. The extent to which teacher behavior in the classrooms conformed to the new model would, therefore, indicate the degree to which the innovation was actually being implemented in the school in May.

We present in Tables 5-2 through 5-7 the percentage of classroom time, both on a daily and weekly basis, that each teacher gave to efforts to implement the catalytic role model. In Table 5-8 we report on a weekly basis the proportion of time that the total staff devoted.

Table 5-2. *Amount of Classroom Time Devoted to Performing in Accord with the Traditional Role Model and the Catalytic Role Model (Daily, Weekly, and Overall Percentages for Primary Class #1)*

	Minutes Available	Minutes Monitored	Traditional Role Model Behavior (in minutes)	Traditional Role Model Behavior (in percent)	Catalytic Role Model Behavior (in percent)
April 24	250	250	250	100.00	0.00
25	250	250	205	82.00	18.00
26	250	210	165	78.57	21.43
27	250	250	175	70.00	30.00
28	250	205	205	100.00	0.00
Weekly Total	1250	1165	1000	85.84	14.16
May[a] 1	250	250	180	72.00	28.00
4	250	250	175	70.00	30.00
5	250	205	160	78.05	21.95
Weekly Total	750	705	515	73.05	26.95
May 8	250	250	135	54.00	46.00
9	250	250	205	82.00	18.00
10	250	250	175	70.00	30.00
11	250	250	145	58.00	42.00
12	250	220	175	79.55	20.45
Weekly Total	1250	1220	835	68.44	31.56
Overall Total	3220	3090	2350	76.05	23.95

[a]On Tuesday and Wednesday of this week all students were taking tests required by the school system in all its schools. For the most part, instructional activities were suspended during this period. Also, on Wednesday afternoon the teachers completed our questionnaire needed for the project. School was dismissed at noon.

Table 5-3. *Amount of Classroom Time Devoted to Performing in Accord with the Traditional Role Model and the Catalytic Role Model (Daily, Weekly, and Overall Percentages for Primary Class #2)*

	Minutes Available	Minutes Monitored	Traditional Role Model Behavior (in minutes)	Traditional Role Model Behavior (in percent)	Catalytic Role Model Behavior (in percent)
April 24	250	250	250	100.00	0.00
25	250	250	250	100.00	0.00
26	250	250	250	100.00	0.00
27[a]	—	—	—	—	—
28	250	250	250	100.00	0.00
Weekly Total	1000	1000	1000	100.00	0.00
May 1	250	250	250	100.00	0.00
4	250	250	250	100.00	0.00
5	250	250	250	100.00	0.00
Weekly Total	750	750	750	100.00	0.00
May 8	250	250	250	100.00	0.00
9	250	250	250	100.00	0.00
10	250	250	250	100.00	0.00
11	250	250	190	76.00	24.00
12	250	130	130	100.00	0.00
Weekly Total	1250	1130	1070	94.69	5.31
Overall Total	3000	2880	2820	97.92	2.08

[a]Teacher absent on this day.

Table 5-4. *Amount of Classroom Time Devoted to Performing in Accord with the Traditional Role Model and the Catalytic Role Model (Daily, Weekly, and Overall Percentages for Primary Class #3)*

	Minutes Available	Minutes Monitored	Traditional Role Model Behavior (in minutes)	Traditional Role Model Behavior (in percent)	Catalytic Role Model Behavior (in percent)
April 24	250	250	190	76.00	24.00
25	250	250	190	76.00	24.00
26	250	250	250	100.00	0.00
27	250	250	250	100.00	0.00
28	250	250	250	100.00	0.00
Weekly Total	1250	1250	1130	90.40	9.60
May 1	250	250	250	100.00	0.00
4	250	250	190	76.00	24.00
5	250	220	220	100.00	0.00
Weekly Total	750	720	660	91.67	8.33
May 8	250	220	160	72.73	27.27
9	250	250	190	76.00	24.00
10	250	250	190	76.00	24.00
11[a]	—	—	—	—	—
12[a]	—	—	—	—	—
Weekly Total	750	720	540	75.00	25.00
Overall Total	2750	2690	2330	86.62	13.38

[a]Teacher absent on this day.

Table 5-5.   *Amount of Classroom Time Devoted to Performing in*
Accord with the Traditional Role Model and the
Catalytic Role Model (Daily, Weekly, and Overall
Percentages for Primary Class #4)

	Minutes Available	Minutes Monitored	Traditional Role Model Behavior (in minutes)	Traditional Role Model Behavior (in percent)	Catalytic Role Model Behavior (in percent)
April 24	250	250	220	88.00	12.00
25	250	250	220	88.00	12.00
26	250	250	220	88.00	12.00
27	250	250	220	88.00	12.00
28	250	250	250	100.00	0.00
Weekly Total	1250	1250	1130	90.40	9.60
May 1	250	250	150	60.00	40.00
4	250	210	180	85.71	14.29
5	250	220	220	100.00	0.00
Weekly Total	750	680	550	80.88	19.12
May 8	250	250	250	100.00	0.00
9	250	250	250	100.00	0.00
10	250	250	250	100.00	0.00
11	250	250	190	76.00	24.00
12	250	250	250	100.00	0.00
Weekly Total	1250	1250	1190	95.20	4.80
Overall Total	3250	3180	2870	90.25	9.75

Table 5-6. *Amount of Classroom Time Devoted to Performing in Accord with the Traditional Role Model and the Catalytic Role Model (Daily, Weekly, and Overall Percentages for Intermediate Class #1)*

	Minutes Available	Minutes Monitored	Traditional Role Model Behavior (in minutes)	Traditional Role Model Behavior (in percent)	Catalytic Role Model Behavior (in percent)
April 24	250	250	130	58.00	42.00
25	250	250	145	58.00	42.00
26	250	250	250	100.00	0.00
27	250	250	85	34.00	66.00
28	250	250	85	34.00	66.00
Weekly Total	1250	1250	695	55.60	44.40
May 1	250	250	90	36.00	64.00
4	250	250	145	58.00	42.00
5	250	250	250	100.00	0.00
Weekly Total	750	750	485	64.67	35.33
May 8	250	250	150	60.00	40.00
9	250	250	190	76.00	24.00
10	250	250	90	36.00	64.00
11	250	250	205	82.00	18.00
12	250	250	130	52.00	48.00
Weekly Total	1250	1250	765	61.20	38.80
Overall Total	3250	3250	1945	59.85	40.15

Table 5-7. *Amount of Classroom Time Devoted to Performing in Accord with the Traditional Role Model and the Catalytic Role Model (Daily, Weekly, and Overall Percentages for Intermediate Class #2)*

	Minutes Available	Minutes Monitored	Traditional Role Model Behavior (in minutes)	Traditional Role Model Behavior (in percent)	Catalytic Role Model Behavior (in percent)
April 24	250	250	190	76.00	24.00
25	250	250	250	100.00	0.00
26	250	250	250	100.00	0.00
27	250	250	250	100.00	0.00
28	250	250	250	100.00	0.00
Weekly Total	1250	1250	1190	95.20	4.80
May 1	250	250	250	100.00	0.00
4	250	250	250	100.00	0.00
5	250	250	250	100.00	0.00
Weekly Total	750	750	750	100.00	0.00
May 8	250	250	190	76.00	24.00
9	250	250	180	72.00	28.00
10	250	190	190	100.00	0.00
11	250	250	250	100.00	0.00
12	250	250	250	100.00	0.00
Weekly Total	1250	1190	1060	89.08	10.92
Overall Total	3250	3190	3000	94.04	5.96

The teachers in Primary Class #1 devoted 14 percent of their time the first week to making efforts to carry out the innovation, 30 percent the second week, and 32 percent the third week. In Primary #2 the weekly percentages of time teachers spent were zero, zero, and 5 percent; in Primary #3—10 percent, 8 percent, 25 percent; in Primary #4—10 percent, 19 percent, 5 percent; in Intermediate #1—44 percent, 35 percent, 39 percent; in Intermediate #2—5 percent, zero, 11 percent.

The *quantity* of overall weekly staff effort recorded in Table 5-8 tends to be constant; compare 14 percent, to 15 percent, and to 19 percent. The slight rise in effort during the week of May 8-12 can largely be explained by two circumstances. First, during the entire week in Primary Class #1 an employee of the bureau was taking movies of the class "doing the innovation." This activity led these teachers to give more time to the innovation than they had during the two previous weeks. Second, because the fieldworker was having difficulties in obtaining data about the quality of the innovative efforts in four classrooms, he asked the teachers in these classrooms during the week whether they were going to try to conduct "the activity period" (one of their terms for the innovation) that week, and when they planned to do so, so that he could observe it. This undoubtedly led them to spend more time that week trying the innovation than they normally would have. Those two factors probably account for the slight rise in total staff effort.

If we view percentage scores of 76-100 percent as very high innovative effort, 51-75 percent as moderately high, 26-50 percent as moderately low, and 0-25 percent as very low effort, the findings reveal that (1) general overall teacher innovative effort, quantitatively, was very low (16 percent); (2) that the weekly overall school efforts were very low (14 percent, 15 percent, 19 percent); (3) that with one notable exception (Table 5-8, Intermediate #1, 40 percent) overall individual classroom efforts were very low; (4) that a few daily (and fewer weekly) efforts in individual class rooms were moderately low (Tables 5-2—5-7); and (5) that only

Table 5-8. *Amount of Classroom Time Devoted by the Staff Performing in Accord with the Traditional Role Model and the Catalytic Role Model (by Class and Week)*

By Class and By Week	Minutes Available	Minutes Monitored	Traditional Role Model Behavior (in minutes)	Traditional Role Model Behavior (in percent)	Catalytic Role Model Behavior (in percent)
By Class:					
Primary #1	3250	3090	2350	76.05	23.95
Primary #2	3000	2880	2820	97.92	2.08
Primary #3	2750	2690	2330	86.62	13.38
Primary #4	3250	3180	2870	90.25	9.75
Intrmdt #1	3250	3250	1945	59.85	40.15
Intrmdt #2	3250	3190	3000	94.04	5.96
By Week:					
April 24-28	7250	7165	6145	85.76	14.24
May 1-5	4500	4355	3710	85.19	14.81
May 8-12	7000	6760	5460	80.73	19.22
Grand Total	18750	18280	15315	83.73	16.22

four daily efforts, all in Intermediate #1, could be judged moderately high. No daily classroom effort was ever very high (Tables 5-2—5-7).

The evidence thus reveals that during the three-week assessment in May the staff as a whole was devoting most of its time (84 percent) to behavior that tended to conform to the traditional role model and that it was giving minimal time to efforts to implement the catalytic role model.

We now turn to the *quality* of teachers' performance when they attempted to implement innovation. Table 5-9 reports average scores of the total staff and of individual teachers. The classrooms and their teachers are presented in order of the quantity of effort made, and the criteria are listed according to the magnitude of their scores for the

Table 5-9. *Quality of Innovative Effort: Average Scores of Individual Teachers and of the Staff for the Assessment Period (N = 10)*

Criterion[a]	Intmd #1[b] Teacher		Prmry #1 Teacher		Prmry #3 Teacher	Prmry #4 Teacher		Intmd #2 Teacher	Prmy #2 Teacher	Intmd-S Teacher	Overall Staff Scores
	A	B	A	B	A	A	B	A	A	A	
1. Make available all materials	3.00[c]	3.00	2.33	2.33	3.00	3.00	3.00	3.00	—[d]	2.00	2.74
2. Permit student interaction	2.73	3.00	2.40	2.00	2.00	2.00	2.00	2.65	1.00	1.00	2.08
3. Permit free movement	2.73	3.00	1.00	1.00	3.00	1.00	1.00	3.00	3.00	1.00	1.97
4. Permit shift in activities	2.73	3.00	2.20	1.67	3.00	1.00	1.00	2.30	1.00	1.00	1.89
5. Permit choice of subjects	3.00	3.00	1.67	1.67	3.00	1.00	1.00	1.35	—[d]	1.00	1.85
6. Permit choice in number of learning mates	3.00	3.00	1.80	1.00	3.00	1.00	1.00	1.65	1.00	1.00	1.75
7. Teacher movement in room	1.62	1.62	3.00	2.20	1.00	2.33	1.00	2.65	1.00	1.00	1.74
8. Arrange room into areas	3.00	3.00	1.00	1.00	1.00	2.33	3.00	1.00	1.00	1.00	1.73
9. Utilize the areas	1.36	1.36	1.00	1.00	1.00	2.33	3.00	1.00	1.00	1.00	1.41
10. Interact with students	1.62	1.00	2.20	1.40	1.00	1.00	1.00	2.65	1.00	1.00	1.39
11. Try to act as a catalyst between children	1.00	1.00	1.60	1.00	1.00	1.00	1.00	2.65	1.00	1.00	1.23
12. Try to act as a catalyst between child and materials	1.00	1.00	1.60	1.00	1.00	1.00	1.00	2.65	1.00	1.00	1.23
(Quantity of Overall Effort)	(40.15%)		(23.95%)		(13.38%)	(9.75%)		(5.96%)	(2.08%)	—	(16.22%)

[a] The criteria are presented in ranked order according to overall staff scores.
[b] Classes are presented in descending order according to quantity of innovative effort.
[c] Teacher performance scored as follows: 3 = high; 2 = moderate; 1 = low
[d] Insufficient data to score the teacher.

entire school staff. Two findings of special interest emerge from an examination of Table 5-9. The first is that during those periods when the teachers did make some attempt to implement the innovation, most engaged in activities that required them to expend little effort. The last column in Table 5-9 reveals that the teachers most often permitted their pupils to use all materials in the classroom (criterion #1, staff score = 2.74). The second most frequent activity in which they engaged was permitting students to interact (criterion #2, staff score = 2.08) and the third was allowing students to move freely in the classroom (criterion #3, staff score = 1.97).

The second finding is that most teachers did not try to act as catalysts or guides during the period when they were making innovative efforts. This is evidenced by the 1.23 scores on criteria #11 and #12, and the 1.39 score on criterion #10 of the staff at Cambire. It is important to note that on the four criteria (#9-12) requiring the greatest teacher effort, teacher performance was, on the average, relatively low. Even on criteria #6-8, which required a slight amount of effort, their average performance scores were "below moderate." The teaching staff had "nearly moderate" scores on only four of the twelve behavioral criteria (#2-5), and as noted, only on #1, "permitting use of all materials," was the staff's average performance relatively high.

The data in Table 5-9 thus reveal that during the time when teachers made efforts to implement the innovation, they generally did little more than allow their pupils to do what they wanted to do, short of physical harm to each other, or directed the children in multi-activities. The majority (six out of ten) paid little attention to the room arrangement, and most were unconcerned about how they could maximize space in their rooms (eight

---

[4] The two teachers whose behavior is described in the last two columns of Table 5-9 had substantially lower scores compared to the other eight; one teacher, Primary #2, devoted only one hour to the innovation during the assessment; the other, Intermediate Special, made no observable shift in classroom behavior between November and May in order to judge quantity of innovative effort.

out of ten) or about steps they could undertake to serve as catalysts to pupil learning (nine out of ten). In short, the staff exhibited, qualitatively speaking, a minimal degree of implementation of the catalytic role model.

Variations did occur, however, among teachers at Cambire in their classroom performance (Table 5-9), and they deserve some comment: (1) the classroom teachers in Intermediate #1 devoted the most time to the innovative effort; however, they did little more than permit the children at certain times each day to do what they wanted; (2) the two teachers in Primary #1, who devoted nearly a quarter of their time to the innovation, made little effort to act as catalysts. Teacher A made more effort in this respect than Teacher B, but both were primarily directive and tried to limit the students' freedom of movement, choice of subjects, and choice of learning mates. Teacher A engaged in a great deal of "individualized instruction" engaging students in worksheet activities usually in connection with reading and math; (3) the Primary #3 teacher during her innovative efforts granted pupils considerable freedom, but did not serve as a catalyst in any respect; (4) in Primary #4 the performance of the two teachers was highly similar; they generally did not allow the children to select the subjects they wanted to work on; although all materials were used, they were tightly controlled. The Teachers simply were supervising pupils in a structured multiple-activity classroom, with one of the teachers "standing by" and the other seeing to it that the students kept "their noses to the grindstone"; (5) during the small percentage of the time that the Intermediate #2 teacher devoted to innovative effort, he tried to get all children to do "constructive" things; indeed his attempts "to help" were so strong that at times he acted as a traditional director, rather than as a catalyst, hence, the 2.65 rather than 3.00 ratings on criteria #10, #11 and #12; (6) the single in-depth observation made of the Primary #2 teacher did not provide adequate data to complete a full set of ratings. During this observation, however, she continually told the children from a corner of the room to "sit down," "keep

quiet," "stop doing that"; her activities focused primarily on con-
trolling pupil behavior; (7) the performance of the Intermediate-
Special teacher was essentially the same as that of the Primary #2
teacher. He basically tried to keep his students "contained."

Our assessment of the overall *quality* of innovative effort thus
revealed that it consisted primarily of the teachers' insertion into
traditionally scheduled, self-contained classrooms varying "chunks"
of free time for their pupils each week. During these periods we
found little evidence of behavior reflecting the basic notion of
teachers serving as "catalysts." Most teachers used these periods
essentially as "free play" sessions, periods when children were free to
do as they wished, short of harming each other; they did little more
than see to it that their pupils did not get hurt and when activity
time ended, they resumed their traditional schedules. Teachers, in
short, tended to behave as guards rather than guides. They failed to
use this time to enrich a child's educational experience in ways that
would encourage him to learn in accord with his own individual
style and interests. Therefore, we conclude that the quality, as well as
the quantity, of the innovative effort of teachers in May was minimal.

Evidence from other sources support our two major assessment
findings: (1) that teachers devoted only a small proportion of their
time to efforts to perform in accord with the new role model, and
(2) their performance when they made such efforts was of low
quality. The following excerpts represent a sample of the large body
of evidence we obtained from our interviews with staff members and
teachers-in-training to support the conclusion that there was minimal
implementation of the innovation in May:

(1) "They [the children] haven't really been choosing . . . we've
just had forced multi-activities. The room is not being run as
Williams wants it."; (2) "I kept hearing about the great experimental
Cambire School, I had high hopes; I was told, 'Don't mind the high
noise level'; then, I was greeted by a silent class in rows being yelled
at by an authoritarian teacher."; (3) "In the morning before recess
. . . kids were allowed to do different things after completing their

work, but it was like play time . . . so I've even had to structure this."; (4) "I think teachers . . . still are giving what you might call lip service to the innovation . . .; many have the wrong impression of it. They have the feeling that since it is to be materials oriented, all you have to do is put the materials in the classroom and just make sure the kids don't knock each other out."; (5) ". . . her [the full-time teacher's] reaction is, 'I'm really tired, I think I'll have an activity period'! I don't know whether it's because she doesn't understand it [the innovation] or resists it! Obviously she isn't doing it, but I don't know why."; (6) "He [the full-time teacher] doesn't think I should be trained according to the innovation so he has me teaching the whole class most of the time, he, himself, spends little time on it."; (7) "I have to admit . . . I am failing to make as much effort as I was in the past because of my doubts about the assumptions and values . . . and also the effect of this thing on the kids when you let them go."; (8) "Report cards are due; I have to grade these kids; now on some things I can fudge around but not reading and math, if I have to make out report cards I've got to try to teach them this stuff; let them get rid of report cards and sell the parents on it and then I'll sit back and let them play all day."; (9) "He [Williams] told me out in the hall, 'Boy the program is really falling apart and another group is supposed to come visit here on Monday.'; so I told him, 'Don't worry the teachers will put on a show for them.' I guess he thinks it's too quiet around here"; (10) . . ."I am just going to settle back and let August ease on in; if they don't act up in class, I'll let 'em [the children] do whatever they damned well please—Williams is using us, and I'm not going to 'break my ass' now that he doesn't want me back!"

In light of this body of evidence which corroborates data obtained by systematic techniques used in the classroom observations by a trained observer, we feel confident in the findings and conclusions of our assessment.

Summary

We found in this chapter that the educational innovation, the catalytic role model, announced in November was not being implemented in May despite a set of apparently positive antecedent and prevailing conditions in the school system, community, and school.

After a brief discussion of the rationale underlying the evaluation methods employed, we presented the data-collection and data-reduction procedures used to determine the extent to which the teachers had changed their performance in the classroom from a traditional role definition in November to behavior that conformed to the catalytic role model in May. Analysis of the evidence gathered showed that the staff, in May, was still behaving for the most part in accord with the traditional role model, and was devoting very little time to trying to implement the innovation; moreover, we presented evidence that showed that the staff's performance, when efforts were made to conform to the catalytic role model, was of low quality. These findings led us to conclude that the degree of implementation of the innovation in May was minimal.

Barriers to the Implementation of the Innovation: Obstacles Encountered by the Teachers

Why were teachers at the Cambire School making so little effort to implement the catalytic role model in May 1967, six months after the announcement of the innovation? Our analysis of the case study data led us to conclude that this condition could primarily be attributed to five circumstances: (1) the teachers' lack of clarity about the innovation; (2) their lack of the kinds of skills and knowledge needed to conform to the new role model; (3) the unavailability of required instructional materials; (4) the incompatibility of organizational arrangements with the innovation; and (5) lack of staff motivation. Our findings revealed that the first four conditions existed at the outset, persisted throughout the period of attempted implementation, and that the fifth emerged during the latter part of this period.

In this chapter we shall present evidence to support these conclusions. In the following chapter we offer an analysis of the underlying factors that accounted for the existence of the five obstacles

122

that were associated with the minimal implementation of the innovation.

Lack of Clarity about the Innovation

The first circumstance that acted as a major barrier to the implementation of the catalytic role model was that the teachers never obtained a clear understanding of the innovation. We asked the teachers[1] whether they had a clear picture of what they were expected to do in order to implement the catalytic role model in November, when it was announced; in January, just before they were asked to make their first efforts to conform to the new model; and in May, just prior to our assessment of implementation.

During our formal interviews with the teachers, we asked them to describe their understanding of the innovation in November. We focused our questions on their interpretation of the innovation after it was first described to them and on their perception of the behavioral changes that would be required of them. Table 6-1 indicates their responses. Most teachers mentioned both new types of behavior that would be expected of them and role behavior that would no longer be appropriate. Several mentioned only new types of behavior. A majority (six out of ten) of the teachers indicated that the innovation required abandoning formal lessons and group recitations, while a few (three out of ten) mentioned that the

---

[1] Data were available at the time of the assessment of all eleven full-time teachers. However, it was brought to the attention of the fieldworker on several occasions by different teachers that "one of the teachers" had indicated privately, to them, that "I am telling him what I think he wants to hear." The information this teacher provided is, therefore, open to serious question. With such a small number of teachers, the omission of such information is serious. By the same token, however, given such a small sample, questionable information if used might substantially distort the findings. The decision was made, therefore, to exclude information offered by this teacher from the analysis in this chapter.

Table 6-1.   *Types of Behavior that Teachers Reported They Would Need to Abandon or Adopt in Order to Conform to the New Role Model (N = 10)*

Types of Behavior:	Teachers									
	1	2	3	4	5	6	7	8	9	10
Behavior to be abandoned:										
1. Teach formal lessons with group recitations		x			x	x	x	x	x	
2. Serve as an authority figure	x						x		x	
New types of behavior:										
1. Give pupils freedom to choose activities	x	x	x	x	x	x	x		x	
2. Offer multiple activities, and individual attention		x	x		x	x		x		x
3. Saturate room with "self-instructional, high interest," materials for pupils		x	x	x			x	x		x
4. Tolerate noise	x		x		x		x			
5. Act as an advisor or offer support						x	x	x		x
6. Work with other teachers and subject specialists in the room		x	x			x	x			
7. Move about the room		x			x			x		

teacher would be required to cease acting as an authority figure. Nearly all (eight out of ten) said that the innovation would require them to "give pupils freedom to choose their activities," while six out of ten said that the innovation would necessitate both "a multiple-activity classroom with individual attention to pupils" and "self-instructional, high interest materials." Slightly less than a majority (four out of ten) mentioned "tolerating noise," "acting as an advisor or supporter," and "working with teachers and subject specialists" as necessary behavioral requirements. Three teachers noted that "moving about the room" was also an essential element of the innovation. The majority (six out of ten) mentioned four or five "new types of behavior." No teacher mentioned all seven of the behavior items listed in Table 6-1.

In addition to the responses presented in Table 6-1, one teacher said that "teaching by a curriculum guide" would no longer be appropriate, and another mentioned that teachers should not "follow the guide *too closely*." A third said that "teachers would no longer be held to a tight schedule all day." Three teachers mentioned one of the following new types of behavior which they thought would be required: "toleration of visitors," "a great deal of inter-action with pupils to find out what they know," and "keeping individual records"; two other teachers mentioned "setting up the room into areas" as new behavior required by the innovation.

Most, but not all, of the requirements they described deal with very general aspects of the innovation. The *key* idea of the innovation, namely that the teacher should serve as a catalyst to pupil learning, was only touched on by four of the ten teachers who mentioned "being a guide or supporter"; furthermore, these teachers could not, in spite of persistent probing, specify what it meant to be a "guide" or a "supporter."

We would maintain that, while it is appropriate to use the twelve general behavioral indices specified in Chapter 5 to assess degree of implementation of the innovation, the catalytic role model must be reduced to more specific actions required of a teacher in attempting to determine how clear the innovation was to the teachers. If they had a clear conception of the innovation, teachers should have been able to answer questions such as "What are you expected to do when you act as a catalyst?" and "How would a catalyst handle this type of situation?" We reasoned that they would not have a clear conception of their new role in the classroom unless they were capable of specifying behavioral requirements at this level. In spite of our continual attempts during the interviews to get teachers to make statements about specific behavioral requirements of the catalytic role model with respect to their performance, we found that they could not talk about the new role in this manner. Instead, they usually described the innovation in terms of the pupils, perhaps in large measure because Williams' documents focused heavily on what pupils should be doing, and gave slight attention to what teachers would be required to do to get pupils to behave accordingly. Teachers talked about an activity period for the pupils or a comprehensive classroom for them. It is, therefore, not surprising that when they were asked, "After you first heard about the innovation did you feel you had a clear picture of what you were expected to do in carrying out the innovation?," nine of the ten responded "No."[2]

Here are some typical responses when they were asked the follow-up question, "In what respects was it [the innovation] unclear?": (1) "At that time, and still, what methods would best implement it . . .?"; (2) "It's unclear in most ways; how are you supposed to get a new idea across to children when he [Mark] didn't want us to call children together; I am unclear as to my role!"; (3) "How should the classroom teacher behave in this situation? The brochure never spelled out the teacher's job!"; (4) "What is the teacher's role? Should she outline daily activities?; Should she spur children on?; Would the activity period be all or part of the day?"; (5) "At the meeting [when the innovation was announced] it wasn't clear whether he wanted a qualitative or quantitative change

---

[2] Initially one of these teachers said, "In organizing the room, watching the children maybe, I guess I did, sort of. . . ." However, later when asked if the innovation implied behavior Williams had not written down, she responded, "No! I think it's because I didn't know anything about it—I couldn't have any idea until I tried it." Then when asked, "Did you think you could make the changes?" she replied, "Since I didn't know what it was, I could not know how to!" This teacher's response was, therefore, coded as a, "No."

in education; I got no definite answer although I asked Williams directly, 'Do you expect, as a result of this program, more traditional excellence or different learning?' His answer was circular, nondirect. I assumed he wanted something."

The teacher who, during her interview reported that she had a clear picture of what she was expected to do described the new role in a manner similar to those who replied that they did not have a clear picture of it. When pressed for what one would do when acting as a guide (which was one of her responses) she said, "That's the question I can't answer!" Thus, the data indicate that no teacher in November had a clear picture of the catalytic role model in specific operational terms. Instead, they had a partial conception based on a few of its more general notions.

The teachers were also asked about how clear their conception of the new role model was *just before* they were requested to make their first efforts to implement the innovation by the administration. This was done in order to determine whether any changes had occurred in this respect between November and January. When asked (after reviewing their statements about the clarity of the innovation in November), "As a result of what went on during this period (between its announcement and just prior to your first efforts) did your feelings change about the clarity of [what] you would be expected to [do]?," eight of the ten teachers said, "No." A "no" respondent commented, "I still really don't have a clear understanding of the innovation, and I can assure you that I'm not the only one!" Two responded, "Yes." When we explored this matter with these two teachers through "probe" questions, neither could indicate a specific change in their conception of the innovation. We, therefore, concluded that there was no difference in the clarity of their conceptions of the innovation in November and at the end of January.

When we asked about the clarity of the new role model just prior to the assessment of the innovation, we repeated to the teachers exactly what they had said their conceptions of it were at the time of announcement. We, then, asked them whether they had a clearer conception in April of the changes expected of them than in November, when it was announced. Their responses are recorded in Table 6-2. Only two of the ten teachers said, "Yes." The others responded, "No."

Table 6-2.   *The Extent to Which Teachers Were Clear about the Changes Required in Their Behavior by the Innovation Just Before the Assessment as Compared to Their Clarity When It Was First Announced (N = 10)*

Clarity at the time of Announcement		Number of teachers responding just prior to the assessment:	
		"Yes, clearer"	"No clearer"
Clear about the requirements when announced	(0)	—	—
Unclear about the requirements when announced	(10)	2	8

Six of the eight, who said they were "no clearer," reported being unclear at the beginning. A typical follow-up statement to these "no clearer" responses was: "... it's still hazy, I still don't know how to act in this type of classroom. I am still hazy about what the role of the teacher in the classroom should be." Another said:

> ... they [the administration] were side-stepping the main issue; I don't think anyone has a clear idea of what the innovation is all about; no one, not even Williams, would let them [the pupils] come in and just move around after a couple of days. It's the vagueness of how far things should go, like the amount of noise in the classroom or the amount of noise on the stairs we should tolerate. Williams with his brain trust should have set up a room and had kids go into action and stay with them; they should do it, stop talking about it and do it. . . . He should have gotten more

involved in classes; if a kid acted up and started punching and Williams said, "That's OK," then it would be clear; but, if he saw it in action, he might not like it.

One of the eight teachers coded as "no clearer" initially said, "Yes it is clear, I think so, but don't ask me how!" Because she subsequently was not able to add anything to her original statement about her conception of the new role model in November, she was coded as "no clearer." Another teacher who was coded as "no clearer" also at first responded that she was clearer about the new behavior to be required, but she, too, was unable to specify in what ways she had a clearer understanding of the innovation. The ninth and tenth teachers coded as "yes, clearer" said that the innovation was less ambiguous as a consequence of their rereading of Williams' documents. However, their responses revealed that they had a clearer idea about the assumptions underlying the innovation such as "interest will lead to motivation to learn," and "primary school pupils do not have to be 'taught' how to read," but not about the role expectations for their performance.

To summarize: the data supported the conclusion that staff members were not clear in November (at the time of the announcement of the innovation) about the kinds of role performance required to carry out the innovation and that they were no clearer in January (just prior to their first efforts to implement it) or at the time of our assessment of its implementation in May.

Lack of Capability to Perform the New Role Model

The second circumstance that blocked implementation of the innovation was that the teachers did not possess the capabilities needed to perform in accord with the new role model. By capabilities we mean skills and knowledge, not the capacity *to learn how* to perform the new role. One possible way to determine their capabilities would have been to ask the teachers whether they thought they had the skills and knowledge needed to conform to the catalytic role model. However, we rejected this procedure for two reasons. First, the findings would be based on teachers' self-assessments and the accuracy of evaluations of this kind is problematic. Second, as noted earlier, the teachers did not have a clear conception of the requirements for their role performance, and, therefore, they would hardly be in a position to know what capabilities were required to perform the new role.

We used a way of assessing the capabilities of the staff that was based on the following rationale: the extent to which individuals possess the capabilities to behave in accord with a new set of specifications for their performance will be reflected in the number and kinds of problems they are not able to cope with in attempting to conform to it. If teachers reported and our observations corroborated that they could not cope with a large number of problems, we would conclude that they were incapable of performing the new role; if they reported and we observed few problems of this kind, then we would draw the opposite conclusion.

It seemed reasonable to expect that when teachers made their initial attempts to implement the innovation, they would encounter numerous problems. If their capabilities increased over time, they could be expected to report fewer problems with which they were unable to cope during the later phases of the period of attempted implementation. In the case of the innovation introduced at Cambire, the kinds of problems that we anticipated that teachers incapable of performing the new catalytic role model would report included the effective use of new materials, how to maintain pupil interest under a different basis of classroom organization, and how to foster pupil interaction. The findings presented in Table 6-4 shed light on the extent to which they reported encountering these and a number of other types of problems during their innovative efforts. Before considering them it is relevant to examine (Table 6-3) the number of teachers reporting that they were exposed to serious problems in their attempts to perform the new role at different time periods.

Table 6-3. *Responses of the Teachers to Questions about Whether They Faced Serious Problems during Their Innovative Efforts (N = 10)*

Question Asked Teachers	Number of Teachers Responding:	
	Yes	No
1. At the beginning did you find any serious problems in trying to carry out the innovation?	10	—
2. Was there any help or advice that you needed during the period when you made your first attempts which you didn't get?	9	1
3. Did any of the problems that arose during your first attempts to implement the innovation continue to persist?	9	1
4. Have any new problems arisen?	7	3
5. Has there been help or advice that you have needed that you haven't gotten during your subsequent attempts to implement the innovation?	10	—
6. Do any of these earlier problems continue today? (just prior to the assessment)	10	—

During our interviews with the teachers we asked them whether they had encountered any *serious* problems when they made their first efforts to implement the innovation. All ten replied "Yes." Moreover, nine of the ten said that they failed to get the help and advice they needed at that time. We then inquired whether any of the earlier problems continued to exist subsequent to their first attempts, and nine out of the ten replied that "earlier problems had continued to persist"; nearly all of them added, parenthetically, that *most* continued. When asked whether new difficulties had arisen, seven of the ten responded, "Yes." Moreover, all ten teachers responded "Yes" to the question, "Did you need help or advice which you did not receive during your subsequent attempts to implement the innovation?" When asked if the problems they had encountered previously continued to exist for them at the point just prior to our assessment, all ten teachers replied, "Yes." When asked, "Which ones?" seven of the ten responded, "All of them."

Their informal remarks suggest the extent to which the problems they encountered persisted. One teacher said, "They are mostly continuations of original problems in varying degrees. Most of them do exist, some to a lesser extent, others to a greater extent." Another responded, "All the problems at the beginning have continued to exist today—especially discipline!" A third commented, "All of 'em do; I want to know, how are you supposed to motivate a child in this type of classroom so that he will automatically do work without having to chase him?" A fourth exclaimed, "All of them: discipline, evaluation, motivation; children seemed to have lost the ability to sit and work on assignments by themselves for any period of time; how do you get them to do this?" A fifth teacher in retrospect said, "I never was able to instigate [sic] enthusiasm in these kids while keeping the noise level down, and I never knew how to get them to use their time for learning instead of playing. The children were beginning to abuse freedom; they wouldn't do any work; they wouldn't record what they had done; many became discipline problems who weren't in the beginning. I just didn't know what to do."

Table 6-4 presents the number of teachers who reported that they had been exposed to specific kinds of serious difficulties during their efforts to implement the innovation. All ten teachers indicated that maintaining discipline had been a serious problem. They said that pupils fought for desks, materials, and for personal reasons. Nine out of the ten reported that the pupils did not appear to be learning very much; they felt that large numbers of pupils were "wasting their time," "just playing around with the materials," or "not making efforts to learn something from the materials," and that they did not know how to cope with this problem without

Table 6-4.   *Serious Problems Teachers Reported They Encountered in Their Efforts to Implement the Innovation (N = 10)*

Serious Difficulties Arising:[a]	Teachers Responding Affirmatively:									
	1	2	3	4	5	6	7	8	9	10
1. Pupil discipline problems (ineffective child interaction)	x	x	x	x	x	x	x	x	x	x
2. Minimal pupil learning	x	x		x	x	x	x	x	x	x
3. Lack of continued pupil interest and motivation	x	x	x		x	x	x	x		x
4. Pupil misuse of materials	x	x	x	x		x	x	x		x
5. Minimal awareness of the ways of using materials to encourage pupil learning	x	x	x		x	x	x	x		x
6. Insufficient contact with all pupils	x	x	x	x				x	x	x
7. Ineffective interaction with partner in room		x		x	x	x		x		x
8. Inability to evaluate effectiveness of personal behavior during this period		x		x	x	x	x			x

[a]Difficulties presented in order of frequency of teachers reporting them.

"requiring children to learn" or without restricting their freedom. Eight out of the ten teachers also reported related problems: difficulties in keeping pupils interested and motivated in pursuing their own interests and in getting other pupils to help those having learning problems. They reported that large numbers of the pupils were continually demanding "direction" from them. Others were at a loss as to how one applies "subtle coercion," a term used by Williams to describe the teacher's expected performance in relating to pupils who would not work on subjects or in areas in which they should be actively involved. Put another way, the teachers found that many pupils continued to do only those things that they did well, and they were perplexed about how to get them to do other things without "forcing them." One teacher said, "How are you supposed to guide a child to work on skills or subjects with which he is having trouble but without requiring him to do so?" Other teachers mentioned that there were many pupils in their classrooms who would not spend any concentrated period of time working on anything that the teachers considered educational, in spite of their efforts to influence these pupils.

A large majority of the teachers (eight out of ten) were disturbed by the extent to which pupils were not "caring for" the available instructional materials. Several were upset about stealing, others about waste, and still others mentioned deliberate destruction of materials and failure to return them to where they were obtained so that the next user could find them easily. Eight of the ten teachers also reported that they did not know how to make effective use of the instructional and other materials that were available. This was mentioned as a particularly acute problem by the primary classroom teachers who did not know how to help pupils to learn how to read and do math without giving them any instruction. Seven of the ten teachers were very concerned with the problem of inadequate contact with the pupils. Most maintained that they were not able to "keep on top of all children, know what they're doing, and know what they are learning." Their expression of concern about their inability to be able to get around to all pupils was usually followed by the statement that "there are just not enough people in the room to do this job." Furthermore, a majority of the teachers also noted that they had difficulties in developing an effective working relationship with the other teacher in their room. The major source of these problems, the teachers reported, was conflicting ideas about what constituted "appropriate" classroom activities. Finally, a majority of the teachers indicated their uncertainty about whether what they had done during their innovative efforts had any positive effect on the pupils. Many teachers complained that "nobody ever tells me whether what I am doing is right or wrong!"

Of the eight problems presented in Table 6-4, eight teachers mentioned at least six of them. One teacher mentioned five, and only one mentioned as few as three of them. In addition, teachers discussed other difficulties but with less frequency: three were concerned with the ineffective way rooms were set up; five indicated that they were having trouble restraining the class from continually making an overwhelming amount of noise; three reported uneasiness about determining the appropriateness of available instructional materials.

The findings, in short, indicate that teachers faced serious difficulties with which they were unable to cope at the time of their first efforts to implement the catalytic role model and that these problems, plus new difficulties that arose later, were in evidence at the time of our assessment of the innovation. We, therefore, concluded that the staff never developed the capabilities to perform according to the new role model.

Unavailability of Necessary Materials

A third circumstance that served as an obstacle to the implementation of the innovation was the unavailability of the necessary instructional materials. As noted earlier, Williams' conception of the innovation[3] specified ". . . transferring as much of the instructional and 'motivational' responsibilities as possible from the teacher to the total classroom environment—and to the greatly enhanced . . . materials with which the rooms should be filled." He also stated:

> . . . we would like these materials to be such that *they* can generate the intrinsic interest of the children and thus relieve the teacher of much of the need to "motivate" children. In addition, we would hope that many of the materials can be self-instructional, that they can be used by students with a minimum of

---

[3] See Appendix B-3, January Document, p. 270.

guidance from the teachers. . . . If the teacher has adequate assistance and adequate amounts of high-quality, self-instructional
materials, perhaps she will have a great deal more time to spend
helping individual students who need her attention while other
students can progress at their own speed and largely on their own.

The director thus maintained that in order for teachers to act as
catalysts, they *must* make available to their pupils curriculum materials that are "highly motivating" and self-instructional in nature for
two reasons: first, in order to "free" the teacher from group instruction, and second, to permit the teacher to act as a catalyst in relating
to the pupils. To what extent were these necessary, highly motivating,
self-instructional materials available in the classrooms to teachers?

The question of available appropriate materials is really double
barrelled: Are the materials available to teachers, in fact, highly
motivating and self-instructional? and are there enough to go
around? If highly motivating refers to the quality of the materials
in terms of their ability to hold a child's interest and attention for
relatively long periods of time while he progresses in his learning,
then clearly such materials did not exist at Cambire. The teachers
stressed that one of the basic problems they faced was that pupils
were not spending adequate time with materials nor learning very
much in connection with them. Self-instructional can mean materials which allow a pupil to learn through his own efforts and to
advance through a set of progressively more difficult learning stages.
It can also mean materials from which a pupil can learn something,
although what that something is may not be apparent prior to the
learning experience. Indeed, if one uses this latter definition, it is
apparent that any set of materials can be viewed as self-instructional.

With these thoughts in mind, we now examine two lists of
"available materials," one for a primary class and one for an intermediate class[4] that were in the classrooms at the time the teachers

---

[4] With a few minor exceptions, the amount and types of materials seemed to
be the same in the primary grades and intermediate grades.

first made efforts to implement the innovation. The primary list consisted of the following kinds of reading materials: independent worksheets, word games such as "Spill and Spell," vocabulary flash cards, riddles, and a large variety of library books. For mathematics there were Cuisenaire Rods, an abacus, Count the Beads, a scale, a math card game, math flash cards, and a printing set for numerals. For art the available materials consisted of paper and various media like crayons and water paints; and for writing, a typewriter was available.

The intermediate list contained the following types of materials in reading: a controlled reader, the SRA Program, worksheets, flash cards, Scrabble, Probe, Password, Anagram, and paragraph puzzles. For mathematics there were worksheets, a controlled reader, flash cards, Solitaire, "21," Concentration, Bingo, and a T.M.I. Grolier machine for fractions. For science there were microscopes, mirror cards, pendulums, mystery powders, batteries and bulbs. In social studies the following materials were in evidence: Geography Lotto, Wide World, map clue sheets, and a globe.

Most of these materials represent the type of supplementary materials that could be found in a well-stocked suburban elementary school. They hardly represent instructional materials that would permit a pupil to progress very far in a meaningful way on his own, without instruction from the teacher.

What about the quantity of these materials available to teachers? Eight of the ten teachers complained bitterly that the amount of curricular materials placed at their disposal at the time they made their initial efforts to implement the innovation was inadequate.

During the period between the time of the announcement of the innovation in November and just prior to its assessment in May, administrators and staff, independently and in concert, frequently commented on the inadequacy of the available instructional materials in terms of both their quality and quantity.

When we talked to Rudy just after the announcement of the innovation, he said: "The whole idea of the teaching process is

an important goal . . . the big problem is getting the proper materials." Early in December we asked Faith, the teacher who had
unofficially been designated to be the first to carry out the innovation, "When do you think you'll try. . . . I'd like to visit . . .?" She
replied (angrily): "At this rate I'll never get it going, I just don't
have the materials and they can't get the money through the regular
channels for it."

At an afternoon staff meeting early in January, discussion centered
on helping this teacher prepare for her first effort. The "lack of
materials" theme permeated the discussion:

Rudy: "What do you envisage might happen on Monday?"

Faith (very concerned): "I'll tell them what to do, what materials they should use, but I need materials."

A subject specialist then noted: "I think we probably have enough
materials for *one* day. After you've tried it, Faith, then we can decide
better what we'll need in the future."

Near the end of the meeting Rudy asked Faith, "Do you think we
have enough materials?" She responded, "Yes, I think I'll have
enough for the one day."

During the period when teachers were making their first efforts
we had a conversation with Williams about his conception of the
innovation. He noted that "the right kinds" of materials were not
available at Cambire. In his words, "I'd expect to see corners [in
each room] with the same kinds of materials, say for science, math,
art, reading, and children in these corners working independently or
in small groups—lots of self-instructional materials, *but these are
hard to develop*." Later in a conversation he observed: "We *have*
noticed a number of problems with materials, finding materials that
kids can really work with on their own."

In a private document he submitted to the Bureau of Educational
Change, a subject specialist made the following comment:

At this point I would have to say that some teacher-directed
activities appear to be essential. This is perhaps a reflection of

both our knowledge of the ways children learn and of the kind of curriculum materials which are presently available. . . . It has been suggested that the quality of the materials is an important factor. We must seek games, toys, and other kinds of equipment which are open-ended in nature, which stimulate thoughtful exploration and which are innately attractive to pupils. In evaluating the potential effectiveness of materials, we should always consider their value in terms of the tool skills and operational competencies which can be developed through their use. Selection and use of materials should be one of the primary topics explored in this coming summer's program. . . . A danger inherent in attempting to establish the Comprehensive Classroom is falsely equating quantity of materials with quality.

We have presented evidence obtained at different points in time during the period of attempted implementation from the teachers, specialists, and the administration about the instructional materials available to the teachers in the Cambire School. This evidence supports the following conclusion: the quality and quantity of materials required for teacher implementation of the catalytic role model were not available during the entire period of attempted implementation, beginning with the announcement of the innovation in November and continuing through the six-month period that ended at the time of our assessment.

Incompatible Organizational Arrangements

The fourth circumstance that constituted a barrier to the implementation of the innovation was the existence of organizational arrangements that were incompatible with the catalytic role model. At Cambire, at the time of the announcement of the new role model, three practices existed which were incongruent with the new role model and, therefore, required alteration: the rigid scheduling of school time, the assignment of pupils to classrooms according to age, and the use of subject-oriented report cards.

As we noted at the end of Chapter 4, the school, just prior to the announcement of the innovation, was departmentalized. This meant that different teachers were required to direct the learning of groups of pupils in specific subject areas during particular periods of the day. This practice needed to be changed if the innovation were to be implemented because the innovation required that teachers allow pupils in their classes to pursue their own interests *throughout* the day.

At the time of the announcement of the innovation the school also engaged in the practice of grouping pupils on the basis of their age. If teachers were to "act as catalysts between children and promote the teaching of children by children," then a different basis for grouping the pupils was required. Creating classrooms with pupils of varying ages is especially important in connection with their learning how to read in primary school, as is indicated by the following excerpt from a description of a school in an English county in which an innovation similar to the one at Cambire had been introduced:

> . . . . a lot of rich material is needed, according to the teachers, but the best stuff is often homemade. . . . A child might spend the day on his first choice, or he might not. . . . How they learn reading offers a clear example of the kind of individual learning and teaching going on in these classrooms. . . . At first it is hard to say just how they do learn reading, since there are no separate subjects. A part of the answer slowly becomes clear, and it surprises American visitors used to thinking of the teacher as the generating force of education: children learn from each other. They hang around the library corners long before they can read, handling the books, looking at pictures, trying to find words they do know, listening and watching as the teacher hears other children's reading. It is common to see nonreaders studying people as they read, and then imitating them. . . . A very small number of schools. . . have adopted what they call "family," . . . grouping, which further promotes the idea of children teaching children. In these schools, each class is a cross-section of the

whole school's population, all ages mixed together . . . older
children help teach the young ones to clean up and take first
steps in reading. [Featherstone, August 19, 1967, pp. 18-19]

At the time the innovation was announced, the school used a
report card system that required teachers to "give grades" to each
pupil for his mastery of different skills and subjects. However, the
innovation specified that teachers should focus on the *process* of
learning and on the "operational competencies" involved, such as
defining problems, organizing evidence and information, comparing
and differentiating phenomena, and developing hypotheses. The
report card system, therefore, required alteration if teachers were
to be expected to encourage these new types of learning in their
pupils. However, the old report card system was retained. The
impact of the failure to abandon the old system upon implementation of the innovation is suggested by the following incident. In a
routine manner Rudy announced at the April 3rd staff meeting
"report cards are due the 10th of April." Many of the teachers
looked somewhat uncomfortable; Stan gave out a loud guffaw.
Later a teacher confided, "We are using the old report cards, if
I were really carrying it out [the innovation] I'd have no basis for
grading; I'd have to 'use' the old card, but would grade on involvement and interest."

To what extent were the other two school practices that were
incompatible with the innovation at the time of its announcement
altered? At the end of January there was a return to self-contained
classrooms unencumbered by a tight classroom schedule. However,
the old school schedule that included the following practices
was present at the time of the assessment: all pupils were kept out
of the building in the morning until the 8:30 bell rang and released
in the afternoon by the 2:20 bell; a second bell rang in the morning
before classes began. Bells were also rung for recess and lunch; all
classes were expected to participate in recess from 10:30 to 11:00
and lunch from 12 to 12:30 as evidenced by the distribution of

milk to all classes just before noon. Teachers were expected to adhere closely to this schedule. Pupils were taken in groups to lavatories at lunch and recess; they were required to walk up and down stairs in single lines, and were dismissed at the end of the day in a similar fashion. Moreover, pupils were required to participate in certain types of activities, regardless of their interests. These included the following: reading, art, music, sewing, gym, and field trips. The continuation of these school practices served to block, as did the full departmentalization plan, the implementation of the catalytic role model by teachers.

Although the innovation specified that teachers should encourage the teaching of pupils by other pupils, the practice of homogeneous grouping of pupils on the basis of their ages was retained throughout the period of attempted implementation of the innovation.

In short, two of the three organizational arrangements that required changes to make them compatible with the new teacher role model were never altered during the period of implementation, and the third although adjusted to some extent, was still restrictive to a considerable degree. Thus, we concluded that incompatible aspects of the environmental setting that existed at the beginning of the period of attempted implementation and that were never altered, constituted a major barrier to teachers' efforts to carry out the innovation.

Lack of Motivation to Make Efforts to Implement the Innovation

The fifth circumstance that constituted a major obstacle to the implementation of the catalytic role model by teachers in May was their lack of motivation to expend the time and effort required if it were to be successfully carried out. We shall consider first the initial response patterns of the teachers to the announcement of the innovation in November 1966, and then examine their willingness to make efforts to carry it out in November and in May 1967.

Our interviews with the teachers revealed that they had varied and mixed reactions to the innovation when they first heard about it. Three of the teachers had general reactions that could be classified as positive, three as essentially ambivalent, and four as somewhat negative. Table 6-5 contains a cross-classification of the teachers, categorized on one hand by their general feeling toward the innovation, and on the other, by their reactions to a number of its dimensions.

The findings reveal that nine of the ten teachers reported that they agreed with the objectives of the innovation. As one staff member put it:

> I don't think you can disagree with the objective that we want to make thinkers out of the kids. We want to make them enjoy school, we want to make them intellectually more powerful, we want to give them a better self-image. I would say I definitely agree with his [Williams'] goals.

Table 6-5 also shows that all of the teachers felt that there was a need for basic changes in the operation of their school.

The four teachers classified as having negative responses to the innovation at the time it was announced held the belief that it was not very practicable or feasible for Cambire and that it would not be beneficial to the pupils. As one of these teachers put it: "Children are supposed to have maturity and discipline which they need in order to do the required stuff; I think they needed a more traditional classroom."

It is not surprising that three of the four teachers who maintained that the innovation would not work at Cambire anticipated no positive consequences for pupils and all four teachers saw negative consequences for the pupils. While some of the "positive" and "ambivalent" teachers reported possible adverse effects for them and their pupils, all anticipated that there also would be positive consequences. Some positive, ambivalent, and negative teachers perceived detrimental consequences for themselves; only negative

Table 6-5. *Teachers' Initial Responses to the Introduction of the Innovation and Their Reactions to Selected Issues Related to It (N = 10)*

Issues Related to the Innovation	Teachers with Initial Positive Response			Teachers with Initial Ambivalent Response			Teachers with Initial Negative Response			
	1	2	3	1	2	3	1	2	3	4
1. Need for basic change at Cambire	Y	Y	Y	Y	Y	Y	Y	Y	Y	Y
2. Need for *this* change	Y	AMB	Y	Y	AMB	Y	N	AMB	N	N
3. Perceived priority of:[a]										
director	E	E	E	E	E	E	DK	E	E	G
assistant director	M	M	M	G	E	N	DK	N	L	E
subject specialist A	E	M	M	DK	DK	DK	DK	N	L	L
subject specialist B	E	M	M	DK	M	DK	DK	N	M	M
"downtown"	DK	DK	DK	L	N	DK	N	N	N	N
4. Perceived workability	Y	Y	AMB	DK	AMB	AMB	N	N	N	N
5. Agreement with objectives	Y	Y	Y	Y	Y	Y	Y	Y	Y	N
6. Perceived capability	Y	Y	Y	Y	DK	Y	DK	Y	Y	N
7. Perceived consequences:										
positive for self	Y	Y	Y	Y	Y	Y	Y	Y	N	N
negative for self	Y	Y	N	Y	N	Y	Y	N	Y	Y
positive for students	Y	Y	Y	Y	Y	Y	N	N	N	Y
negative for students	Y	Y	AMB	Y	Y	Y	Y	Y	Y	Y

[a]Y = yes; N = No; Amb = Ambivalent; E = Extreme; G = Great; M = Moderate; L = Little; N = None; DK = Do not know

teachers, however, perceived no positive effects for themselves. These findings suggest that the teachers' initial reactions may have been partly the result of their comparisons of the anticipated positive and negative consequences for themselves and students

Another finding of interest in Table 6-5 is that the "negative" group perceived the top echelon of administrators as giving a lower priority to the innovation than the director. In fact, all four of these teachers believed that the central administration gave no priority to this innovation at Cambire. In addition, most of the teachers perceived that the assistant director placed less priority on the innovation than the director. The only teacher who believed that the assistant director placed more priority on it than the director said, "Rudy is actually doing more than Williams because he wants to please him. He puts more emphasis on it than Williams."

It is especially important to note that all the teachers, even those who were classified as "negative," reported a willingness in November to make efforts to try to implement the innovation.[5] As one of the teachers who was classified as "negative" put it:

> Williams came down . . . and wanted to see our reactions, he expected arguments. He was surprised when he saw we were all willing. . . . We figured that if he wanted it, let's give it a try.

We found, however, that at the time of our assessment the situation with respect to the teachers' willingness to make efforts to

---

[5] Our data provided no support for the notion that tend to be teachers resistant to changes introduced by their administrators. No teachers indicated their resentment of the fact that the innovation was introduced in a unilateral manner by their superiors. What they did resent was the lack of follow-up by the administration once the innovation had been announced. Thus, the evidence leads us to conclude that the pattern of initiation "from the top," that is, by the director, did not have any apparent impact on the initial reactions of teachers to the innovation at Cambire. We suggest that the assumption that teachers tend to be resistant to changes proposed by their administrators needs to be tested, rather than assumed, in any empirical case.

implement the catalytic role model had changed drastically. Teacher responses to questions in the formal and informal interviews revealed that strong resistance had developed to making efforts to implement the new role model. The following comments of teachers, obtained just before and during the period of our assessment, reflect the unwillingness of the staff to devote time and effort to the innovation. One teacher expressed her feelings this way, "Sometimes I am really negative, at other times I am just confused; I just don't see anything positive coming out of it!" Another said, "As a result of the way things have been run around here, I am really doubtful; it needs a lot of rehashing, discussion, communication between teachers; it needs organization, both general and specific, about details of the classroom, timing, organizing and teachers' time, getting used to materials. If these things aren't done, I am skeptical." A third put it this way, "I have to admit that I really feel less willing and *maybe* (pause) well *I am* failing to make as much effort as I was in the past because of my doubts about the assumptions and values implicit in this innovation and also the effect of this thing on the kids when you let them go." A fourth commented, "I wonder whether it's worth the effort one has to put into it [the innovation] . . . . I can't really tell how much they're learning nor how many are learning." A fifth divulged the following, "I'm just getting tired; I can't take it with the kids anymore; I can't see what good it [the innovation] is doing; it's not worth the effort. . . . I go home and I've got a headache; I bite my nails; and why should I do anything if it's not appreciated? Why should I go home and work myself to the bone preparing and not even getting the slightest acknowledgement of appreciation?" A sixth complained, "Why bother, I'm not coming back, I'm just going to settle back and let August ease on in; if they don't act up in class, I'll let 'em [the pupils] do whatever they damned well please—Williams is using us, and I'm not going to 'break my ass' now that he doesn't want me back!" A seventh left little doubt about his feelings, "The kids aren't taking to it so why go home and plan these things, and also I don't feel like doing anything because of the *raw deal* and the *run around* we're getting from Williams. . . . I don't like his idea, I don't think it will work. I question *his* assumptions about interest and self-motivation for these kids; maybe for a gifted class it's OK but most of my kids are around 100 I.Q." An eighth teacher reacting to the lack of discipline of her children which she felt was caused by their response to the innovation exclaimed, "The kids are getting really fresh now. . . . Yesterday I had to go home and take two tranquilizers. The worst class is the second grade. . . . What one child said to me I couldn't repeat. . . . I really hated coming to school today; I am sick of this place." After a brief absence from school, another teacher noted sardonically, "Ya know, I was sitting home the last two days saying that it can't really be that way, and that this school can't be as bad as I think it is; then I came back. Ya know, it really *is* that mixed up, confused, and nutty!"

The data, in short, revealed that in November the staff had mixed reactions to the announcement of the major innovation by the director and that while some teachers were positive, others somewhat negative, and still others ambivalent in their responses to it, all teachers were willing to attempt implementation of the catalytic role model. By the time of our assessment in May, however, we found that a noticeable shift had occurred in staff willingness to devote time and effort to trying to implement the innovation. Resistance to making efforts had developed during the period of attempted implementation and was in strong evidence at the time of our assessment.

Summary

In this chapter we have examined the following major question: What conditions could account for the degree of implementation of the catalytic role model that we observed six months after it had been introduced in to the school? The findings presented in this chapter showed that five basic factors were involved in the minimal implementation of the organizational innovation at Cambire at the time of our assessment in May: the teachers' lack of clarity about the innovation, their lack of needed capabilities, the unavailability of required instructional materials, the incompatibility of organizational arrangements with the innovation, and the lack of staff motivation. Moreover, the findings revealed that the first four factors existed at the outset and persisted throughout the period of attempted implementation whereas the fifth, lack of staff motivaton, developed during the period between the announcement of the innovation and our assessment of its implementation.

7

Obstacles Encountered by Teachers: Roots of the Difficulties

What accounted for the continued existence or development of the five major barriers during this period of attempted implementation? More specifically, (1) Why did the staff never receive a clear conception of the new role requirements for their performance? (2) Why did the staff fail to develop the capabilities needed to implement the innovation? (3) Why were the instructional materials essential to the implementation of the innovation never made available? (4) Why were organizational arrangements that were incompatible with the innovation never modified? (5) Why was there a sharp decline in staff motivation to make efforts to implement the innovation? In this chapter we examine data that emerged from our case study that bear on these questions. However, it is relevant first to present a brief chronology of major events bearing on these issues, that occurred between the announcement of the innovation at Cambire and our assessment of its implementation in May.

At the end of November 1966, copies of a ten-page document about the innovation were passed out to teachers and subject specialists. At a meeting, shortly thereafter, Rudy presented the idea of the new model to the staff in Mark Williams' presence. This was the first effort to bring the innovation to the attention of the teachers. In the middle of January 1967, Faith Bailey made the initial attempt to implement the proposed change. Later in the month copies of an expanded version of the earlier document were distributed to the staff. At the end of January the departmentalized organization of the staff, initiated in October, was discontinued; the self-contained classroom was reinstated, but now each room was double-staffed with either two regular teachers or a regular teacher and a practice teacher from a nearby university. Teachers at this time were "urged" to make efforts to implement the innovation.

In the middle of March, Rudy officially announced that he was leaving Cambire the next month to take over the principalship of a school in the "regular system." Teachers received forms in the latter part of March to reapply for their positions at Cambire next year and simultaneously were given forms to apply for a transfer to other schools in the regular system for the following year. At the beginning of April the first wave of three student teachers left the school and another set arrived. Just before spring vacation, in the middle of April, Rudy left the school. After spring vacation John Helman, subject specialist, took over as temporary head of the school. Our classroom assessment began April 24 and lasted through May 12, 1967.

We now turn to an examination of those conditions that appeared to account for the continued existence or development of the major barriers to the implementation of the catalytic role model at the Cambire School.

Lack of Clarity about the Innovation

We have seen that the staff at Cambire, between November and May, never developed a clear picture of the role performance that was expected of them with respect to the innovation. What accounted for this state of affairs?

The teachers were unfamiliar with the innovation before its announcement in November, and their first exposure to it occurred when they read the November document. What did it say about the innovation? It contained a very general statement of its purposes and a brief discussion of the physical layout of the classroom and what the children would be doing in it. The document discussed in vague and in the most general of terms what was expected of teachers; it did not specify precise types of role performance teachers should engage in to obtain the "desired behavior" from their pupils.

Our evidence indicates that the teachers' ambiguity about the innovation was not recognized or dealt with by the administration in November or later. A number of teachers expressed the sentiments indicated in the following comments of two members of the staff. The first noted, "Williams was there at the first meeting, but he didn't say anything"; the second stated, "We didn't talk about it very much. This was Williams' philosophy, this is what he believed. I took it [the document] home and read it." We asked teachers whether at the time of the announcement of the innovation they believed that Mark and Rudy had really thought it through carefully and had specific plans for putting it into effect. To both questions all the teachers answered, "No." Their informal remarks reveal their perceptions of why these conditions prevailed. One teacher commented, "Williams has no classroom experience so he can't think it through; his philosophy is that it's an idea that the teacher has to work out." Another said, "Williams knew where he wanted to go; he had a diagram of the room, but he didn't know how to get there; outside of this, no more." A third teacher stated, "The document was all jumbled up and it wasn't clearly presented." One subject specialist said, "Williams wanted a materials oriented classroom, where kids should have a choice. He wasn't too clear about it; Rudy wasn't clear either about what Williams wanted. Rudy 'sat' on the innovation; he didn't tell us much." When another specialist was asked, "Did you get the impression from the way it

was first proposed or announced that Mark and Rudy had really
thought the innovation through carefully?," he replied:

> I think this was a vague idea of a type of classroom that Mark
> would like to see. . . . He was speaking in generalities . . . and we
> didn't get down to specifics before we tried to put this into
> operation and really talk about what we would like to see going
> on in classrooms, what the teachers' role would be; I think more
> preparation should have gone into this, for my part as well as
> everybody else's. . . . I think the only plan they had was that we
> were going to have a variety of materials in the classroom and the
> kids would be given the freedom to choose what materials they
> would like to work with, and then the teachers would walk
> around the room, doing what, I'm not sure; I don't think Mark
> made it very clear.

We also asked the teachers about the activities they had engaged
in with respect to the innovation between November and the end of
January, when they made their first efforts to implement it. Most
teachers indicated that they had given the innovation considerable
thought during this period. Their responses revealed that they had
thought about numerous aspects of it including the types of instructional materials that would be required and how students would
react to them. A typical response was, "I thought about everything,
for example, how you'd set things up; how to program it; would they
[the pupils] be free all day; how many materials you would need;
how would you control the children. *There were so many things.*" For
most teachers, the extent of their reading about the innovation was
limited to the documents prepared by Williams. When questioned
about discussions of the innovation, most teachers reported talking,
either formally or informally, about it at staff meetings. The discussion usually centered on child discipline problems or the paucity of
curricular materials. One teacher said, "Unfortunately talking was
done in bull sessions; we never came up with a guide for future
action." When asked if he had any serious questions he said,
"Whether it was planned well enough; someone must have done it

before somewhere; we should know. I am sure there is information, but it hasn't been provided [for us] yet!" Another said, "I talked a lot [to administrators], but thought about it even more. . . . I wanted to know where it had been tried; I wanted to know, if it had been tried anywhere else, why."

The subject specialists were more detailed in their discussions of Rudy's activities. One commented:

> I don't know, you'll have to ask him; he was more concerned with the daily handling of the school. He had to do this, he had lost his Assistant Principal (Phil Jackson) so he was busy entertaining visitors; he says he wrote reports to Mark; I didn't see them, so I don't know what he said.

The other, equally critical, said:

> Rudy came back [from a session with Williams] with a drawing, but there was no real communication. Either Williams wasn't communicating or Rudy wasn't communicating it to us. I knew that whatever happened at BEC meetings, we weren't getting the information. He would tell us only what he wanted us to know. It was being discussed somewhere because Tanner and Aldem [assistants at BEC] seemed to have some knowledge about it. Rudy made a mystery about everything. . . . Williams should have read his statement to us, spent a week or two with us just discussing questions and answers; notes should have been taken and at the end of this a summary set forth in which Mark would say, "I want certain things done or there is nothing I want done."

When asked whether they had tried to raise questions about the innovation with either Mark or Rudy, the responses presented here are typical:

> No, there wasn't enough time given our schedules; too many bull sessions. . . .

> Not with Mark, because he wasn't there; not with Rudy, because he didn't have the answers; no one had the answers because they didn't do their own research work on it!

I don't think they knew how to resolve them!

Their lack of knowledge wouldn't permit them to answer my questions.

If we asked them questions at the meetings, they always left things in the air. They'd say, do it yourself, try it out! Everything was so indefinite.

The subject specialists responded in a similar vein when asked why their questions were not handled effectively. One said:

We needed experience to get some answers, we didn't have any answers yet, . . . if we are basing this on Leicestershire, then I should have gone to see what they were doing; they should have done what we will be doing next summer [bringing someone over from England with experience].

The teachers were asked whether the administrators had tried to find out how they felt about the innovation. The majority said that the administration had tried to ascertain their feelings. A teacher who responded yes said, "They asked us what we thought of the catalytic role model and if *we* had any plans." A teacher who responded no said, "I don't think so except at the first meeting. They asked, 'What did you think of the idea?' – this was in respect to Williams' booklet." Another said, "No, aside from a perfunctory, 'What did you think of it?' "

The observer's field notes revealed that little effort was made by teachers to obtain a clearer image of the innovation during December or early January. He reported that discussions in the teachers' lounge seldom touched on the innovation, and when it did it was usually with respect to (1) Can you give a child such freedom? or (2) Can we get the materials? Their lack of effort to obtain clarification can be explained in part by their understanding that Faith was the one informally designated to try the innovation first.

We also asked the teachers questions about the extent to which the director and assistant director attempted to clarify the innovation after the teachers had made their first efforts at implementation, that is between January and May.

In describing Mark's activities most teachers indicated that he had been of slight or no value in this respect. The following remarks were typical: "Very insignificant"; "I don't know what he does up there"; "I don't know of anything — he came to a few meetings, maybe once a month"; "I don't have any idea"; "Mark? Nothing"; "Williams came down once in December and January and wanted to see our reactions"; "We didn't see him that much — he was kind of vague when we did see him, he never commented on our activities"; "Once he came with the superintendent of schools; his activities were limited to giving the documents out; he came into my room, kids would flock around him; he was very happy; but, he didn't contribute anything." One subject specialist noted, "He wrote up his description and assumptions for the catalytic role model, but there was no communication after that"; another said, "Other than mentioning it once to me, nothing I know of!"

Rudy's activities in connection with clarifying the innovation during this period were seen as somewhat more varied, but still minimal; as one teacher put it, "He conducted meetings and presented us with lists of materials that were available"; another said, "looked for materials, ordered materials, asked my opinion; he was a big help, he left the plans for the innovation up to me"; a third reported, "Rudy? Nothing!" A fourth teacher commented, "Gault was always asking what kinds of equipment *we* thought we would need; he would search through books, and he would try to get them"; a fifth reported, "Asked for lists of materials *we* thought might be useful in carrying out the innovation; he ordered some of them. In the meetings we talked about projects already in process and a little about our reactions to Williams' objectives." A sixth teacher, in an unenthusiastic tone of voice, offered, "Not much, we had meetings and we discussed certain things; he'd pass out certain things he read in magazines; he would always say we were doing a wonderful job."

What were Mark Williams' views about the clarity of the innovation between January and May? In answering a question about how clear he thought the innovation was in the minds of the teachers, subject specialists, and assistant director, Mark revealed in February 1967 that *he* was not clear about the specific behavior that the new role would require of teachers. When he was asked, "How clear do you think the innovation is in the minds of the teachers and Rudy?," Mark replied:

> Different teachers have different ideas; therefore, the innovation can be different in some ways to different teachers; but, I felt that when this was first presented the objectives were clear to everyone. . . . I can't say the same for the plans for doing it. . . . Here, all of us will have to find out what we are talking about.

His answer to a question about the source of the innovation also indicates his lack of clarity about it:

> Oh, we sort of robbed Bruner; we robbed everybody . . . we had all sorts of hypotheses that if you create this kind of environment you *will* get kids to read better and read more, and you will get them going on interesting and really fascinating topics, and to some extent you can sort of subjectively test this out at least in that you *do* find yourself continually in situations where you *can't* supply what a kid *wants* and that's very bugging; and I don't know what the answer is to how to keep kids going and how to get yourself in a situation where you can supply exactly what a kid wants just when he wants it.

Rudy's view of the clarity of Mark's documents in January after their distribution was:

> . . . actually how to go about it was our job. But his job was what the philosophy should be. . . . You must understand that he would admit to us that *he* didn't have *all* the answers. He wasn't sure that it was going to work, and he didn't know where we were going to get this manipulative equipment; getting those materials experts in there was one attempt at trying to develop

them. . . . He was heading in that direction without having all the answers, too.

Rudy, himself, during this period was uncertain about what would be required of teachers in performing the new role:

> . . . I had heard about permissive classroom situations, but it didn't include the idea of children being free for almost the *total* day . . . ; I was very worried about reading and math. I wasn't quite sure how they would fit into this.

In addition, both Mark and Rudy held the belief that "really creative" teachers could "discover on their own" what the appropriate role performance of the teacher would be as they attempted to conform to the catalytic role model. Mark stated:

> What I want are top teachers, not regular teachers who have to be dragged along. . . . The introduction of these new materials and the Tuesday afternoon activity period was all done as part of a strategy of treading water and building confidence in the teachers. . . . What we have wanted is a bunch of really creative, innovative teachers and administrators who could eventually take this idea and make something out of it.

Rudy noted that he felt the type of teacher required for this innovation was missing at Cambire:

> . . . there was a kind of professional orientation which I didn't see in some of those people. I think you had to be bright, . . . dynamic, . . . well-read and interested, . . . imaginative! And it wasn't enough to say, what do you want me to do? This kind of a person doesn't belong in the innovative school. The kind of person needed is the one who makes things happen.

To summarize: during the period between the time of announcement and just *before* the teachers were urged to try to implement the innovation at Cambire, there was a failure to clarify the ambiguities teachers had about the catalytic role model. The November document contained only a general statement of the aims of the innovation and described it primarily in terms of the physical layout of the classroom and the behavior to be expected of pupils. It glossed over the standards to be applied to the teacher's role performance. The January document did not expand on the earlier limited description of the teacher's new role. It simply specified the assumptions underlying the innovation and speculated about individual differences among pupils and the process of learning. When discussions about the innovation occurred during staff meetings held within the period between the announcement of the innovation and the staff's efforts to implement it, they centered primarily on the kinds of materials that would be needed and how the pupils might react to them.

During the period between the end of January and our assessment in May, the administration continued to ignore the need to clarify staff ambiguity about the innovation at Cambire. Both administrators not only held ambiguous views of the catalytic role model, but also thought that it was the teacher's responsibility to develop a clear conception of their new role for themselves.

Our analysis suggests that the failure to clarify the new teacher's role may be attributed to the four following conditions. The first was the failure of the staff to communicate its lack of clarity about the catalytic role model to their administrators. This circumstance can be attributed in part to the administration's failure to communicate to the teachers that they would be asked to try to implement the innovation within a relatively short period of time; it also appeared to be a consequence of the staff's belief that the administration did not have a clear conception of the catalytic role model, and hence, efforts to obtain clarification would be of little value. The second condition was the lack of clarity on the part of the administrators themselves about the specification of the new teacher's role. The third was that both the director and assistant director were operating on the assumption that creative teachers, if given maximum freedom, would "figure it out" for themselves. This assumption probably accounts for the minimal effort made by the director to clarify the reservations of the teachers about the innovation. Finally, the fact that the assistant director was not fully committed to the total implementation of the new role model appears to have played an important part in his lack of effort to clarify it for the teachers.

The Staff's Lack of Capability to Perform the New Role

We described in the preceding chapter the numerous problems that teachers continued to encounter throughout the entire period in which they made efforts to implement the innovation; for example, discipline problems, low pupil motivation, and lack of pupil interest in the new instructional materials. The fact that these difficulties persisted throughout this period suggested that the capability of the teachers to perform the new role did not improve between January and May. What accounted for this circumstance?

Teachers began making their first efforts to implement the innovation in a state of basic ignorance about how they should behave because of the failure of the administration to present a clear picture of the innovation before "urging" the teachers to try it. During our interviews we asked teachers to describe their first and subsequent efforts to implement the innovation. One teacher reported her initial effort as one of "offering the children a one-hour Tuesday afternoon activity period in which they could choose from a variety of activities — from playing games like Rook to using reading, science, and math materials." Another said that her initial efforts consisted of the following activities: rearranging the room, trying to get along with the other teacher, and except for the reading period, recess, lunch, and giving students complete freedom. A third reported giving children an activity period from 11:15 to 12:00 noon or from 1:35 to 2:15 P.M. two times a week. All teachers, with one exception, indicated that they spent most of the time during their initial efforts to implement the innovation in carrying out directed classroom lessons in math, literature, social studies, science, art, was well as in reading.

In discussing their later efforts to implement the innovation, six of the ten teachers said they had altered their earlier performance; four said they had not. It is *critical to note* that all six of the teachers who had made changes in their performance reported more structured subsequent behavior, that is, greater control of their classes and less open-ended activity. One put it this way, "We've cut down on their free time because we found children were wasting their time away"; another said, "We spend less time on multiple classroom activities and more on group instruction and on individual worksheet activity. Then we let them go for some time each day." A third reported, "We found that the children couldn't use the free time, so both Arthur and I agreed not to give them complete freedom; they don't know the difference."

Thus, we found that those teachers who initially tried to create a great deal of free time for children later reported shifts back to a more structured classroom environment. The others who made little or no effort to change their performance continued to conduct highly structured classrooms. Reversion to the traditional patterns by the six teachers who had made efforts to alter their performance appeared to be a consequence of the problems they had encountered, but which they were not able to overcome, in trying to carry out the new role.

Our field observations revealed that teachers received little help within or outside of their classrooms as they attempted to implement the innovation, and that there was little communication between teachers and administrators about the problems to which the teachers were exposed during this period. The teachers' responses to questions about these matters corroborated our observations.

We asked teachers first to indicate the amount of effort that the director, assistant director, and subject specialists expended in trying to help them; then we asked them to indicate the degree to which these individuals were a help or hindrance to them in coping with the problems they faced in implementing the innovation. We also asked them to respond to these questions with reference to the period during which they made their subsequent efforts, which ended with the beginning of our assessment. The findings are summarized in Table 7-1.

Table 7-1. *Teachers' Evaluations of the Director, Assistant Director, and Subject Specialists on Three Criteria When They Attempted to Implement the Innovation (N = 10)*

	During Initial Attempts[a]					During Subsequent Attempts[a]				
	5	4	3	2	1	5	4	3	2	1
1. *Director:*										
Amount of effort	—	—	—	—	10	—	—	—	—	10
Amount of help	—	—	—	1	9	—	—	—	—	10
Amount of obstacle	1	—	—	—	9	1	—	1	1	7
2. *Assistant Director:*										
Amount of effort	1	2	—	1	6	1	—	—	2	7
Amount of help	1	2	—	2	5	1	—	—	1	8
Amount of obstacle	1	1	—	1	7	1	1	—	1	7
3. *Subject Specialist A:*										
Amount of effort	2	1	3	2	2	1	—	—	4	5
Amount of help	1	1	3	1	4	1	—	1	2	6
Amount of obstacle	1	—	1	—	8	1	—	—	1	8
4. *Subject Specialist B:*										
Amount of effort	2	1	3	3	1	1	—	1	3	5
Amount of help	1	1	3	2	3	1	—	2	1	6
Amount of obstacle	1	1	—	—	8	1	—	—	1	8

[a]Code: 5 = Great; 4 = Considerable; 3 = Some; 2 = Little; 1 = None.

All the teachers reported that the director made no effort to help them during both time periods. One said, "The only thing Mark did was to give me the feeling that I could do anything; there was no pressure, no help; he was nebulous in the background"; another remarked, "Mark came to a couple of meetings, said a few things, he was like a phantom, an overseer with no practical help to offer."

A large majority of teachers reported that the assistant director offered little or no help during the time they made their initial efforts to implement the innovation; moreover, a still larger majority reported this to be the case during their subsequent efforts. In commenting on her relationship with the assistant director, one teacher said, "He never came into the classrooms to observe what was going on. As assistant director, he did nothing that I saw; occasionally in meetings he would throw out ideas but never in a planned way, they were 'off the cuff' 'occasional remarks.' " Another commented, "Rudy would say 'How's it going?'; he had nothing to do with the programs; at meetings he led discussions." A third noted, "You could go to him with any problem; he would try to talk it out; he listened to you . . . , but he didn't tell you how to do it; he didn't know."

Table 7-1 shows that the teachers reported that the subject specialists made more effort to help them with the innovation during their initial attempts to implement it than during their subsequent efforts. The kind of help provided by the specialists, however, was restricted largely to providing materials. One teacher in commenting on subject specialist B said, "He had no sense of place; he'd come into the middle of an intense teaching lesson and want to tell me about some new game he had; he did come across with one concrete thing, balance units, but didn't help me to learn how to use these units." Another staff member commented, "One [subject specialist] came up with paper work for the kids, phonic sheets, stories cut up and rearranged; the other brought new science stuff, some new games, not much else."

Few of the teachers perceived any of the administrators or staff specialists as obstacles. Typical comments were: "None were obstacles; how could they be, they didn't do anything"; "They weren't obstacles; they didn't come in. They should come in every day not once every two weeks." In short, the two administrators were mainly perceived as neither help nor hindrance, while the subject specialists were seen in a slightly more positive light.

Two teachers reported that they viewed their teaching partners as one of their serious obstacles. With only one exception, no teacher reported that other teachers offered help or had been of service to them in their attempts to cope with the problems they faced in their classrooms.

We asked teachers, "Who should be giving you help?" They mentioned with approximately equal frequency the director, assistant director, and the two subject specialists. Some felt that all four should have worked as a team to be of service to the teachers. A typical comment reflecting this feeling was: "Rudy as assistant director should have set this up with John and Alex, and Mark should have been around, asking questions and taking a decisive leadership role; it should have been a group effort, it wasn't!" Another statement reflecting teacher sentiment was:

> . . . he [Mark] should come into the classrooms *by himself* to observe; he only comes in when he wants to bring in a visitor and show off. . . . Evaluators should be in rooms constantly; they don't even read our reports; one admitted this; they made us think up seventy questions; that's not my job, that's their job; Mark should be making them evaluate us; we're too close to it.

At the end of February, during an interview Mark stressed that the ideas for new role model for teachers came from a number of sources including Educational Services Incorporated, John Holt, Jean Piaget, but mainly from Leicestershire. When asked how change in the teacher's role would take place he responded:

> I want the teachers to give themselves the idea that they can change themselves, I want to give the teachers the idea that they are professionals doing what each one wants to do. . . . I also wanted a school where the head of it took on the job of educational leadership, who felt free to experiment and change. We've had some problems here, too; we wanted a situation where the teachers would feel free to go to Rudy to get stuff and Rudy would feel free to do things. . . . [adding parenthetically that] The teachers were virtually fighting to try this thing in November;

I didn't expect them to be so enthusiastic about it; I was really happy about this.

The preceding excerpt suggests that Mark felt that the teachers, if they were willing to change and given the freedom to do so, could make the change without assistance, and that if any help were needed from someone "at the top," he expected Rudy to provide it. How did Rudy feel about the ability of the teachers to change their role performance?

In response to the question, "Do you think the teachers made the efforts they could have made at Cambire to implement the innovation?," he replied:

Of equal importance to the idea of the novelty of the innovation is the performance of the teacher. In other words what I'm saying is if you put it on a mimeographed sheet and give it to some people, you'll have sheer disaster. Give that very same program to people who have a talent for that kind of program, you'll have a very successful program. So you cannot say that an innovation in itself is going to be successful. What you've got to say is an innovation with high performing teachers for *that* program will be successful.

Rudy therefore felt, that able teachers would be required if the innovation were to be implemented. In addition, he appeared to be convinced of the importance of providing help to staff members. Acknowledging the importance of helping teachers to implement the innovation, he added:

. . . I think the teachers themselves could have done more; but, I'm not putting the blame on them. I'm putting the blame on the orientation of these same teachers. If these teachers had been more properly oriented . . . even during the summertime. They could have used the summer for greater orientation; if at the same time we had the support of the subject specialists, if they knew what their role was, and if they carried it out, then they could take a teacher with inhibitions, they could take a teacher

with frailties, they could take a teacher of mediocrity, and make
that teacher perform better in her new role.

In response to the question, "Why didn't the specialists do these
things?" he replied:

> Role expectations! I would have loved to have said to them that
> now that the program has reached this stage this is what we need
> and this is what I think we should do for these teachers. I'm talk-
> ing about the subject specialists. But I couldn't say that because
> they were there under certain apprehensions and in all fairness to
> them they were fulfilling the role that may have been expected
> of them when they were first engaged, when they first volunteered
> to come in; and I'm not quite sure what they were told.

Rudy's remarks suggest that he expected the specialists to act as
advisors to the teachers. However, this expectation was unreasonable
since we have noted that the subject specialists did not have any
clearer idea about the new teachers' role than did the teachers. As
one specialist put it:

> He [Mark] doesn't have any answers. If he can tell me how we
> can do it all day long, fine. I mean it's easy to say, math and read-
> ing will be a concomitant result of all these activities. It's one
> thing to say you won't have to take kids and have a formal reading
> or math program but the next question is, How? He hasn't said
> how to do it.

Thus, the subject specialists did not believe that they were in a
position to coach teachers or to give them advice about how to cope
effectively with the new problems they were encountering in their
classrooms. They gave the only help they were capable of giving:
obtaining and distributing supplemental education materials. In short,
the director perceived the helping role for teachers as part of the assistant director's job; he, in turn, expected the subject specialists to
assume this role. The specialists, however, were not capable of providing the kind of help the teachers needed.

The administration could have employed several methods to help the staff develop its capability to implement the innovation, but they were never used. First, since the innovation, according to Mark, was an amalgam derived from many sources, but primarily from Leicestershire, someone from its schools could have been contacted and brought to Cambire to demonstrate the new role and to show teachers how to cope with their role problems. Second, staff meetings could have focused on analyzing the problems that teachers faced; they could have been set forth clearly and examined in depth. This was not done. Third, help was never requested of people residing in the metropolitan area where Cambire was located and who were knowledgeable about the central ideas involved in the innovation and how they might be made operational. Why were no attempts made to enlist the aid of such individuals? The reasons Rudy failed to make these kinds of efforts after teachers began trying the innovation in February are suggested by his comments when interviewed after leaving Cambire:

> Now in February I knew that I was going to leave and so I was determined at that particular time that I wasn't going to rock the boat too much; I felt that they had shown some effort and that it was off the ground a little bit. I'd be leaving soon and John Helman would be taking over. He need not agree with what I was doing, and maybe he had another way of doing it, maybe he was entitled to do it his way and so from February till the time that I left [the middle of April] I went to the meetings and so forth, but I must admit that I had let up with the little bit of strength that I could have to push the innovation.

Before most teachers at Cambire could conform to the new role model they needed to develop the skills and acquire the knowledge required to serve as a catalyst or guide to their pupils. They needed help from persons qualified to demonstrate what constituted effective performance in the new role and from individuals who could help them acquire the techniques and behavioral skills needed to conform to its specifications. Because the innovation was based on a set of assumptions about the nature of the child and the learning process different from those held by most of the teachers, they not only needed to obtain new skills but also a set of new educational attitudes and values and a new way of viewing the phenomenon of schooling. Nothing short of a complete program of teacher retraining was required. However, Rudy believed (Appendix B-4) that a teacher who had difficulties in conforming to the new role model need only "revert to traditional classroom procedures so that he can rethink *his* plan." Mark held the view that "teachers can change themselves." The director and assistant director were thus apparently unaware of the need for the retraining of the staff if it were to be expected to implement the catalytic role model.

Teachers at Cambire, therefore, did not develop the capabilities needed to perform in accord with the new definition of their role because they were not exposed to a retraining process and were never given the help and advice they required. Our findings suggest that this circumstance was a function of three basic conditions: (1) the administration was unaware of the need for retraining the teachers and did not establish procedures to initiate such a process; (2) the few efforts that were made to provide help to the teachers were marked by lack of frank communication and erroneous expectations. Mark delegated the responsibility of dealing with problems encountered by the teachers in their efforts to implement the innovation to Rudy, but Rudy believed that "the helping" function was part of the subject specialists' role, although they reported a lack of understanding of the new definition of the teacher's role; (3) Rudy discontinued his efforts to provide help to the staff when he was informed in February 1967, that he would soon be promoted to a principalship, and therefore, would be leaving Cambire. As a consequence of these conditions, the staff received little or no help in developing the competencies needed to implement the innovation.

The Unavailability of Instructional Materials

To implement the catalytic role model the teachers at Cambire required special educational materials that were never made available to them during the period between the announcement of the innovation and our assessment of its implementation. Why were they not provided?

The director appeared to define the problem as one of constraints placed on the school by the larger system. Because Cambire was both part of the BEC and also of the regular school system, the director did not have the authority to spend funds allocated to the school for the purchase of instructional materials. He had to order them through the purchasing office of the school system which, however, permitted only the purchase of equipment and materials specified on an "approved" list. The list did not include "innovative" materials of the kinds necessary for use by teachers trying to implement the catalytic role model.

Williams noted this bureaucratic constraint on his purchasing of materials in a private document sent to the superintendent's office during the middle of February 1967, several weeks *after* teachers were urged to make their first efforts:

> Difficulty in obtaining supplies and materials quickly enough has often hindered the experimental program from operating with desired efficiency. Experimental programs cannot be planned in detail sufficiently ahead of time to order supplies in conformity with procedures currently in effect. The needs of these programs cannot be predicted in the usual fashion, since, in most cases, succeeding phases of a program depend upon the results of the first experiments. A long lapse of time between the end of a first phase and the arrival of materials for a second phase can destroy the effectiveness of an entire program. The establishment of procedures that would enable the staffs of the experimental schools to order and to purchase materials directly and quickly would be highly desirable.

Thus, Williams appeared to define the unavailability of materials needed by teachers to perform the new role largely in terms of a constraint imposed on Cambire by the larger system, a condition that the director apparently had difficulty in removing.

We think, however, that a more fundamental reason for the failure to provide the kinds of materials needed for implementing the innovation was that few instructional materials of the type required existed. We noted in the last chapter the comments of the administrators and subject specialists about the lack of "highly motivating, self-instructional materials" and about the need for their development levels for children of different ages and varying achievements. The director's attempts to enlist the aid of outside curriculum and educational media firms in developing such materials suggests that he was aware of this problem and had made efforts to cope with it.

Despite the constraints placed on the bureau to purchase materials required for the innovation, it appears that even if this agency had been given complete freedom in this respect, the types of materials teachers needed did not exist. The administration, in effect, was requesting teachers to carry out an innovation that required unique types of instructional materials that were not available.

Failure to Adjust Organizational Arrangements

We noted in the last chapter that three school practices that were incompatible with the innovation existed at Cambire prior to its announcement: rigid scheduling of school time, age-grouping, and the report card system. The last two were never altered and the first, the school schedule, although altered, remained rigid in many respects. Why were the needed changes in organizational arrangements never made?

One possible explanation is that the willingness of school administrators to change long-standing practices to make them congruent with an innovation will depend in part on the extent of their commitment to it: the less their commitment to the innovation, the less they will be willing to institute changes in these practices. Data collected at Cambire revealed that the staff's immediate superior, the assistant director, had serious reservations about the innovation. He had mentioned earlier in his interview some of his basic reservations about the innovation and had stressed his uneasiness about the way pupils were expected to learn to read. The interviewer first summarized his earlier remarks:

> Your feeling was that although basically you *liked* the idea of trying out the innovation, you weren't convinced about *all* of its aspects, especially [its value in teaching] reading; you also didn't think that it was something that ought to be done all day with all kids. It was something that maybe should have been done only part of the day. Is this a *fair* statement of your views?

Rudy replied:

> Well. My feeling was that we wanted to try to make the innovation work as one of the projects of the school. . . . I think his [Williams] idea was to require the teachers to follow the new role model all day long. . . . I don't know, I don't think we've reached that stage where the innovation *should* be followed all day long at the Cambire School. You've got to think of kids, too. You're dealing with children, living children who deserve a good shake in education, and I wasn't confident enough to say that we could have good learning go on and find out all we can about it [the new role model] by giving them exposure to it all day long.

These sentiments are also reflected in his memorandum (Appendix B-4) to the teachers at the end of January in which he announced that the former practice of self-contained classrooms would be reinstated. His suggested schedule indicates his concern for maintaining a routine in which children are regularly exposed to formal instruction in reading and math, regardless of their interests.

An allegiance to the traditional teacher-directed classroom with its focus on the teaching of specific subjects was also held by the subject specialists, as this excerpt from an interview with one of them reveals:

> I initially thought we'd have to modify it [the catalytic role model] and I still think we do in terms of materials and programs that are available; we have to go back to the so-called "meaty" subjects such as reading, language, and math. I still think once we got to reading and math anyway we'd have to have more directed teaching. Well, maybe I'm misinterpreting the new model, but I envision some directed teaching going on, and I think I envision more than he [Mark] does.

The most reasonable explanation to account for the lack of change in the report card system and in age-mixing appears to be that the administrative personnel at the school were not aware that such alterations constituted prerequisites for implementation.

Our evidence suggests that there was little recognition of the need for altering these traditional organizational arrangements at Cambire that were incompatible with the innovation. The extent to which this was due to a failure to recognize the importance of these conditions, to a failure of communications, or to an unwillingness to make changes by an administrator not fully committed to the implementation of the innovation, is an open question. The administration had the authority to make the required changes, but it did not do so. The continued existence of this barrier may be attributed, therefore, to the failure of the administrators of the Cambire School to institute the required changes.

The Decline in Staff Motivation to Implement the Innovation

Data presented in the preceding chapter showed that all of the teachers at Cambire were willing to make efforts to implement the innovation immediately after it was presented to them in November, but that during the following months their motivation or willingness to attempt to conform to the new role model steadily declined. What conditions accounted for the hardening of the teachers' resistance to make efforts to implement the innovation in May?

Our evidence strongly suggests that the increasing resistance of the teachers could primarily be attributed to their increasing disenchantment with the innovation and its sponsorship, a disillusionment that grew out of a set of disappointments and frustrations that they began to experience shortly after the announcement of the innovation and that continued to multiply during the ensuing months. Serious difficulties arose between December and February. They focused on the four obstacles considered in detail in Chapter 6 that the teachers were never able to surmount. They became aware of ambiguities in the innovation and the unavailability of appropriate curriculum materials in December and early January, before they had even attempted to implement the innovation. In late January and February, when they were asked to make their first efforts to implement the innovation, they began to realize their inability to perform in accord with the new expectations for their behavior and that existing organizational arrangements were incompatible with the new role model. During this period, the staff began to experience serious reservations about the director's decision to introduce the innovation during the middle of a school year; they also began to experience interpersonal tensions in relationships with their teaching partners as well as considerable strain and fatigue because of the role overload to which they were exposed.

In March and early April, the director was unwilling to make a commitment to the teachers that they would again be assigned to Cambire the following year; this fact and their growing belief that the director was "using them" in an unprofessional manner to promote "his" innovation added to their mounting frustrations and feelings of disillusionment.

In addition to being exposed to these experiences, the staff at the end of April became aware that the director had rejected the application of the school's informal leader for the position of assistant director of

Cambire next year, and most teachers unofficially learned that they were not going to be invited to return for the following year.

We now examine in more detail these conditions as they emerged and multiplied, and how, through their accumulation, they led to growing staff disenchantment with the innovation and its sponsorship. We also will show how this combination of circumstances accounts for the emergence, "snowballing," and congealing of the resistance to the implementation of the innovation that was manifestly evident in May.

Obstacles That Were Never Removed

Our observations in the school and interviews with the staff provided abundant evidence of the teachers' initial frustrations over their inability to overcome the obstacles they encountered after the innovation was announced in November and of their mounting frustrations during the period beginning in late January, when they attempted to implement it. The teachers' growing bitterness toward the administration because of its failure to clarify ambiguities in the new role model and its inability to demonstrate how it could be implemented is evidenced by the following comments of one teacher:

> Everybody kept saying that they don't understand how to do it. Mark *never* gave us definite plans; there was a lot of resentment that they were asking us to do something that they didn't understand themselves.

The teachers' growing anger over the unavailability of required instructional materials is illustrated by this excerpt from an interview with a staff member who was initially highly motivated to attempt to conform to the new role model:

> He [Williams] made it so flowery; I'd like to see him with these kids; he wrote it up in such a way that he gave me the impression that it was an easy thing to do. It isn't! I didn't have any equip-

ment; I had to make up my own new games; they didn't give me what I needed.

The frustrations of the teachers resulting from the failure of their superiors to adjust organizational arrangments that were incompatible with the innovation, such as the method of reporting grades, is indicated by the words of this teacher:

> Report cards are due; I have to grade these kids; now on some things I can fudge around but not reading and math; if I have to make out report cards I've got to try to teach them this stuff; let them get rid of report cards and sell the parents on it and then I'll sit back and let them play all day.

The strong feelings of the teachers about the unwillingness or inability of the director to help them with the numerous problems they had encountered, or to see to it that they were provided with the types of assistance they needed, were expressed by one of the teachers as follows:

> ... Williams, they were his ideas; we were trying to work them out for him and he was nowhere in sight. I am surprised that people didn't lose interest earlier or take a "who cares" attitude; now this is so, but it wasn't this way in the beginning.

In addition to the teachers' continued frustration over the four barriers that were never removed, in late January and February they also began to express serious reservations about the director's decision to introduce the innovation during the middle of the school year. Interpersonal tensions between teaching partners in the same classroom also began to emerge at this time. Teachers began to experience considerable fatigue and mental strain during this period as a consequence of role overload. At one and the same time they had been asked to continue to learn the new role, to carry it out. and to maintain important aspects of the traditional classroom environment as well.

The Way the Innovation was Introduced at Cambire

Contributing to the emergence of staff resistance to implementing the innovation in late January and early February were the teachers' feelings that the administrative decision to introduce the innovation at the end of January was ill-timed. As one teacher put it:

> At a meeting, Rudy announced Williams thinks it's a good idea for all of us to do it; I guess if you didn't like it, tough! I guess everyone wanted to; I didn't think one could refuse, I was surprised; we had been told to help Faith, now all of a sudden we were asked to do it!

Another said:

> When the brochure was passed out Faith was told she was the one [who was] to try it out. But, four weeks later we were all told, "You are going to try it out." I had everything worked out in my classes at that time; now, everything was to be upturned. We should have tried it either in October or waited for the next year; it was just too much work to try in the middle of the year.

Another staff member noted:

> The lack of communication was hindering. We should have had a meeting. Williams should have sat down with Rudy, Alex, and me and found out what we thought about the idea, about our positive or negative feelings, asked our reactions. He railroaded it. We should have had at least a weekly meeting. Williams by nature has a lack of organizational strength. Perhaps he was so busy with a myriad of problems and duties up there at BEC that he couldn't see the need for this. His idea was sound but he's not a strategist or tactician in implementing a program. This is because of his lack of experience. Maybe Mark expected Rudy to do it. Rudy didn't. But maybe Mark didn't communicate this to Rudy.

When the assistant director was asked whether the decision to request all teachers to try the innovation in January was made by the director, Rudy said:

The decision to introduce the innovation was made by Williams.
. . . He said to put it into Cambire; he didn't tell me exactly how
to do it; he didn't give me that kind of direction.

In January one subject specialist commented as follows about
Rudy's role in the introduction of the innovation:

I don't think Rudy moved until he got a mandate to do so. It had
to be a clear-cut order. I know he had a great many misgivings
about the innovation.

The director was questioned about this matter in May 1967. He
noted, "Maybe I did say something about that to Rudy."

The basis of the decision in January to request all teachers to
carry out the innovation was the administration's belief that the
teachers were willing to make the efforts to implement it as far back
as when it was announced in late *November*.

In an interview with the director in December 1966, he said, "We
were really surprised in November when all of the teachers said that
they would be willing to try it [the innovation] out." In February
1967, subsequent to the decision, the director expressed this
view: "The teachers were virtually fighting to try this thing out in
November; I didn't expect them to be so enthusiastic about it; I
was really happy about this.

The assistant director also believed that all of the teachers
were willing to try the innovation. In discussing this matter,
he reported:

. . . as we began to talk about the innovation, it was after I
handed out these books, [the November Document] I said, "Now
who would like to try it?"; everybody's hand went up and I said,
"Fine." Then we began to redirect our energies toward it.

A subject specialist recalled telling the assistant director that he
had misinterpreted what the teachers' reactions were in January:

I mentioned to him the next day that many teachers felt, you
know, they were being compelled to try this at this time, and he
said he thought he had made it clear that this was strictly a voluntary task. So, somewhere communications broke down.

Evidence presented in the preceding chapter showed that the
teachers at Cambire were initially willing to try the innovation when
it was announced in November. Because all teachers expressed a
general willingness to try out the innovation in November, the
director and assistant director assumed that the entire staff would
also be positively predisposed to trying it out at the end of January.
It is problematic whether the director would have postponed his
decision to ask all teachers to make implementation efforts if the
director had had a clearer understanding of the teachers' feelings
about the introduction of the innovation in January. What is clear is
that the administration did not make efforts to ascertain the opinions
and feelings of teachers about the new role model before making the
decision in January to ask them to conform to it, and that the
teachers did not feel free to express their honest reactions to their
administrators about the innovation.

Interpersonal Tensions between "Teaching Partners"

When the teachers attempted to conform to the catalytic role
model in February, they encountered additional difficulties. The
administrators had instituted double staffing of classrooms on the
assumption that a smaller teacher-pupil ratio would facilitate the
likelihood of implementing the innovation. However, this arrangement led to two new serious problems: interpersonal conflicts
between "teaching partners" and disagreements between student
teachers who were to serve as "second teachers" in the classrooms
and the regular staff.

One of the teachers described the strains and tensions that had
developed in her relationship with her teaching partner and its
effects on her willingness to continue to make efforts to try to implement the innovation as follows:

Somehow this whole thing is catching up with me, and I am losing
interest; part of it is Arthur; he says, 'let's not do it today,' and
I go along; I am a jerk for doing it, but I go along. Ya know the
new games?; Arthur took them home for his kids.

When asked whether she had discussed this matter with Arthur, she
replied:

I just can't tell him. It's really my fault. Arthur came in initially
and took over. I think he thinks he knows more than I do. He
interrupts me constantly; he makes me ashamed.

When asked whether she had discussed this problem with the assistant director, she complained:

He would have put me off like he did in November when I complained about Arthur because he was too loud with his reading
group and we were in the same room. Rudy's reaction was,
"He's trying."

The following episode illustrates the tensions that existed
between teaching partners in the spring. A parent was in the office
of the acting assistant director, John Helman, and was complaining
about conditions she had observed in the classroom in which Stan
and Linda were teaching partners. Both teachers were in the office
when the parent asserted:

. . . the class was *very* loud, completely out of control and several
boys were on the floor fighting; now I want to know, is this the
kind of *new* program these kids are getting?

At the close of this tense session Stan assured the parent that
such an incident would not occur again. After Linda left the office
Stan blurted out:

The minute I leave that goddamned class, it falls *apart*. If I had
that class by myself, I would have it so that I could *stroll* around
the block and come back without it being noisy, . . . , but with

her, what the hell can I do? She lets them do whatever they want
and expects me to pick up the pieces. . . . (As he stormed upstairs
he asserted) 'there will be no play time today!'

The field observation notes for that day showed that Stan
punished the whole class by forcing them to spend the remainder
of the day sitting at their desks with their hands folded. The children
ate lunch in silence and were not permitted to read or do anything
else.

The administrators wanted to make use of the student teachers
to facilitate the implementation of the innovation. The regular
teachers, however, felt that they had an obligation to give the
teachers-in-training the chance to learn a great deal about the
traditional role model and required the student teachers to conduct
group instruction in specific subject areas. When we interviewed the student teachers, all of them told us that they had wanted the opportunity to attempt to behave in accord with the catalytic role model
and had expressed their desire to do so to the regular teachers.

However, the regular teachers felt differently about the matter.
As one put it:

> The student teachers must gain experience teaching regular
> classes. . . . When they get out of here they aren't going to teach
> in this kind of atmosphere; they must learn to handle thirty kids
> by themselves, in a traditional setting!

A student teacher put it this way:

> . . . he [the regular teacher] didn't think I should be trained
> according to the innovation so he had me teaching the whole
> class most of the time; he himself spent little time on it.

The administrators introduced double staffing because they
anticipated that this arrangement would speed up the implementation
of the innovation. However, this new practice had unanticipated consequences that contributed to the teachers' frustrations and their

growing unwillingness to make efforts to implement the innovation. The difficulties created by double staffing and by the ambiguity of the role of student teachers were never brought out in the open as problems that required solutions, and, therefore, were never resolved during the period of attempted implementation.

Strain and Fatigue from Role Overload

In early January teachers were behaving in accord with the traditional role model. In late January, without prior training or orientation, they were asked to carry out the innovation at Cambire. This required teachers to make efforts of the following kind: explore how to use "innovative" materials in new ways; develop new materials; become adjusted to a teaching partner and in the case of teachers who had student teachers as partners, help them adjust to the experiences of working in a school; develop and use new procedures to monitor the directions in which children were progressing; help children to adjust to the new expectations for their behavior; prepare traditional lessons for reading and math. They also had to do a great deal of paper work, including weekly reports to the assistant director and monthly reports to BEC. It is not surprising, therefore, that the teachers experienced a heavy degree of role overload especially during February and March.

One subject specialist described the teachers' situation as follows:

> The change was just too much for them to handle. . . . Their role is twice as difficult now; not only do they have new curricula and materials, but also a new classroom organization and a new role as a teacher. More planning, more research should have been done; consultants should have been brought in. . . .

During February and early March our field observations indicated that many teachers were becoming exhausted and short tempered and that these characteristics were not in evidence when they reverted to their traditional patterns of performance.

At Cambire, the administration not only failed to anticipate the role overload to which teachers would be exposed when they attempted to implement the innovation, but in addition, they did not cope with the problem once it was very apparent. This unquestionably contributed to the teachers' frustrations and the increase in staff resistance to the implementation of the innovation.

Staff Uncertainty about Reappointment to Cambire

In March and April a number of events occurred that added to the teachers' growing feelings of disillusionment about the innovation and its sponsor. Two of these events concerned whether the teachers would be reappointed to Cambire the following year.

At a faculty meeting in the middle of March, Rudy Gault distributed *formal* reapplication forms to the teachers so that they could request that they be assigned again to Cambire the following year. The teachers knew that positions at Cambire were to be filled on a yearly basis, that is, no permanent teaching positions had been allocated to the school. Teachers had been told earlier that if their efforts during the year were assessed positively they would be invited to return the next year; if not, they would not be asked back. The teachers interpreted Rudy's request to fill out the official forms to mean that their year of experience at the school would be disregarded when decisions were made about who would be invited to teach at Cambire the following year. The fact that Williams never personally came to talk to them about their work and did not waive the *formal* reapplication procedure also concerned them greatly. Moreover, at the meeting at which Rudy gave out the reapplication forms he also distributed forms to them to apply for a transfer to another school in the regular system the next year. The teachers informed us that they perceived this as meaning that Mark really did not want them back next year. The following short conversation among three staff members after the meeting indicates their feelings:

John sardonically said, "What we need is a cadre of teachers with nerves of steel." Fred replied sarcastically by pretending to be unconcerned, "I am just looking over my release." "Who is going to continue to try, if they know they're leaving?" interjected Ruth.

This meeting touched off a barrage of rumors about Mark, led to numerous discussions about the schools to which teachers at Cambire probably would be assigned next year, and created considerable anxiety about the impact of their year at Cambire on their own careers. During the ensuing weeks the teachers spent a considerable amount of time discussing these matters. Their anxieties about their future status at Cambire are reflected in this conversation:

Have you heard anything from Williams about next year?

Are you kidding? Rudy is leaving shortly and I can't get him to make a final decision about me, let alone for you next year.

Well, if he doesn't want us back, why doesn't he just come out and say so?

That's what I'd like to know!

What's all the secrecy about? Why can't he just tell us?

The career anxieties of the teachers is evidenced by the following dialogue:

Did you hear anything about next year?

We'll know come about September 1st!

I'll be damned if I'll wait that long before getting another position. I can just hear Mark on August 31, 'Well we've found someone else to fill your position who has more creative ideas'; then you'll end up in some hole in this system with some nut as a principal cracking the whip over you.

Not me, I won't wait that long, I'm looking now!

Me, too.

The continued concern and rumors about Mark's intentions are illustrated by the following interchange:

He's going to get rid of all of us!

He wants to make it look like he's giving everyone a chance to be rated, but he really doesn't want most of us back.

I don't think Mark knows what he wants!

Rudy realized that something had to be done to allay the mounting anxieties and hostile feelings of the teachers. He invited Mark to meet with the teachers on April fifth, nearly three weeks after the meeting at which Rudy gave out the application forms, to discuss their future status. In answering a question about the number of people from the "regular" system who were applying for positions at Cambire, Mark commented:

> . . . we will now want to look at the whole batch. . . . We won't know yet for some time how many teachers we will need; we won't need to interview you, but those we don't know, must be. I can't say who will be here; our program is based on a completely voluntary, carefully selected basis terminated either at the will of the teacher or the administration. (long pause) I realize this is awkward for you and me. (long pause) Are there any questions?

Stan responded, "When will we know whether we're coming back or not?" Mark replied, "Oh probably in a month or so." Almost in unison, the teachers responded in a tone of disbelief, "A month?"

A great deal of heated discussion ensued. The teachers demanded that they be notified by the following week whether they would be asked back. Mark immediately told them that he could not give them an answer that soon. He agreed, however, to phone the Office of Personnel immediately. As soon as he returned to the meeting he reported that the following decision had been made:

The Director of Personnel says it's OK for each of you to pick as first choice another school; if you are selected for Cambire the other application will be dropped and you'll have no obligation to it.

The meeting ended shortly thereafter. The teachers were not only disappointed with the outcome of their meeting with Mark; most of them were furious about the way they had been treated:

Mark is nothing but a big bag of wind!

What did he tell us? If I can find better people, you'll leave, if I can't get anyone else you'll stay.

What principal in his or her right mind would wait for Mark to decide whether he wanted us?

Gee, I'm not sure Mark really knows what he is doing now.

You know in business and politics I expected double talk, but in education, I didn't; this is what makes me mad; most of us like the freedom here but not this kind of crap. Who is he kidding; what principal will let you tell him you will take a job in his school, but that he must wait to see if Cambire wants you first. If he does and then you tell the principal you can't take his job, . . . you'd be committing suicide in this system.

If he doesn't want me that's OK, but why doesn't he tell us? That's what gets me mad, he won't tell me; maybe he's afraid we won't do anything the rest of the time we're here!

The Feeling of "Being Used"

The mounting difficulties and frustrations of the teachers were further exacerbated by certain events that took place in March and April that led teachers to believe that there was some foundation to the rumor that they were being used by the director to "feather his nest." In spite of promises made as early as November by the administration that it would sharply curtail the number of visitors permitted in the school, more persons visited Cambire in April than in

November. Moreover, in early April the administration asked teachers on several occasions to rearrange their schedules so that they would be sure to be engaged in the "activity period," that is, making efforts to implement the innovation when the visitors arrived at the school. One staff member remarked after receiving such a request:

> What bugs me is that they just call and *tell* us that they are coming. And we have to put on a show [the activity period] all of the time until they leave. The teachers are beginning to think that Williams is using them.

This statement of a teacher, made after one of these requests, demonstrates the type of impact they had on the attitudes of teachers toward attempting to carry out the innovation. One said:

> I had to pull them back into a traditional class today; they got *wild* yesterday because of that activity period Rudy wanted for those visitors; I don't like putting on a show!

Another said:

> Last week I was really disturbed when we were told to put out new games for that visiting group even though we had never seen the games prior to their visit.

Before the arrival of two prominent visitors one morning, the assistant director went to each classroom and requested teachers to begin activity period immediately after reading. They were asked to continue it until the visitors, who would be accompanied by Williams, left. In the hallway just prior to the beginning of the activity period, the following exchange was heard between two teachers.

> Time to put on the show!

> Christ, he's [Mark has] got everyone upset! Who the hell is this guy that's visiting? OK, if he wants a show I'll put one on; I don't care. But I don't understand it; this is Rudy's last week.

Why is he so shook up? Why doesn't he tell Mark to go jump?
[pleadingly] They can't all be that important; last week it was
that urban group, then Mrs. Pierce, now these guys.

A teacher being interviewed that morning observed:

Why must we continually cater to visitors? Who is it now? I'm
sorry we have to break up our interview; I guess I have to go
perform! The only time Williams comes down here is when he
brings visitors or wants something!

Williams and the two visitors arrived late. They first met with the
assistant director and the subject specialists in the school office. The
following episode about this meeting was related to the fieldworker
and most of the other teachers.

The assistant director began speaking to the visitors about the
different parts of the curriculum at Cambire. He pointed to a set
of plastic weighted numbers and a scale children used for arithmetic. Visitor A, an unusually outspoken person, interjected,
"This is really stupid, most of this stuff is useless."

A few minutes later the assistant director started explaining with
great enthusiasm his idea of a school in the round . . . about the
way the teacher would sit in the middle of this circular room in
a glass encasement with a set of microphones. . . . Visitor A interjected, "Sounds like 1984 is here!" The assistant director,
wrapped up in his enthusiasm, failed to grasp the negative con-
notation of the comment. Interpreting this to mean that education is advancing very rapidly, he responded, "Isn't it great?"
Visitor A retorted, "No." The assistant director became very
embarrassed. Williams sat silent during this period; shortly thereafter, he said abruptly, "Let's go see the classes!"

Because the visitors and Williams had arrived late and had spent
considerable time in the office, when they emerged from the
meeting the school was having recess. The children were on the
playground and were being supervised by a number of teachers;
most of the remaining teachers were in the lounge having coffee.
The classrooms were empty. The director in an astonished tone

said, "Where are the kids?" "It's recess time; they're all outside
having recess," a staff member responded. Williams retorted
angrily, "Why? Why do they *all* have to be outside at the same
time?" Another staff member responded, "That's the only way
they can get physical exercise and at the same time give the
teachers a break from their classrooms." "Why," the director
replied sharply, "do the teachers need a *break*. . . . The hell with
the teachers!"

Walking upstairs toward a primary room, Visitor A interjected,
"It doesn't matter, I don't have to see the kids to know if some-
thing worthwhile is going on; all I have to do is look at the rooms."
Walking into the first room they reached on the second floor,
Williams advised, "Let's get out of here, this room isn't any good!"
Moving into another primary room, Visitor A, pointing to the
built-in book cabinet, said to Visitor B, "All these books do is
take up space!"

The rest of the tour went no better; the visitors and Williams left
the building as the children were returning to their classes.

Detailed accounts of this episode circulated among all of the
teachers during the rest of the day and their reactions to it were
bitter. Teachers were especially disturbed because Williams indicated
no approbation for their efforts. The following statements reflected
their feelings at the time: "Williams is after a big job somewhere else;
that's why he's 'kowtowing' to this guy"; "he wants a big name and
doesn't care who he has to step on to get one"; "Why the hell should
I break my back if that's the attitude he takes toward us"; "he's
feathering his own nest; he's not stupid; he doesn't care about us";
"If that's the way he feels the hell with him; I'll do just what I have
to, to keep things going and *no more*!"

Two Final Blows to Staff Morale

Two occurrences during the last week in April contributed
materially to the teachers' disenchantment with the director and the
innovation. The first was the rejection of John Helman's application

for appointment as assistant director at Cambire. The second was the announcement that most of the teachers would not be reappointed to their positions at the school for the following year.

Rudy left Cambire to assume his new job in the middle of April, just before spring recess. When school reopened a week later, Williams invited John Helman to serve as acting assistant director for the remainder of the school year, but at the same time informed Helman that he would not be recommended as the person to fill this position next year. Helman wanted the job very much and he and the other teachers had anticipated that he would get it. The teachers' reactions to this decision are revealed in the following conversation between two teachers:

> John is the only one who really tried to help us get together . . . ; he's the only one who has kept the spirits of the teachers up and kept this place together . . . ; it's not right.

> I have no feelings of loyalty anymore; this is bad. How can you be loyal to a guy who does something like this, . . . a guy who isn't honest with the people who work for him. . . . I just don't have any feelings about Williams anymore and I know he doesn't care about us. (long pause) If I can get another job I'm going to take it.

In a meeting with the teachers at the end of April Helman told them that Williams had hired, or was about to hire, new staff for nearly all the teaching positions at Cambire, a decision which most teachers had anticipated. Helman ended the meeting with the following remarks:

> I know these last few months have been positively insulting; why, one handling a crew at the docks wouldn't handle them the way he's handled us; anytime you take one's dignity away! All that was talked about at the meetings were first and second choices and qualifications; now he's picking them out of a black hat; it's too bad because this could have been a good thing next year. . . . It's almost 4:00 P.M.; before we break up let's get one thing

straight; as long as I am in charge we're going to have order around here. I don't care how you run your classes but I want order, none of this running up and down stairs, fighting, and wandering from one room to another, in and out of classes; I want these last few weeks to be as pleasant as possible for both you and me, OK?

The sentiments expressed by the acting assistant director reflected the solid resistance that had developed by this time among nearly all of the staff to making further efforts to implement the innovation. When Helman was asked whether he planned to hold any meetings to discuss the innovation now that Rudy was gone, his response was blunt and direct:

We're not having any formal meetings on Mondays or Wednesdays. . . . I won't call any, and if I do, they won't be to talk about the innovation. They were never called before to talk about it, so why should *I* do it now? Hell no! Why should I set this job up for someone else in the fall? Besides, I can't push teachers who have been given such a bum deal. How can I make teachers who know they're not coming back and who got such a rotten dumping make any effort to do anything?

To summarize: our findings showed that the teachers' lack of motivation to make efforts to implement the innovation in May was the result of steadily increasing disenchantment with the innovation and its sponsorship, a disenchantment that began soon after the announcement of the innovation by the director and reached its peak of intensity as the year drew to a close. The evidence revealed that this disillusionment grew out of a set of serious obstacles and frustrations that teachers began to experience shortly after the announcement of the innovation and that continued to multiply during the ensuing period. Obstacles first appeared in December and included a number of barriers that teachers were not able to surmount. They recognized ambiguities in the innovation and became aware of the unavailability of appropriate curriculum materials in December and early January; during the latter part of January and early

February after they began to make efforts to implement the innovation, they began to realize their inability to perform in accord with the new role model and began to recognize that existing organizational arrangements were incompatible with it. Also during late January and February, the teachers began to have serious reservations about the director's decision to request all of them to make efforts to implement the innovation so late in the year. They were also feeling stress and tensions in their relationships with their teaching partners and strain and fatigue from role overload as they made efforts to perform in accord with the new role model.

The director's unwillingness in March and early April to make decisions about the retention of the staff and the teachers' growing belief that the director was "using them" in an unprofessional manner to promote "his" innovation contributed to their mounting frustrations and disillusionment. The congealing of the teachers' disillusionment came at the end of April. It resulted from the staff's learning that Mark had rejected the application of the school's informal leader to serve as assistant director at Cambire the following year and from their securing unofficial information that most of them were also not going to be invited to return.

An Explanation of the Obstacles to Which Teachers Were Exposed: The Implementation Strategy of the Director

To this point in the chapter we have focused on the question: What accounted for the emergence and persistence of each of the five major barriers that served as obstacles to the teachers' implementation of the innovation at the time of our assessment in May 1967?

We now enquire whether the emergence and persistence of these five conditions can be attributed to a more fundamental organizational condition. Our analysis suggests that each of them is linked to a common root: *the failure of the administration* to recognize or to resolve problems to which it exposed teachers when it requested them to implement the innovation. This condition, we contend, was a consequence of the director's failure to recognize the complexities of the process of implementing organizational innovations and his lack of awareness of his role obligations to his subordinates when he initiated this process.

The director's view of the steps required to implement the innovation, as evidenced by the strategy he employed, may be briefly described as follows: (1) explain the philosophy and objectives of the innovation to teachers through several written documents; (2) give teachers maximum freedom to carry it out; and (3) delegate responsibility to an administrative subordinate (the assistant director) to see that the innovation is implemented. Williams' conception of how to promote educational change stressed making additional funds available to schools so that new ideas could be tried out and providing teachers with maximum freedom so that they could carry out an innovation as "professionals," that is, independent of the bureaucracy of the school system. In his words:

> . . . We began to pick up a lot of the new ideas . . . drawn from or coincidental with a lot of the work that has been done over the last nine or ten years in Leicestershire in England which means essentially getting the teachers off the kids' backs, getting the administration off the teachers' backs, and saying to the teachers . . . , "you're adult professionals, you said you wanted to experiment, you said you were full of ideas, go to it." That's not exactly how we did it because actually we came in and said, "We'd like to try some of the ideas at Leicestershire."

In February, in response to a question about his perception of how the staff at Cambire viewed him, Williams said, "I would guess probably as the agent for setting up the situation at Cambire; an originator of ideas; they shouldn't, but I think they see me as their boss."

In April 1967, Williams commented as follows on a copy of a proposal for an innovation submitted to him by a teacher at Cambire:

Fred—I think this is excellent—It catches the spirit of what we
are trying to do at the Cambire. It also is a good example of the
thoughtful professionalism we are trying to release in our teachers.
It's there—but we all have to convince ourselves that we can let
it out and make it work—Good Job—(Signed) Mark

The assistant director's appraisal of Williams' approach corroborates our interpretation of his orientation to educational change:

... Mark felt that getting the teachers together, providing the
funds, and expressing his ideas, even though they were not fully
crystallized for himself, was an *initiative* which would propel us
into innovation, you see. And his thinking was, "If it's worth
doing, you're going to do it yourself. You're not going to do it
because I tell you to do it. If you're really interested, you'll
evolve it for yourself."

The director's strategy was inadequate for two basic reasons. First
it failed to take account of difficulties that could have been anticipated when the teachers attempted to implement the innovation.
Second, it contained no provisions for mechanisms to identify and
cope with problems that could not be anticipated but that might
emerge during the period of attempted implementation.

The director's strategy for implementing the innovation gave prac-
tically no consideration to the potential obstacles that were likely to
arise when the teachers would attempt to implement the new role
model. Since the director's model for change essentially ignored these
potential problems, no efforts were instituted prior to the introduction of the innovation to remove or minimize these barriers, nor was
attention focused on ways to cope with them if they emerged during
the period of attempted implementation.

The second major deficiency in the director's strategy was its
lack of feedback mechanisms. We noted that the assistant director
had a number of reservations about the innovation, as did the subject specialists and a number of the teachers. But the assistant director was not given adequate opportunities to communicate his feel-

ings to the director about this matter. When discussing Williams' lack of help in promoting the implementation of the innovation, he added:

> . . . he was too busy, I was lucky to get a chance to corner him to tell him what was happening. . . . I had to use my own insights. . . . He was concerned about staffing the school for the fall, in other words, he was learning about the city, the system, the people, how they got there, and so forth; he was very much interested in what would happen *next September.* (Italics ours.)

Furthermore, provisions were not made for the teachers to speak frankly to their superiors about their reservations with regard to the innovation and the difficulties they encountered as they attempted to implement it. In addition, the other interpersonal and organizational problems to which they were exposed during the period of attempted implementation, additional sources of their frustration, were never discussed openly and frankly.

The director made numerous assumptions about the innovation and the operation of the Cambire School that were in fact tenuous. He assumed that the assistant director and he were in agreement about the nature of the innovation. He assumed that the teachers would not experience any serious problems in carrying out the innovation, and that those that would arise could be effectively handled by the assistant director or the subject specialists. However, these and other assumptions he made were erroneous, and since he did not provide for feedback mechanisms in his strategy of implementation, he had no way of obtaining the facts therefore identify or take steps to cope with these barriers to implementation.

Summary

The evidence gathered during the case study led us to conclude that the most plausible explanation for the conditions that blocked the implementation of the innovation could be located in two fundamental deficiencies in the strategy used by the director:

(1) it failed to identify and bring into the open the various types of difficulties teachers were likely to encounter in their implementation attempts, and (2) it failed to establish and use feedback mechanisms to uncover the barriers that arose during the period of attempted implementation.

8

Conclusions and Implications

In his incisive paper on "The Bearing of Empirical Research on Social Theory" Merton (1957) points out that one of the ways in which empirical inquiry invites the extension of theory is through observation of neglected facts. In his words, "When an existing conceptual scheme commonly applied to a subject-matter does not adequately take these facts into account, research presses insistently for its reformulation. It leads to the introduction of variables which have not been systematically included in the scheme of the analysis" (p. 108).

Our case study identified a set of facts that were of critical importance in explaining why the effort to implement a major organizational innovation in a school failed, facts that have been overlooked in the explanation most frequently invoked to account for the success or failure of efforts to implement changes in organizations. These findings supported our reservations about explanations that assume the problem of implementing organizational innovations is essentially one of overcoming organizational members' *initial* resistance to change.

In this chapter we first examine the findings of the case study in terms of their theoretical implications. We then consider several kinds of inquiries suggested by this research experience that we view as especially important. In the final part of the chapter we will dis-

195

cuss several practical implications of our investigation for the management of change in schools.

Theoretical Implications of the Study

Barriers Encountered by Organizational Members

One of our basic reservations about the "resistance to change"
explanation was that it ignores the whole question of barriers that
may be encountered by members of organizations in their efforts
to carry out innovations.

Our findings showed that the failure to implement the innovation
was attributable essentially to a number of obstacles that the
teachers encountered when they attempted to carry it out that were
never removed. What were these barriers that were of critical importance in accounting for the failure of the implementation effort we
studied, but that existing conceptual schemes disregard?

One barrier that blocked the teachers' efforts to implement the
innovation throughout the six-month period was their lack of clarity
about the new role model. Our observations of teachers indicated
that most of them did not have a clear image of the role performance expected of them. Our formal interviews confirmed these
field observations. They revealed the teachers never had a clear
understanding of the innovation. When the teachers were asked
about their understanding of the innovation just before they were
requested to make their first efforts to implement it in January,
most teachers still indicated confusion about it. And when we asked
the teachers about the clarity of the innovation in May, just prior to
our assessment of its degree of implementation, most teachers again
indicated that they still had an ambiguous notion of what was
expected of them. These findings suggest that the *clarity of an
innovation to organizational members* needs to be taken into account
in conceptual schemes designed to explain the success or failure of
implementation efforts.

A second barrier to the implementation of the innovation uncovered by our inquiry was the teachers' lack of the skills and knowledge required to carry it out. All teachers reported that serious problems arose that they were unable to resolve when they made their initial efforts to implement the innovation in January. They all indicated that these unresolved problems persisted during the following months as they made subsequent efforts to carry out the innovation, and furthermore, that new problems, with which they could not cope, also arose. We concluded that the minimal efforts of the teachers to implement the innovation in May were in part attributable to the condition that they lacked the skills and knowledge required to perform the new role. These findings underscore the need to include the variable, *capability of members of an organization to implement an innovation,* in formulations designed to account for the success or failure of efforts to implement innovations.

A third barrier to which the teachers were exposed was the unavailability of required materials and equipment. In a brochure prepared for the teachers by the administration, they were told that teachers should "transfer as much of the instructional and 'motivational' responsibilities as possible from the teacher to the total classroom environment—and to the greatly enhanced materials with which the room should be filled." But our observations in the classrooms revealed that "highly motivating self-instructional materials" were never made available to the teachers. Most of the materials that were available represented the kind of supplementary materials that could be found in a well-stocked suburban elementary school. They did not represent instructional materials that permitted pupils to progress very far in a meaningful way on their own, that is, without instruction from the teacher. These findings stress the importance of including a third variable, the *availability of necessary materials and equipment,* in explanations designed to account for the success or failure of efforts to implement innovations.

A fourth obstacle that blocked teachers in their efforts to imple-

ment the innovation was a set of organizational arrangements existing prior to and during the innovation's introduction that were
incompatible with the innovation, for example, the rigid school
schedule. Another incompatible organizational arrangement was the
system of evaluating pupils, one that required teachers to "give
grades" to each child for his mastery of different skills and subjects.
These findings argue for the inclusion of a fourth variable, *compatibility of organizational arrangements,* in theoretical formulations
designed to account for the implementation of organizational innovations.

The Possibility of the Development of Resistance

What we have stressed to this point is the failure of the "resistance
to change" explanation to take into account a number of obstacles
to which organizational members can be exposed when they attempt
to implement an innovation. A second major reservation we had
about this explanation was that it overlooked the fact that resistance,
certainly an important condition, can *develop* among organizational
members who are positively oriented to change *after an innovation
has been introduced* into the organization as a consequence of
frustrations they experience in attempting to implement it. We
observed such a development at Cambire.

In November 1966, there was general acceptance of the need for
change at the school, and despite the fact that four of the teachers
indicated somewhat negative reactions to the innovation at the time
of its announcement, all of them reported a willingness to try to
carry it out. However, at the time of our assessment in the spring,
most staff members were no longer willing to make such efforts.

These findings emphasize the necessity for theoretical formulations to recognize not only that organizational members' initial
resistance, or lack of willingness, to make efforts to implement an
innovation is important; but in addition, that resistance can develop
after its introduction, that is, *during* the period when members
attempt implementation.

We have now specified two major ways in which our empirical case study invites the extension of theory with respect to the implementation of organizational innovations. First, it suggests that formulations applied to the problem of implementing proposed changes must take into account, in addition to initial staff resistance as a potential obstacle, the following conditions: the clarity of an innovation, members' capability to perform it, the existence of necessary materials and resources, and the compatibility of organizational arrangements with the innovation. All of these variables had a bearing on the failure of the implementation effort we studied; we would argue that they constitute a set of conditions that may need to be viewed as *desiderata* for the maximum implementation of most organizational innovations. Second, the study reveals that the degree to which each of these conditions prevails may vary over time.

The Role of Management in the Implementation of Innovations

Our final major reservation about current theories concerned the limited attention they give to the influence of management, as an important segment of a subordinate's role set, on the implementation process. We do not question the proposition that if organizational members are resistant to change, power equalization efforts by management may be one means by which their resistance can be reduced. However, the performance of management can have a critical bearing on the implementation of innovations in many other ways, most notably in establishing and maintaining the conditions that will facilitate subordinate implementation of innovations.

The importance of the role performance of management became particularly evident in our case study when we asked why the major barriers teachers encountered when they attempted to implement the innovation were never removed. The evidence indicated that the teachers' lack of clarity about the new role model could largely be attributed to the following conditions: ambiguities in the minds of the director and his administrative subordinates about the specific nature of the new role requirements for teachers; the failure of the administrators to provide effective mechanisms for teachers to obtain clarification about their role expectations; and the failure of the staff to secure clarification about the innovation, because of their lack of confidence in the capabilities of their administrators. In attempting to account for the staff's lack of the skills and knowledge required to implement the innovation, we concluded that this condition was primarily attributable to the failure of the administration to recognize that the teachers needed to be resocialized if they were to be able to conform to the new definition of their role and to its failure to provide them with the type of retraining they required. The unavailability of the self-instructional materials that the teachers needed to implement the innovation was attributed to the failure of the administration to face up to the reality that such materials did not exist at the time, and that teachers had neither the skills nor the time required to develop them on the job. The failure to make modifications in organizational arrangements was traced back to two circumstances: the administration's unawareness that certain organizational arrangements were incompatible with the implementation of the new role model and to reservations of the director's key administrative subordinate, the assistant director, about the innovation. The sharp decline in the teachers' motivation to attempt to implement the innovation and the development of their resistance to it between November and May were attributed to their growing disillusionment with the innovation and its sponsorship that resulted from an accumulation of obstacles that were never resolved and to the mounting disappointments and frustrations they experienced during this period. Our findings, reported in detail in Chapter 7, indicated that the teachers' growing disenchantment with the innovation and the administration was a result of many conditions that the administration did not recognize, ignored, or dealt with in inept ways.

These findings led us to conclude that the teachers were unable

to implement the innovation largely because the administration
failed to recognize or to cope effectively with the problems, difficulties, and uncertainties to which it exposed teachers when it asked
them to carry it out. This condition we would contend, was a consequence of the director's restricted view of the process of the
implementation of organizational innovations and his lack of awareness of his role obligations to his subordinates when he initiated
this process.

The director's strategy of implementation was deficient in two
important respects: (1) it failed to take account of *difficulties* to
which teachers would probably be exposed when they attempted
to implement the innovation, and (2) it contained no provisions for
feedback mechanisms to identify and cope with barriers and problems arising during the period of attempted implementation.

This suggests that subordinates may be unable, or find it difficult,
to make changes in their role performance unless management conforms to a set of expectations that subordinates "have a right to
hold" for its performance. More specifically, subordinates have a
right to expect management (1) to take the steps necessary to provide them with a clear picture of their new role requirements; (2) to
adjust organizational arrangements to make them compatible with
the innovation; (3) to provide subordinates with necessary retraining
experiences, required if the capabilities for coping with the difficulties of implementing the innovation are to develop; (4) to provide
the resources necessary to carry out the innovation; and (5) to provide the appropriate supports and rewards to maintain subordinates'
willingness to make implementation efforts.

Furthermore, we would maintain that subordinates have a right
to expect management to be committed to an innovation it expects
them to implement, and to provide effective mechanisms and decision-making procedures to cope with anticipated and unanticipated
problems that may arise. Our findings, in short, suggest that the
extent to which these expectations are recognized by management,
built into its strategy, and conformed to, will have a direct bearing

on the degree to which subordinates implement organizational innovations. The role of management in the implementation process needs to be brought to center stage in theoretical formulations of the problem.

Toward a Theory of the Implementation of Organizational Innovations

We maintain that the *starting* point for an explanation of the differential success of organizations to implement innovations needs to be based on the assumption that if members of an organization are resistant to change, then overcoming this barrier constitutes an initial prerequisite for the implementation of innovations. Our second assumption is that the degree to which an innovation is implemented will be a function of the extent to which five conditions are present during the period of attempted implementation. The first condition is the degree to which members of an organization have or develop a clear understanding of the innovation. Clarity, we assume, will be positively related to their ability to implement it. If they have an ambiguous understanding of the innovation, then they will be unclear about what is expected of them. If they have an erroneous interpretation of the innovation, then their efforts at implementation will be misguided. The second condition is the extent to which the members of an organization possess the capabilities needed to carry it out. If they lack the skills and knowledge required to perform in accord with the demands of the innovations, then it will be impossible for them to implement it. The third condition is that their ability to carry out the innovation also depends on the availability of the materials and other resources it requires. The fourth condition is the compatibility of existing organizational arrangements with the innovation. If arrangements in existence prior to the introduction of the innovation are incompatible with it and are not changed, then it will be more difficult for members of the organization to carry it out. However, if each of these four conditions is fulfilled, it does not follow that staff members will implement an innovation. The staff must also be willing to expend the time and effort required for its implementation, and hence, this condition also must be operative.

Our third assumption is that the extent to which these five conditions are present during the period of attempted implementation will be a function of the performance of management. If ambiguity or confusion exists in the minds of the staff, management is in the best position to clarify the situation. Furthermore, the authority to establish training programs and provide the materials and other resources required by the innovation is lodged with management. In addition, only management has the power to make changes in organizational arrangements that are incompatible with the innovation. And it, too, is the agency that can offer the types of rewards and punishments required if the staff is to be continuously motivated to expend the time and effort required to implement an innovation. Moreover, management can most effectively handle difficulties that arise and that inhibit the development or maintenance of these conditions. For example, at Cambire managerial actions could have alleviated conditions such as teacher role overload, interpersonal strain between teaching partners, and teacher frustrations from lack of managerial support, circumstances which played an important part in the emergence, development, and congealing of staff resistance to the innovation and its sponsorship.

If, as we have assumed, one condition that will preclude the implementation of an innovation is staff resistance to change, then when it exists it must be initially overcome by management. If, as we have further assumed, the implementation of an innovation by the staff is also a function of the degree to which the five conditions previously specified are present, and if as we have additionally assumed, the extent to which these conditions prevail will be a consequence of the performance of management, then it follows that the degree of implementation of an organizational innovation will be a function of the extent to which management creates and/or maintains these conditions.

Some Research Implications of the Study

The Assumption of Initial Resistance to Change

In reviewing the literature on organizational change we noted that it is usually assumed that organization members are resistant to the introduction of innovations. The rationale for this assumption seems to be that members of an organization are generally satisfied with the existing state of affairs in their work situation and hence, any proposed change in it will be met with resistance. We submit that this "resistance-to-change" assumption needs to be challenged. We would contend that in many organizations the empirical reality is that a number of their members are exposed to irritating problems and needless strain, and consequently would welcome innovations that appeared to offer solutions to their difficulties.

We believe that it will be more heuristic to assume that in most organizations members will vary in their degree of resistance or receptivity to innovations. Moreover, for a specific organization some members may be positively predisposed to certain kinds of innovations and negatively predisposed to others. Our research experience leads us to conclude that investigators of the introduction or the implementation of an innovation would be well advised not to treat the degree to which members of an organization are initially resistant to change as "an organizational given," but as a matter requiring empirical examination.

When we treat resistance to change as an organizational variable, a number of important research questions may be raised. For example, what impact do higher administration officials have on the receptivity or the resistance of their staffs to innovation? What types of social relationships between superordinates and subordinates and among subordinates promote positive attitudes toward organizational change? Are firms whose employees are characterized by a positive orientation to change more productive than firms whose employees are negatively predisposed to change? This is a small sample of the many questions that are open to empirical inquiry when we treat resistance-to-change as a variable.

The Need for Replication Studies

Case studies, of course, can generate, but do not test, theories. Our study was designed to isolate factors that influence the implementation phase of organizational change. It led to the development of a theoretical framework that conceptualized the successful implementation of a major innovation as a complex process involving a set of dynamic and interrelated circumstances. Investigations of successful and unsuccessful implementation efforts need to be conducted to ascertain the validity of the explanatory scheme we have proposed. Only systematic research can determine whether the circumstances blocking the implementation of the catalytic role model at Cambire will also be in evidence when post-mortems are carried out in organizations that have experienced failure in their efforts to implement innovations. Furthermore, in implementation attempts that are successful our theory would lead us to predict that effective steps had been taken to remove or overcome the obstacles that arose at Cambire. In short, replication studies will need to be conducted and their results carefully analyzed before we can make judgments about the generality or limitations of the theory we have proposed.

The Need for Conditional Inquiries

In the literature on organizational innovations little consideration has been given to the way in which they vary in their complexity and how this variable influences their implementation. A possibility that deserves serious consideration is that different patterns of obstacles may emerge in efforts to implement different kinds of innovations. Empirical investigations are needed to determine if there is any support for this idea. Furthermore, studies are needed to determine if particular strategies of implementation are more or less effective depending upon the extent to which they take into account the magnitude of the behavioral change required of organizational members if they are to carry out the innovation.

Such proposals suggest the need for a typology of innovations and the possibility that different explanations may be required to account for the successful implementation of different types of organizational innovations. In this connection, it is important to note that the theoretical explanation proposed in this chapter to account for the implementation of organizational innovations may be applicable to only certain kinds of organizational innovations, for example, those involving major changes in the role performance of organizational members.

We have raised the question of whether the type of innovation being implemented has any consequences for the kind of obstacles that arise during the period of attempted implementation. We also need to consider the possible impact of organizational variables on the process of implementation. To explore this issue studies will need to be designed that introduce the same innovation into a number of organizations that vary on one or more organizational characteristics, for example, average age of the staff, degree of staff autonomy, or the influence of the external environment on the functioning of the organization. Through an analysis of the types of obstacles that arise in the organizations examined, valuable data would be obtained on organizational conditions that may influence the implementation process.

The Evaluation of Innovations

Our findings imply that an assumption usually found in evaluative studies of innovations needs to be challenged. The assumption is that the innovation under consideration has in fact been implemented. The strategy used in most of these studies is to obtain before and after measurements on one or more criteria variables for the con-

trol and experimental groups. If the gains in the experimental group
are significantly greater than those of the control group on the
criteria variables, the innovation is viewed as a success. If the differences between the two groups are not significant statistically
or if the control group achieves a greater gain on the criterion variable than the experimental group, then the innovation is viewed as
unsuccessful.

Now, assume that the catalytic role model was the innovation
that was being evaluated and that a control group was used. There
is little doubt that a comparison of the cognitive and affective learning outcomes in the control and experimental groups would indicate
that the innovation had little or no positive educational consequences
at Cambire. The investigator in this case might readily conclude that
his findings indicated that the catalytic role model did not appear
to be a promising educational innovation.

Such a conclusion, however, would be inappropriate because it
would be based on an erroneous assumption, namely that the innovation had been implemented at Cambire. Our findings showed that
teacher's performance did not conform to the catalytic role model.
It would be unfair and illegitimate for the evaluator to describe the
innovation as a failure when the "treatment," had not taken.

The major implication of our inquiry for educators and social
scientists who conduct evaluative studies is that it underscores the
need to ascertain whether the innovation under examination has in
fact been implemented before they attempt to make assessments
about its effects. If they fail to take into account the extent to
which the innovation was implemented, they can readily fall into
the trap of making erroneous judgments about the utility of innovations that have never been given a fair trial.

Practical Implications of the Study

We now turn to a discussion of the implications of our findings that
may be of greatest utility to school administrators concerned with the
promotion and management of educational change in their organizations.

Implementing Educational Change: A Complex Process

Educational administrators typically conceive of the process of
promoting successful change in schools as including three requirements: first, locating or developing a promising new educational
idea; second, obtaining the funds needed to carry it out; and third,
convincing the staff that the innovation has educational value. If the
innovation does not take hold, the failure is generally ascribed to the
absence of one or more of the following circumstances: the idea
itself may have been found wanting, the anticipated financial support
may not have been forthcoming, or the staff may have resisted the
educational change. Most school administrators appear to hold the
view that if the *initiation* phase of the educational change process—
getting the "right" idea, securing the required funds, and overcoming resistance to change—is well handled, innovations will be readily
implemented.

Serious questions, however, can be leveled at this image of educational change. We would contend that although these conditions
may constitute necessary prerequisites for the successful *initiation*
of educational change, they do not represent a sufficient set of
requirements for the successful *implementation* of innovations. The
inability of schools to demonstrate positive educational effects
from their attempts to institute educational change may be attributed in part to the truncated version of the change process held by
their administrators.

Our case study showed that the obstacles and frustrations to
which the teachers at Cambire were exposed, and that eventually
led to their abandonment of efforts to carry out the innovation,
arose during the period *subsequent* to its initiation, that is, during
the period of attempted implementation. Therefore, we would contend that the following assumption made by many administrators
needs to be challenged: when an innovation is introduced into a
school and teachers are willing to make efforts to carry the change

out, it will then be implemented. Our study suggests that initial acceptance, even enthusiasm for an innovation on the part of a staff, is not enough to ensure its implementation. Although teachers may start off with extremely positive feelings toward a proposed change, they may encounter frustrations and serious difficulties in their efforts to carry it out that, if not coped with, can snowball into a resistance to the innovation that will be both hard to stop and harder to reverse. Experiences of this kind could readily cancel out their earlier positive attitudes.

In conceiving of educational change as a complex process, administrators will also need to recognize that most innovations require considerable alteration in the usual patterns of teacher behavior. To break away from old modes of behavior and begin to act in new ways is no easy matter and may take considerable time. At Cambire the teachers found the task of attempting to serve as catalysts, rather than as directors of learning, virtually impossible, because the director largely ignored difficulties they encountered as they attempted to change their performance. The teachers became immobilized in their efforts to implement the innovation because the pathways to the very changes they were being requested to make were never opened to them.

Administrators also need to be aware that in the process of their staff's attempts to change from old to new behavioral patterns, some stressful periods are almost sure to occur. Although likely to appear to teachers as setbacks, such periods may actually constitute required forward steps toward the implementation of an innovation. If administrators anticipate these periods, and recognize that they probably are largely functional in "unfreezing" old patterns of behavior, then they will be prepared to provide, at the right times, the types of support and help teachers require if they are to benefit from these experiences. Administrators and teachers need to view such periods as a natural part of the journey from old forms of behavior to new ones, not as stumbling blocks to implementation.

In the case of Cambire, the teachers viewed their pupils' early reactions to their efforts to conform to the new role model as "wild-ness," "rudeness," and "lack of motivation," and being unable to cope with such behavior they began to turn back to their traditional ways of teaching. If this behavior of their pupils had been explained to the teachers as conduct to be expected when a transfer to "control from without" to "control from within" is being attempted, the teachers might have been able to accept this behavior of their pupils as transitional. That is, the pupils, just like their teachers, needed to learn about how to learn in a new way. In other words, it could have been readily anticipated that children would probably need to react in this manner when first exposed to a freer classroom situation in order for them to be able to move on to more self-directed activities.

Obstacles to the Implementation of Innovations

A second idea of considerable importance that emerged from our study, one largely ignored in current educational efforts to implement innovations, is that problems are bound to arise in efforts to carry out the "best laid plans of mice and schoolmen," and therefore, that mechanisms need to be created both to isolate and deal effectively with them. Many educational administrators recognize that they may need to cope with initial resistance to change on the part of organizational members and take steps to overcome it. However, they characteristically overlook critical problems that arise when teachers attempt to implement innovations.

Development and effective operation of workable systems of feed-back are needed to ensure that difficulties will be pinpointed, analyzed, and that steps will be taken to resolve them. At Cambire the lack of feedback mechanisms, for example, largely accounted for the failure to recognize and cope with the ambiguities teachers had about the new role model. And even when limited opportunities were provided for teachers to inform administrators about their difficulties, such as at faculty meetings, management failed to pro-vide an atmosphere which invited and allowed teachers to speak frankly.

Another critical problem that the administrators at Cambire overlooked was the need for the teachers to be resocialized. Teachers
were asked to conform to a new role model but were not provided
with the skills and knowledge they needed. It was assumed by the
innovator that any professional teacher "worth his salt" could read
a document describing the innovation and then, on his own, radically
change his behavior in ways that were congruent with the new role
model. The teachers were exposed to a host of difficulties when
they tried to do just that, and these difficulties were not recognized
by their superiors or resolved. As noted, teachers tried to behave
in accord with the catalytic role model but immediately found themselves exposed to new and unanticipated responses from their pupils.
Neither prepared for this new pupil behavior nor equipped to deal
with it effectively, they quickly reverted to the security of their
previous role behavior. If the innovator had thought seriously about
the new skills that a "willing" teacher needed in order to be able to
shift to a drastically new way of working with pupils, he could have
provided the teachers with retraining experiences they would need
such as role-playing, simulation, micro-teaching, and coaching.
He could have shown the staff films of classrooms being conducted
according to the new role model and exposed them to teachers who
were already educating children in this new way at other schools.
Such retraining was never provided. The frustrations of the
teachers mounted as they found that their difficulties were largely
unrecognized and that no help was, or would be, forthcoming.

Another difficulty that the director never recognized, and that
served as a barrier to the implementation of the innovation, was
the assistant director's lack of commitment to it. Because of his
hesitancy, caused in part by his reservations about the new role
model, he did not offer leadership to the teachers or provide them
with the kinds of help they needed. We submit that the literature
underplays the need for administrative leadership in implementing
educational innovations. We also would contend that the notion,
frequently found in the educational literature, that the professional

teacher on his own will somehow find within himself the ability and drive to carry out new school programs and practices should be questioned. This perspective ignores the need that teachers have for stimulating and professional leadership in learning new behavior. It also overlooks the need for coordination of teacher activities in innovative efforts as well as the fact that there are many classroom and school conditions over which administrators, not teachers, have the greater control.

Administrators, then, need to be aware of the importance of anticipating the difficulties that are bound to develop in the course of change efforts, and of the necessity of creating feedback mechanisms that will ensure that problems being encountered are aired and heard; they then need to work with their staffs to analyze and resolve these problems.

The Role of Management during Implementation

A third idea emerged from our findings that could be of considerable utility to educational administrators: the critical importance of their performance with respect to the success or failure of the *implementation* of innovations. Administrators typically assign the responsibility for carrying out an innovation to subordinates or to an outside change agent. They appear to assume that their own responsibility is terminated when they make the decision that the organization will adopt a new educational program or practice. Our study implies that there is great need for a critical reevaluation of their responsibilities during the period of implementation. As noted, since management is in the position to command an overall view of the organization and of the complex set of forces that influence it, only it can give general direction to the *entire course* of implementation efforts. Administrators need to recognize that educational change typically is a difficult and complex process and that teachers can encounter many obstacles over which they have little control in their efforts to implement innovations. It is management that is in the best position to anticipate these problems and to set forces in motion to minimize or overcome them. It is management's responsibility to develop an overall strategy for change.

Our study suggests a number of different tasks that management will need to address itself to as it becomes centrally involved in the innovation process. The fact that few difficulties were reported by teachers, although they were in fact experiencing many, suggests a strong need for management to keep in close touch with the process after the wheels of implementation efforts have been put in motion. It needs to see that immediate feedback mechanisms exist and that they are operating effectively. At Cambire, the director essentially disregarded the need to ascertain the reactions of teachers to the innovation and the problems they were exposed to in their efforts to implement it. He apparently assumed that no news is good news. This is a highly tenuous assumption for administrators to make in guiding their organizations.

Another task of management will be to assess the special types of problems that can be expected to arise when different types of innovations are introduced into their organizations. Many administrators assume that all innovations are cut from the same cloth and that the same general strategy will fit almost any proposed change. They need to give careful consideration to the unique qualities of a proposed change and its implications for planning its implementation.

In designing an implementation strategy, a number of decisions will be required. One is whether the innovator, when he is willing and available to direct implementation of his own idea, or another person, should be given the responsibility for directing the change process. Although the qualities needed to develop promising innovations and those required to put them into effect may be found in the same individual, we suspect that this combination of abilities in the same person is rare. Decisions will also need to be made about whether outside assistance will be required, how needless strain can be minimized, and how potential interpersonal conflicts can be dealt with most effectively.

Our study suggests that the strategy used by administrators to institute major educational changes needs to be based on a careful assessment of the conditions that must be fulfilled for the implementation of innovations. At Cambire the director's failure to consider this matter was of critical importance in accounting for the failure of teachers to implement the innovation. His strategy did not consider the obstacles that confronted the teachers as they attempted to implement the innovation. We contend that most of these problems could have readily been anticipated if he had based his strategy on a more realistic set of assumptions about the complexities of the process of implementation and the potential difficulties subordinates can encounter in attempting to carry out innovations proposed by their superiors. Perhaps the most general value of our study then for administrators is that it suggest a set of basic ideas that may serve as guidelines to be used in assessing their proposed strategies to secure implementation of innovations. These guidelines would specify the special importance of: (1) making the innovation clear to the staff members involved in implementation; (2) providing the training experiences required so that the staff will possess the capabilities needed to perform in accord with the innovation; (3) ensuring that the staff is willing to make the appropriate innovative efforts; (4) making the necessary materials and equipment available for implementation of the innovation; and (5) rearranging prevailing organizational arrangements that are incompatible with the innovation. With respect to the fifth guideline, it is important to add that management, in analyzing existing incompatible elements in the organization, needs to pay special attention to aspects of its own role performance that may be incongruent with the innovation, and therefore, that may have to be altered in order to permit effective implementation. The school, as an organization, consists of a set of interrelated roles, and because of this, basic changes in the teachers' role performance may require major changes in management's, if the changes resulting from the implementation of the innovation are to be maintained. At Cambire, for example, administrators made all of the major decisions about school policies, programs, and the types and amounts of materials needed in the classrooms. However, the nature of the innovation required that many of them be made by teachers. The authority system of the school would require alteration in order to assure that teachers had the right to make such decisions and that management accepted the legitimacy of this change in their role.

We would also suggest that those who advocate the use of T-groups, participation of subordinates in decision making, and the use of change agents, need to assess these activities in terms of their actual contribution to organizational conditions required for effective implementation of innovations. For example, in schools where *teachers* prefer considerable direction from above, it seems unlikely that strategies stressing participation would be most efficacious.

Our case study suggests the importance of the need for a strategy which includes mechanisms for effective feedback between the initiators of the change and those who must implement it, and which maintains efficient problem-solving mechanisms for both unanticipated and anticipated issues which arise during the period of attempted implementation. Our study also stresses the need for management to think through a strategy which emphasizes *its* leadership role not only in setting new goals and initiating innovations, as in the case of Cambire, but in seeing to it that the organizational conditions it specifies as necessary for implementation are established and maintained. At Cambire, during the period of time between announcement and assessment, the administrators' leadership was minimal. Indeed, under the banner of "teaching is a profession," the management failed to conceive of teachers as organizational members who *must* rely on their superiors to fulfill many of their needs when they make efforts to implement organizational innovations. Our findings bring into bold focus the need for leadership in the management of the innovation process and the consequences that follow when it does not exist. The implementation of educational innovations, in short, not only requires alterations in

behavior expected of teachers but also changes in the role performance of management.

One final point: it is our hope that studies of the type we have
undertaken will increase the probability of the effective implementation of educationally promising ideas of administrators such as
those of the Director of the Bureau of Educational Change. Only
when such innovations are fully implemented will we be in a position to assess their educational effects. Currently, we would contend
that many promising educational innovations have been rejected
on the basis of experimental designs that failed to take into account
that the innovations may have been inadequately implemented.
Clearly, when a new program or practice has not had a "fair" trial,
judgment about its educational utility must be held in abeyance.

Specimen Research Instruments

Several formal data-collection procedures, in addition to various informal methods, were employed to gather evidence during our study. Presented below are three instruments which we used, and which are discussed in Chapters 3 and 5:

(A-1)   The Teacher Interview Schedule
(A-2)   The Classroom Observation Schedule
(A-3)   The Self-Administered Teacher Questionnaire

The teacher questionnaire was actually the second half of a two-part battery taken by the teachers in May 1967. The first part, The Edwards Personal Preference Schedule, is a standardized, published psychological test and is not included in the appendix. For a detailed discussion of this test see Buros, 1965.

A-1: Teacher Interview Schedule

Introduction

1. We're very interested, as you know so well by now, in educational innovations primarily from the teacher's perspective. You may think it's corny to say again, but I really appreciate your

willingness to help. Without your openness and frankness we could never hope to understand the effort to innovate in this school, from *your* point of view.

2. While everyone is talking about *introducing* new ideas and programs into schools, we really don't know very much about what *in fact* happens when innovations are brought in.

3. Since it is our belief that this is one of the most important but neglected problems in education, what we have been doing here is trying to get a much better picture of the practical realities and problems arising in schools where innovations are introduced.

4. From our observations and informal talks we feel that we have a very good general understanding of what has been happening here. You may even find me asking you questions which you know you've answered before.

5. However, *now* we want to see this process from the teacher's point of view but in a much more systematic way, what I mean is beginning at the time when you first heard about the innovation up to the present.

6. I've mentioned the matter of anonymity before, but I do want to assure you again about it. (Show that a name doesn't appear on papers you're writing on.)

7. We welcome your afterthoughts about this interview, be they additions, corrections, or deletions, so any time afterward please don't hesitate to tell me about any changes you'd like to make.

8. Do you have any questions? (Make sure questions are handled before proceeding.)

Transition Note 1

Let us go back to when you *first heard* that the innovation was definitely going to be introduced here.

1. When was that?

2. How did you first learn about it? Formally _____
   Informally _____
   (Probe: Meeting? Oral? Individually?)

Time Chart

The time when you
first heard that the
innovation was going to
be tried here.

The *period* of time
between when you first
heard and when you
made your first attempts.

(Month)	J	F	M	A	M	J	J	A	S	O	N	D

1965

The time when you
made your first real
attempt to try it.

(Month)	J	F	M	A	M	J	J	A	S	O	N	D

1966

The *period* of time
between when you
made your first real
attempts and the
present time.

Present Time

(Month)	J	F	M	A	M	J

1967

a. Who presented it?

b. Can you recall the atmosphere?
    (Probe: Casual? Exciting?)

c. Were any reasons given for it?   Y   N   OS
    If yes: What were they?

If first heard formally, go to Question 4

3. Was there a teacher's meeting at which the innovation was
    presented?   Y   N   OS

a. Who presented it?

b. Can you recall the atmosphere?

c. Were any reasons given for it?   Y   N   OS
    If yes: What were they?

4. In general, what was your overall reaction to the *way* the
    innovation was announced or proposed?
    (Use Code A* for teacher's reaction)

    Why did you have this reaction?

5. Let's be a little more specific about your initial reactions.

a. From the *way* it was proposed or announced, did you
    get the impression that:

    1) this was a proven educational ideal _____ or was its value
        still open to question _____ ? Why?

    2) this innovation was being treated as an experiment?
        Y   N   OS   Why did you feel this way?

    3) you *had* to try this out _____ or were given the option
        of doing so _____ ? What gave you this impression?

    4) this had really been carefully thought through?
        Y   N   OS   Why did you feel this way?

    5) there were specific plans for putting the idea into
        effect?   Y   N   OS   What gave you this
        impression?

---

*See p. 235 for response categories included in each code used in the interview.

      6) the timing was right?   Y   N   OS   Why did you
         think this was so? (Probe: Time of Year? Role
         Demands?)

    b. Were you taken by surprise by its announcement _____ or
      did you expect it _____ ? Why?

So far we have been talking about the *way* the idea was introduced
and your reactions to it; now let's turn to the *nature* of the innovation itself.

    6. When innovations are introduced into schools, teachers may
      differ in their reactions to them. How did the nature of
      this innovation strike you when you were *first aware* that it
      was going to be introduced here?
      (Use Code A for teacher's reaction)

      Why did you feel this way? (Probe: Other reasons?)

    7. Now, let's explore this in greater detail. After the innova-
      tion was *first described* to you, did you feel that you had a
      clear understanding of it?   Y   N   OS
      If yes: How would you describe it?
      If no: What was unclear about it? Describe what you
           thought it was all about.

    8. What, at that time, did you think (give names) hoped to
      accomplish by introducing it?

    9. Did you think these were *worthwhile* objectives?
      Y   N   OS
      If yes: Why?
      If no: Why not? (Omit next question)

   10. Did you believe that there was *a need* "for this particular inno-
      vation" (If response to question seven was "unclear" then:
      "for something like this") in this school?   Y   N   OS
      If yes: Why?
      If no: Why not?

11. How much *importance* did you feel the following people
    gave to getting this innovation into your school?
    (List names) (Use Code B for amount of importance)

    What did (give names) do to make you feel this way?

12. Did you feel that the innovation *would work* here?
    Y   N   OS   What were your reasons?

13. After you first heard about the innovation did you feel you
    had a clear picture of what you were *expected* to do in
    carrying out the innovation?   Y   N   OS

    If no: In what respects was it unclear?

14. In order to do this did you think that you would have to
    make *any changes* in your behavior?   Y   N   OS

    If yes: From the initial proposal of this innovation by (give
             names) how did you think (give names again) ex-
             pected you to change?
             (List old behavior)   (List new behavior)

    If no: Why not? (Go to Question 17)

15. Did you think that the innovation would require changes
    that weren't expected by (repeat names used in #14)?
    Y   N   OS

    If yes: What were they?

16. Did you think you could make the changes (repeat names
    used in #14) expected in your behavior, when you first
    heard about the innovation?   Y   N   OS

    If no: Why not?

17. When new ideas are introduced into schools they sometimes
    have *positive consequences* for teachers, sometimes *negative
    consequences*, sometimes both.

    a. Did you think there would be any *positive consequences*
       for you?   Y   N   OS

       If yes: What would they be?

    b. Did you think there would be any *negative consequences* for you?   Y   N   OS

       If yes: What were these?

18. What about the consequences for other teachers:

    a. Did you think there would be any positive consequences for other teachers here?   Y   N   OS

       If yes: For whom? In what ways? (Probe: In general? For specific teachers?)

    b. Any negative consequences?   Y   N   OS

       If yes: For whom? In what ways?

19. How about your pupils?

    a. Any positive consequences?   Y   N   OS

       If yes: For what kind of child? In what ways?

    b. Any negative consequences?   Y   N   OS

       If yes: For what kind of child? In what ways?

20. We have been talking about many different aspects of the initial period when you first heard that this innovation was going to be introduced here. What was your *basic feeling*, how did you honestly react to the *whole notion* of bringing it into this school?
(Use Code A for teacher's reaction)

    Why did you feel this way?

21. How about the other teachers here?

    Let's talk about the ones you respect most. Who are they?

    (List names)

    Let's talk about (add names desired by interviewer) too.

    a. What were their *overall* reactions to the innovation? (Repeat names)   (Use Code A for their responses)

       More specifically,

b. Did they have a clear picture of what this innovation was all about?
(Repeat list of names)   (Use Code C for responses)

c. Did they agree with its objectives?
(Repeat list of names)   (Use Code C for responses)

d. Did they feel the need for this innovation here?
(Repeat list of names)   (Use Code C for responses)

e. Did they believe that this was a top priority in this school?
(Repeat list of names)   (Use Code C for responses)

f. Did they believe that this would work here?
(Repeat list of names)   (Use Code C for responses)

g. Did they think they knew how they would have to change?
(Repeat list of names)   (Use Code C for responses)

   If no: Go to Question i

h. Did they believe that they could make these changes?
(Repeat list of names)   (Use Code C for responses)

i. Did they believe it was really worth their while to do this?
(Repeat list of names)   (Use Code C for responses)

22. In a moment I would like to turn to the period after the innovation was announced, but before we do I want to give you the opportunity to discuss any other matters you think would be helpful for us to know about the way it was announced or your initial reactions to it.

Transition Note 2

Now let's focus on that period of time *between* when you first heard about the innovation and when you first tried it *in any way* in your classroom.

1. How long was this period?

2. During this period how much:

a. thinking did you do about the innovation?
(Use Code D for response)
Why? If any: What? (Use special probe)

b. reading about the innovation did you do?
(Use Code D for response)
Why? If any: What? (Use special probe)

c. writing did you do about the innovation?
(Use Code D for response)
Why? If any: What? (Use special probe)

d. talking did you do about the innovation?
(Use Code D for response)

1) Why? If any: What? (Use special probe)

2) With whom? (Probe: Teachers? Administrators? Others?, specify)

3) How? *Formally*? *Informally*? (Probe: Meetings? Workshops? In-service training?)

4) Where? (Probe: Inside? Outside school?)

3. Did *you* have any serious questions or reservations about the innovation during this period?   Y   N   OS

If none: Go on to 4

If yes: What were they? Why?

4. What were (give name)'s activities in connection with the innovation during this period?
(Use special probe)
(List names)   (List activities)

What did you think of them?
(Repeat activities)   (Probe: Helpful? Hindering?)

5. Why did you feel this way about them?
(Repeat activities)

6. Were you completely satisfied with what was done?
Y   N   OS   (Use special probe)

If no: Why not? What do you think they should have done?

If no efforts were made:

7. Why do you think they didn't do anything? Did you find this silence helpful _____ or hindering _____ ?

    If hindering: What could they have done? (Use special probe)

    If helpful: How was it helpful? What else would *you* have done? (Use special probe)

    If 8, 9, or 10 were mentioned, say:

        Just to make sure I really understand you (then go to question 8)

    If 8, 9, or 10 were not mentioned, say:

        Sometimes what administrators do may not seem like efforts to promote the innovation and yet may be. For example:

8. Did the administration try to find out what your feelings about the innovation were?   Y   N   OS
(Use special probe)

    If no: Why do you think they didn't try to find out?

9. Did they attempt to answer questions you had about the innovation?   Y   N   OS
(Use special probe)

    If yes: How did you respond to their attempts?

    If no: Why do you think they didn't make the attempt?

10. Were the questions or reservations you had effectively dealt with to your satisfaction during this period?   Y   N   OS
(Use special probe)

    If yes: By whom?

    If no: Why in your estimation weren't they effectively handled?

11. Now, as specifically as possible, as a result of what went on during this period did your feelings *change* about:

   a. your understanding of what the innovation was all about?
      Y   N   OS

      If yes: How? Why?

   b. your agreement with what they wanted to accomplish?
      Y   N   OS

      If yes: How? Why?

   c. the need for such an innovation here?   Y   N   OS

      If yes: How? Why?

   d. the priority that this change was given in your school?
      Y   N   OS

      If yes: How? Why?

   e. whether or not it would work here?   Y   N   OS

      If yes: How? Why?

   f. how you would be required to change?   Y   N   OS

      If yes: How? Why?

   g. whether or not you could make such changes in your
      behavior?   Y   N   OS

      If yes: How? Why?

   h. the advantages or disadvantages of trying this out, either
      for you, the pupils, or other teachers?   Y   N   OS

      If yes: How? Why?

12. Just before you first tried out the innovation, what was your
    overall reaction to it? (Use Code A for response)

    If no shift from initial reaction go to Question 14.

13. Is it correct to say then that you had made a shift from your
    first reaction?   Y   N   OS

    If no: Why not?

    If yes: How would you account for the change? Were there
             any particular people who influenced your shift?

14. Is it correct to say that you still felt the same way as you did at first?   Y   N   OS

    If yes: What were the major reasons for keeping your first position?

    If no: Why not?

Transition Note 3

Let's shift our attention now to the period when you first *started* trying out the innovation.

1. First, however, have you in fact started trying to carry it out?   Y   N   OS

   If no: Why not? (Then go directly to the next section)

   If yes: When did *you* begin?

2. How much effort would you say that you put into trying to do it at first? How hard were you trying?
   (Use Code D for response)
   Why?

3. What kinds of things did you do?
   (List activities)

   a. How well did each of these things work out as far as you were concerned?
      (Repeat list of activities)   (Use Code E for responses)

   b. What were the reasons for your feelings?

4. At the beginning did you find any serious problems in try-ing to carry out the innovation?   Y   N   OS

   If yes: What were they? (Probe: Any others?)

5. How much did (Give name of person(s)) really *try* to help you overcome *any* of these problems?
   (List names)   (Use Code D for amount of effort)

6. What did (Repeat list of names) try to do to help you?

We have been talking about the problems you had during the period of your first attempts and the extent to which others had *tried* to help you.

7. Now let's explore the extent to which the following people *really were a help* to you in your *first* attempts to carry out the innovation.

   a. How much help was (name of person) to you?
      (List names)   (Use Code D for amount of help)

   b. Anyone else?

   c. Who was the most helpful? Any others?

   d. How did (Read list of names) help?

8. Now let's talk about the extent to which the following people were *obstacles* or *blocked* you in any way in *your* first attempts to carry out the innovation.

   a. How much of an obstacle was (name of person) to you?
      (List names)   (Use Code D for amount of blockage)

   b. Anyone else?

   c. Who was the greatest obstacle during this period?

   d. How did (Read list of names) block you?

9. Was there any help or advice that you *needed* during the period when you made your first attempts, which you didn't get?   Y   N   OS
   If yes: What kind?

10. Who, in your judgment, should have provided these (this)?

Transition Note 4

We have been talking about your first attempts to carry out the innovation. Now we want to focus on the period between those first attempts and the present time.

1. Have you continued to try to carry out the innovatio...
   Y   N   OS

   If no: When did you stop?

   Why did you stop?   (Then go directly to Section 5)

2. Have you continued to make the same kinds of attempts
   you first made?   Y   N   OS

   If no: Why not?

   If yes: Which ones?

3. Have you tried to do anything new since your first attempt?
   Y   N   OS

   If no: Why not?

   If yes:

   a. What new things have you tried since your first attempts?
      (List new activities)

   b. How well have these things worked for you?
      (Repeat new activities and use Code E for responses)

   c. What are the reasons for your feelings?

4. Have any of the problems arising during your first attempts
   continued to exist?   Y   N   OS

   If yes: Which ones?

5. Have any new problems arisen during the period between
   your first attempts to try out the innovation and the
   present time?   Y   N   OS

   If yes: What have they been? (Probe: Any others?)
            (List activities)

6. How much has (give name) really tried to help you overcome any of these problems?
   (List names)   (Use Code D for amount of effort)

7. What has (repeat list of names) done to try to help you?
   (List activities)

We have been talking about the problems you have continued to have since your first attempts, problems which have arisen after those first attempts and the extent to which others have *tried* to help you with any of these.

8. Now, let's explore the extent to which the following people have really been *any help* to you in the period between your first attempts to carry out the innovation and the present time.

   a. How much help has (give name) been to you?
      (List names)   (Use Code D for amount of help)

   b. Anyone else?

   c. Who has been the most helpful? Any others?

   d. How has (repeat list of names) helped?
      (List activities)

9. Now, let's talk about the extent to which the following people have been *obstacles* or have *blocked* you in any way in the period between your first attempts to carry out the innovation and the present time.

   a. How much of an obstacle has (give name) been?
      (List names)   (Use Code D for amount of obstacle)

   b. Anyone else?

   c. Who has been the greatest obstacle during this period?

   d. How has (repeat list of names) blocked you?
      (List activities)

10. Has there been help or advice that you have *needed* that you haven't gotten?   Y   N   OS

11. Who, in your judgment, should be providing this?

12. Overall, during the period between your first attempts to carry out the innovation and the present time, how much effort have you made in trying to carry it out?
    (Use Code D for response)

13. How do you account for this?

14. Do you think your efforts have been successful in implementing the innovation here?   Y   N   OS

   If yes: Why do you believe this?

   If no: What are your reasons for not believing this?

Transition Note 5 (Final)

In this final section I want to focus primarily upon the situation today with respect to the innovation, and in the process review some of what you told me before about your earlier experiences with the innovation to make sure that I accurately understand what you have said.

1. In regard to the *amount* of effort you have made:

	At First	*Period Between*	*Present Time*
Great	_____	_____	_____
Considerable	_____	_____	_____
Some	_____	_____	_____
Little	_____	_____	_____
None	_____	_____	_____

   How much effort are you now making to carry out the innovation? (Record response under "Present Time" column)

   If shift: Why?

2. In regard to the kinds of attempts you have made:
   (Review schedule: First, then Period Between)

   Are the kinds of things you are doing now different from before?   Y   N   OS

   If yes: In what ways have they changed?

3. In regard to the *problems* you have had in trying to carry out the innovation:
   (Review schedule: First, then Period Between)

    a. Do any of these earlier problems continue today?
       Y   N   OS

       If yes: Which ones?

    b. Any new ones?

Make clear to the subject that there will be a shift in the time periods being reviewed.

4. In regard to the *clarity* of what the innovation is all about:
(Review schedule: Initially, then Subsequently)

    Has the degree of clarity of the objectives of the innovation changed?   Y   N   OS

    If yes: Why? How?

5. In regard to the value of these objectives:
(Review schedule: Initially, then Subsequently)

    Do you feel differently now?   Y   N   OS

    If different: Why? How?

6. In regard to the *need* for the innovation here at the school:
(Review schedule: Initially, then Subsequently)

    Do you feel this way?   Y   N   OS

    If no: Why? How?

7. In regard to the degree of *priority* the innovation has here:
(Review schedule: Initially, then Subsequently)

    Have you changed your mind about this?   Y   N   OS

    If yes: Why? How?

8. In regard to the chances of the innovation *working* here:
(Review schedule: Initially, then Subsequently)

    Have your feelings changed about this?   Y   N   OS

    If yes: Why? How?

9. In regard to what you are *expected* to do to carry out the innovation:
(Review schedule: Initially, then Subsequently)

Do you feel differently now?   Y   N   OS

If yes: Why? How?

10. In regard to *making changes* in behavior:
    (Review schedule: Initially, then Subsequently)

    With the school as it is now, have you changed your mind
    about being able to make such shifts?   Y   N   OS

    If yes: Why? How?

11. In regard to the *consequences* of trying to carry out the
    innovation for you, other teachers, or pupils:
    (Review schedule: Initially, then Subsequently)

    Have your feelings changed about any of these?
    Y   N   OS

    If yes: Why? How?

12. In regard to your overall reaction to the introduction of the
    innovation here:
    (Review schedule: Initially, and Subsequently)

	Initially	*Subsequently*	*Now*
Very positive	_____	_____	_____
Somewhat positive	_____	_____	_____
Ambivalent	_____	_____	_____
Somewhat negative	_____	_____	_____
Very negative	_____	_____	_____

    What would you say your feelings are now?
    (Code response above in "Now" column)

    If shift: Why?

13. In general, do you feel more willing to try to implement the
    innovation _____ , less willing _____ , or about as willing
    _____ as when you first heard about its being introduced
    here?

14. If you were to make an impartial judgment about whether or not this innovation will actually take hold here at the school, what would it be?
(Use the following categories to code response: Eventual Complete Success _____ ; Eventual Partial Success _____ ; Eventual Rejection _____)

15. Have we left out *anything* important in talking about what has blocked or facilitated the teachers' efforts here to carry out the innovation?   Y   N   OS

    If yes: What?

Conclude interview with expression of thanks and reassurance of anonymity and confidentiality.

Codes

Code A: 5 = Very Positive; 4 = Somewhat Positive; 3 = Ambivalent; 2 = Somewhat Negative; 1 = Very Negative.

Code B: 5 = Extreme; 4 = Great; 3 = Moderate; 2 = Little; 1 = None; DK = Do Not Know.

Code C: Y = Yes; N = No; AMB = Ambivalent; DK = Do Not Know; NS = Not Sure.

Code D: 5 = Great; 4 = Considerable; 3 = Some; 2 = Little; 1 = None; NS = Not Sure; DK = Do Not Know.

Code E: 5 = Very Well; 4 = Somewhat Well; 3 = Neutral; 2 = Somewhat Poorly; 1 = Very Poorly; NS = Not Sure; DK = Do Not Know.

Special Probe: The Nature of the Innovation? Plans for the Innovation? Specific Behavioral Changes? Help with the Behavioral Changes?

General Code: Y = Yes; N = No; OS = Other, specified

A-2: Classroom Observation Schedule

Date

Time

A. General Overview

1. Give a detailed description of the on-going classroom activities during the period of observation.

2. Sketch the room arrangement and activities during the period of observation.

B. More Specifically, To what extent did the teacher(s):

1. make the materials existing in the room available to pupils?

    not at all $\overline{}$ completely

              1   2   3   4   5

    Notes:

2. have the room arranged into work areas?

    not at all $\overline{}$ completely

              1   2   3   4   5

    Notes:

3. utilize the room according to these work areas?

    not at all $\overline{}$ completely

              1   2   3   4   5

    Notes:

4. encourage or allow pupils to choose their own activities?

    not at all $\overline{}$ completely

              1   2   3   4   5

    Notes:

5. allow pupils to decide whether they wanted to work individually, in pairs or in groups?

not at all _____ completely

           1   2   3   4   5

Notes:

6. allow pupils to move freely about the room?

not at all _____ completely

           1   2   3   4   5

Notes:

7. allow or encourage pupils to interact with each other?

not at all _____ completely

           1   2   3   4   5

Notes:

8. allow pupils to decide how long they wanted to remain at a particular activity—i.e., move freely from one activity to another?

not at all _____ completely

           1   2   3   4   5

Notes:

9. move about the room?

not at all _____ completely

           1   2   3   4   5

Notes:

10. try to work with as many individual pupils or groups as possible?

not at all _____ completely

           1   2   3   4   5

Notes:

11. try to act as a guide, catalyst, or resource person between pupils?

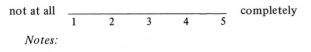

not at all _____ completely
   1   2   3   4   5

   Notes:

12. try to act as a guide, catalyst, or resource person between pupils and the materials?

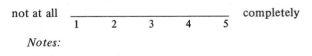

not at all _____ completely
   1   2   3   4   5

   Notes:

Class Schedule

	Monday	Tuesday	Wednesday	Thursday	Week Friday
8:30					
9:30					
10:30					
11:00	R E C E S S				
12:00					
12:30	L U N C H				
1:30					
2:30					

A-3: The Self-Administered Teacher Questionnaire

Instructions

Our purpose here is to obtain background characteristics of teachers. Please answer the following questions by circling the number next to the *one* answer which *best specifies* your reply.

1. How many years have you been a teacher?

   1) 1 year   6) 6-10 years
   2) 2 years   7) 11-15 years
   3) 3 years   8) 16-20 years
   4) 4 years   9) 21-25 years
   5) 5 years   10) over 25 years

2. How many years have you taught in this *school system*?

   1) 1 year   6) 6-10 years
   2) 2 years   7) 11-15 years
   3) 3 years   8) 16-20 years
   4) 4 years   9) 21-25 years
   5) 5 years   10) over 25 years

3. How many years have you taught in *this school*?

   1) 1 year   4) 4 years
   2) 2 years   5) 5 years
   3) 3 years   6) over 5 years

4. In how many *schools* in this system have you taught?

   1) 1 school   4) 4 schools
   2) 2 schools   5) 5 schools
   3) 3 schobls   6) over 5 schools

5. *On the average*, how frequently do you work on school activities at home?

   1) zero nights per week
   2) one night per week
   3) 2 to 3 nights per week
   4) 4 to 5 nights per week
   5) more than 5 nights per week

6. *On the average*, how much of your weekend is taken up with school work?

   1) none   3) some
   2) very little   4) a great deal

7. *On the average*, how frequently are you contacted at home about school matters?

   1) once a week or less
   2) 2 to 4 times a week
   3) 5 to 10 times a week
   4) more than 10 times a week

8. Where were your parents born?

   1) both in the United States
   2) one in U.S. and one foreign born
   3) both foreign born

9. When were you born?

   1) 1941-   5) 1921-1925
   2) 1936-1940   6) 1916-1920
   3) 1931-1935   7) 1911-1915
   4) 1926-1930   8) 1910-

10. What was your *father's major* lifetime occupation?

    1) education
    2) scientific, professional (other than education)
    3) manager, executive, or owner of large business
    4) small business owner, manager
    5) farm owner or renter
    6) clerical or sales
    7) skilled worker, foreman
    8) semi-skilled worker
    9) unskilled or farm laborer
    10) other (specify ____)

11. What was your *mother's major* lifetime occupation (other than housewife)?

    1) none
    2) education
    3) scientific, professional (other than education)
    4) secretarial, clerical
    5) small business owner, manager
    6) skilled worker
    7) domestic or unskilled worker
    8) semi-skilled worker
    9) other (specify ____)

12. What was your *father's* highest educational attainment?

    1) no formal education
    2) some elementary school
    3) completed elementary school
    4) some high school, technical school or business school
    5) graduated from high school, technical, or business school
    6) some college
    7) graduated from college
    8) graduate or professional school

13. What was your *mother's* highest educational attainment?

    1) no formal education
    2) some elementary school
    3) completed elementary school
    4) some high school or business school
    5) graduated from high school or business school
    6) some college
    7) graduated from college
    8) graduate or professional school

14. In what type of a community did you spend the *major* part of your youth?

    1) farm
    2) village or town (under 10,000)
    3) small city (10,000-50,000)
    4) city (50,000 or more)

15. In what type of schools did you receive *most* of your *elementary* school education?

    1) public
    2) parochial
    3) private

16. In what type of schools did you receive *most* of your *secondary* education?

    1) public
    2) parochial
    3) private

17. At what type of college did you do *most* of your undergraduate work?

    1) state university
    2) state teacher's college or normal school
    3) other public college or university
    4) private university or college
    5) private teachers' college or normal school

18. In general, what was the quality of your work when you were in *college*?

    1) graduated with honors
    2) above average
    3) average
    4) somewhat below average

19. At what type of college did you do *most* of your graduate work?

    1) No graduate work
    2) state teachers' college or normal school
    3) other public college or university
    4) state university
    5) private university or college
    6) private teachers' college or normal school

20. What plans do you have for future formal education?

    1) No plans
    2) Will take courses, but not for a specific degree
    3) Will study for a master's but not a doctorate
    4) Will study for a doctorate

21. How many semester hours of education courses did you have as an *undergraduate*?

    1) none
    2) 1 to 10
    3) 11 to 20
    4) 21 to 30
    5) 31 to 40
    6) 41 to 50
    7) 51 to 60
    8) more than 60

22. How many semester hours of *graduate work* have you taken?

    1) none
    2) 1 to 10
    3) 11 to 20
    4) 21 to 30
    5) 31 to 40
    6) 41 to 50
    7) 51 to 60
    8) more than 60

23. What is the *highest* academic degree which you have received?

    1) certificate
    2) bachelor's
    3) master's
    4) master's plus 30 hours

5) doctor's
6) professional degree
(e.g., LL.B.)

24. Which *category* best represents your *current* salary with respect to school?

1) Less than $5,000
2) $5,000 through $7,499
3) $7,500 through $9,999
4) $10,000 through $12,999
5) More than $13,000

25. What is your marital status?

1) single
2) married
3) other

Instructions for Question 26

Please write in the *one* code number [1 = I would not want to; 2 = I am not especially anxious to; 3 = I have some desire to; 4 = I would very much like to; 5 = I am extremely anxious to] which best represents your answer for each of the statements below.

26. How desirous are you of doing the following:

a) Become a specialist attached to a central office. _____

b) Become an assistant principal. _____

c) Become the principal of an elementary school. _____

d) Remain a teacher in this type

of *school* for the rest of my educational career. _____

e) Remain a teacher in this *school system* for the remainder of my educational career, but move to a school in a "better neighborhood." _____

f) Remain a teacher at my present grade level(s) for the remainder of my educational career. _____

g) Obtain a higher paying teaching job in another school system. _____

h) Obtain a higher paying position *outside* the field of education. _____

Instructions for Question 27

For each of the items found below, please write in the *one* code number [1 = very dissatisfied; 2 = somewhat dissatisfied; 3 = neutral; 4 = somewhat satisfied; 5 = very satisfied] which best represents your answer.

27. How do you feel about the following items?

a) The level of competence of most of the other teachers in this school. _____

b) The method employed in this school for making decisions on curriculum matters. _____

c) The method employed in this school for making decisions on pupil discipline matters. _____

d) The attitude of the students toward the faculty in this school. _____

c) The manner in which the teachers and the administrative staff work together in this school. _____

f) The cooperation and help which I receive from my superiors. _____

g) The educational philosophy which seems to prevail in this school. _____

h) The evaluation process which my superiors use to judge my effectiveness as a teacher. _____

i) The level of competence of my superiors. _____

j) The adequacy of the supplies available for me to use in my teaching in this school. _____

k) The academic performance of the students in this school. _____

l) The amount of time which is available to me while I am at school for my personal professional growth. _____

m) The extent to which I am informed by my superiors about school matters affecting me. _____

B

Documents

Many private school documents were collected and examined during the course of our data collection, and several pieces of private correspondence were exchanged between the project and officials of the school system. In this appendix we present several of the most important documents and pieces of correspondence:

(B-1) The Letter to Higher Administrative Officials Requesting Their Permission to Conduct the Study

(B-2) The Director's Initial Description of the Innovation to the Teachers (The November Document)

(B-3) The Director's Expanded Document Subsequently Passed Out to the Teachers (The January Document)

(B-4) The Announcement to the Teachers at the End of January Requesting That They Begin to Make Efforts to Implement the Innovation and a "Suggested Daily Program Schedule"

We have reproduced the original documents, as they stood, adjusting them only to conform to standards for margins and to maintain anonymity. Any irregularities, therefore, were parts of the original documents.

B-1: The Letter to Higher Administrative Officials Requesting Their Permission to Conduct the Study

HARVARD UNIVERSITY
Graduate School of Education

Roy E. Larsen Hall, Appian Way
Cambridge, Massachusetts 02138

October 21, 1966

TO:

FROM: Neal Gross, Professor of Education and Sociology, Harvard University

RE: Study of the process of innovation in schools.

The general objective of the study is to shed light on the process of innovation in schools. There has been considerable speculation about, but little systematic examination of, this process. My associates and I at the Harvard Graduate School of Education believe that research of this kind is needed to obtain a realistic understanding of the kinds of problems teachers and administrators encounter in effecting change and in understanding how they attempt to cope with them. We believe that the most productive way to explore this matter is to observe the day-to-day activities that take place in schools engaged in innovation and to examine the process of introducing educational change from the viewpoint of those participating in it. The innovating environment of the Cambire School, we believe, offers a very valuable opportunity to examine the process of change and to learn from the experiences of those directly involved in it. It will be one of several schools in the area involved in the study. As a consequence of the research encompassing a variety of school situations, we hope to be able to isolate a set of general and common factors which need to be taken into account in efforts of school systems to introduce educational innovations as well as to determine special circumstances that may be relevant to unique situations. It is our anticipation that the conclusion of our research will be of practical value to the participating school systems and also of value to school systems in general in their efforts to introduce change.

Needless to say, any report of our findings will be prepared in a manner that would guarantee complete anonymity to the systems and schools involved in the study; in addition, we can assure all who participate that any information they provide us will be treated in a completely confidential manner and that all necessary precautions will be taken to assure the anonymity of the data they provide. We also would like to assure the faculty that we believe, as they do, that the ongoing education of students is a first concern. For this reason we will attempt to be at all times as unobtrusive as possible. Mr. Joseph Giacquinta, my research associate, who will be at the Cambire School, is well aware of the problems confronting teachers. He is a former teacher and is currently studying for his doctorate in the sociology of education. He will avoid imposing on the time of members of the faculty as much as possible, but I also hope they will be willing to share with him, at their convenience, their insights and ideas and allow him to observe the daily life of the school.

Both of us wish to assure the faculty that our function is simply to learn as much as possible about the process of innovation. We also wish to emphasize that our role in no sense should be conceived as one of evaluating school personnel or programs or as serving as consultants to the staff.

When our study is completed we will, of course, be glad to share whatever findings emerge from the study. We would hope that as a result of your professional cooperation that there will be some addition to the limited knowledge now available about the process of introducing change into schools. Our ultimate objective is indeed the same as yours—the improvement of public education.

B-2: The Director's Initial Description of the Innovation to the Teachers (The November Document)

I. Purposes of the Innovation

1. One basic aim is to build an environment in which children are, within very specific limits, free to follow their own curiosity, to explore as deeply as they are capable of exploring those ideas and areas of learning which are of greatest interest to them, an environment in which, as much as possible, they are not tied to a rigid schedule created for the convenience of the school rather than the children themselves. This does *not* mean (as we shall explain below) that children are simply allowed to do whatever they please or run wild—quite the contrary. But it is, we hope, a place to which children will

want to come and in which they will find it possible to look upon the act of learning as something exciting and pleasurable rather than as some mysterious duty that their parents and the school wish them to undergo.

2. A second basic aim is to create an environment in which children of a fairly wide age range and of heterogeneous achievement levels can become engaged in the process of learning at whatever level of competence they happen to be in the various (loosely defined) subject areas. The children then move at their own best speed and using their own most appropriate styles from where they are to the farthest point they can attain in the course of a year. There is to be no holding a child back because he is moving into material normally considered as belonging to some higher grade or level (such as junior high).

3. A third aim is to create an environment in which, to as large a degree as possible, the children are responsible for their own learning—that is, either alone or in groups they ultimately will be capable of finding their own problems and working their way through to some tentative answers. Thus, in so far as it is possible, the material in the classroom should be *self-instructional, not* in the sense of programmed instruction but in the sense of materials that are tempting and tantalizing, materials that ask questions but do not provide any immediate answers. Games (such as the Dougherty-Lesser Math games), animals, balance beams, microscopes, ESI cartridges and films on the Eskimo, records and cartridge tapes (and tape recorders), intriguing books, as well as art and music materials, cuisinaire rods, printing presses, etc.

4. Another aim is to build an environment in which, as a matter of normal daily routine, *children help other children to learn*—or to put it another way, a situation in which more skilled children become assistant teachers and/or the peer group forms a self-instructional unit, with all children learning from each other. Children teaching other children, clearly, would not always mean older children teaching younger children, since in a heterogeneous group many of the younger children will be ahead of the older ones in some areas. Similarly, not all the teaching will be done by the "brighter" or the verbally talented children, since much of the material will not be verbal but manipulative or will employ the graphic and mechanical arts.

5. Another aim—and just as clearly one of obvious and crucial importance—is to alter the traditional role of the teacher. For far too long now we have been asking teachers to perform an essentially impossible task—or at least a task impossible for all but the most gifted and inexhaustible of human beings (and such paragons are rare). We have been asking a single person to be totally responsible for the education of up to thirty-five children in something called a "class," to handle all of the individual idiosyncrasies of those thirty-five children, their differing abilities, talents, levels of achievement, personality problems and virtues. We have demanded of teachers that they should treat each of these children as individuals and to devise a program that will suit each child's individual needs and capacities.

In the case of elementary teachers, we have not only told them this but we have simultaneously told them that they should keep all of the children gainfully occupied throughout a full six hour day (at best). If they pull a smaller group out of the larger thirty-five, we of course assume that all of the remaining children will not be doing just busy work but that somehow the teacher will invent all sorts of wonderful learning experiences for them while she is tending to that small group. In addition we assume that this teacher is, of course, an expert in every conceivable subject from reading, etc., on down to music, art, and foreign languages. To assist the teacher in doing all this, we provide her with a few battered books and twenty-five dollars per child for all "materials" for one whole school year.

In the secondary schools, we expect a teacher to remain inventive and full of instructional vigor while a succession of 150 students march in and out of his or her room in strict periods of forty-five minutes. And again we provide twenty-five dollars worth of materials for each of those students to learn with. In general we have given these teachers no time at all to think or plan or talk together or to try new and possibly better ways of getting children involved in the process of learning. And as a crowning achievement, we manage to underpay them as well.

True, in recent years, some newer approaches have been invented or reinvented in an attempt to relieve this poor, harassed creature—team or cooperative teaching (or at least the idea that a teacher should not be required to carry all of the burden), the idea of nonprofessional aides, auxiliary and specialist teachers in particular subject areas, etc. But the basic job has still remained in most cases, and thr burden is still primarily on the teacher.

We do not expect that the teacher's burdens will be removed or that the job will suddenly become all fun and games. Nor can we think of any ways by which the role of the teacher could or would be made any less crucial to the educative process than it is now. Indeed under this system the job may become in some ways more demanding. But we do want to make the job much more possible and much more professional by doing the following things:

First, by transferring as much of the instructional and "motivational" responsibilities as possible to the materials with which the room is filled, to force the materials (and the makers of materials) to be intriguing, ingenious, catchy, materials that can be used by children for exploration and learning on their own (not many of these exist as yet).

Second, by building a total classroom environment (including operating procedures) that essentially says to a child, "Here is a place—hopefully a rather fascinating place—full of interesting things to do. There are toys, games, books to look at and read, blocks to build with (for younger types), microscopes to look at small things with, animals to enjoy and wonder about, etc. You are going to have to behave yourself—no nonsense about that. But for a large part of the day, you are going to be able to choose what you want to do. If you want to paint a picture, go ahead and do it. If you want to see things through that microscope, go ahead and do that. If you want to play a card game with several of your pals, do that, or if you want to sit in the library corner and read a book, that's fine too. We would like you to keep busy, but how you do it is going to be largely up to you. Mr. X (Miss Y) is still your teacher, and he'll be in the room to answer any questions you have, to help you get started—help you move along on whatever it is you are doing. There will be a lot of other "teachers" coming in and out of the room. Some of these teachers will be particularly interested in the science material, some in the reading books or the art materials or music. They will be glad to help you and may often suggest things for you to do. If you see any of them beginning to do something interesting, feel free to join whatever group he's working with, and feel free to ask those other kids about what they're doing or ask them questions if you don't understand something. Mr. X and all those other "teachers" will, every once in awhile, suggest something for the whole class to do together—look at a movie and talk about it, go on a trip somewhere, play some math games on the blackboard, or perhaps put on a play.

No one is going to shoot you if you choose not to join in on these activities, but if you give it a try, you might find it's not so bad after all. Now don't get the idea from all of this that you aren't engaged in a serious business. It may seem like a great deal of fun, but Mr. X is also going to be worrying about whether you and the rest of the children are learning to do some of the things that everyone has to do in this world—like how to read and use numbers and what the world is like and how it got that way. So maybe at times Mr. X or one of the other teachers is going to sit you down and suggest that there are some things that you and maybe some of the other children too ought to be brushing up on. Some times you are going to have to take tests as well. So you can't always do just what you want to do. In fact, you will be allowed to do what you want to do only if you are obeying the basic rules—like not hitting the other children or not wandering out of the school or not talking tough to Mr. X. Otherwise, the school is yours.

We would hope that by this means teachers—although still in quite complete control of the class environment—will be able to move freely among a group of busy children, picking out those who need special help in any particular subject either individually or in small groups, to encourage some children to forge ahead, establishing group projects and making sure that children develop a tendency toward finishing what they set out to do. In many ways this will be a harder job for many teachers than just following the lesson plans in the book. But it is also a much more professional and creative job for a teacher to be doing.

II. Some Suggested Operating Procedures

1. No classroom will be set up as prescribed by the innovation unless and until a teacher decides he or she would like to give it a try and until and unless there has been a very careful planning process (including the selection or preparation of materials) involving the teacher(s), the assistant director, the subject specialists (and outside consultants if necessary and desirable) and—very important—the instructional research people who will be attempting to find out what the results of this experiment are.

2. The process of moving into this innovative situation should proceed with deliberate speed. Such a classroom cannot operate

unless and until the materials are ready and in the classroom and unless the teacher feels that the physical set-up of the room is such that the program could begin working.

3. Not only the teacher but the children will have to be moved slowly into this kind of a situation. Children (except perhaps young children who have had no experience with school) will not instinctively be accustomed to or know quite how to handle this kind of freedom. It will be quite a new kind of school experience for them, and they will have much to unlearn. Younger children may well be easier to handle since they can be introduced to this kind of an atmosphere before they have acquired habits and attitudes that will have to be unlearned.

4. A class such as this should have no more than twenty-five children heterogeneously grouped with an age span of two to three years and an achievement spread of two to three grade levels (perhaps even more). There must be *a* teacher who has primary responsibility for the classroom, with the other teachers (art, music) and specialists acting as occasional teachers and wandering consultants to the children (and to the teacher or teacher and assistant teacher).

5. The children should be told that upon their arrival in the morning (hopefully *not* lined up outside and marched in) that they can go directly to whatever they choose as their initial activity (no opening exercises—they just enter the room and start working). Similarly, children should not be forced to go out to recess if they choose not to or to have juice and crackers at some specified time. We might even experiment with letting them eat lunch when they want to. As has been said there will be times during the day when it would be convenient for all of the children to be doing the same thing at the same time—when the music teacher arrives to give recorder lessons, or when a film is around that can only be shown on a conventional projector and therefore requires a darkened room (plus all the noise and confusion that the ordinary projector makes and causes) or when the art teacher arrives to give collage instruction. However, it should be made clear to the children that when this kind of thing happens, they may join in if they want to, but that no one is going to force them to. This then puts the burden on the music teacher or the film maker or the art teacher to make the stuff or the instruction so fascinating that the children cannot help but be drawn into the activity. The same rules should apply if a similar situation

arises, say, in Madison project or Illinois or Cambridge math. If the teacher feels tempted to bring the whole class together and elucidate some fascinating mathematical topic or to give "instruction" in Cuisenaire rods, this temptation should be resisted (at least, let's try to resist it and see what happens). Much better perhaps to ask for volunteers or round up those children who would like to work with math that morning (children have been known to come up to a teacher and plead for such sessions) and let those who wish to join in do so. Those who choose *not* to join in are then treated separately by the teacher—either as a small group coerced into doing some math if they are falling a long ways behind or as individuals "taught" either by the teacher or another child who is eager to pass on the newly acquired skill.

6. There are obviously going to be a strict set of behavioral rules for the children (violations will bring a lessening of the freedom that the more responsible children enjoy—offenders will be forced to sit in a corner and look at old educational films or read "Dick and Jane" or some equivalent torture). Some of these rules would be:

a. You are not allowed to strike, curse at, punch, jab in the ribs or otherwise inflict injury on your classmates or teachers.

b. You are not allowed to interfere with another child's activities, either by grabbing his microscope or yelling in his ear when he is trying to read or by any other means. If all of the microscopes (or cartridge film projector or mathematical games or whatever) are being used, then you will have to wait your turn.

c. If there is a dispute or argument that you cannot iron out quickly by yourselves, the teacher (or nearest adult) will arbitrate and whatever he or she says *goes*.

d. You are not allowed to steal, break, or otherwise damage materials or equipment (unless the teacher specifically says it is yours to take home and do whatever you want with it).

e. Although a basic rule of this classroom is that a variety of activities can all be going on at the same time and therefore you are free most of the time to choose what you want to do, this is a place in which everyone is responsible for being busy and productive. It is not a place for horsing around and wasting your time and everyone else's. We do not mean by "busy and productive" that you have to be bustling around all of the time—sitting quietly in a corner reading a book is being quite busy and productive, and often when you are just sitting and staring out of the window you can be thinking great and useful thoughts. But there *are* serious things going on in this room, and you *are* going to be expected to keep moving intellectually and to be learning all sorts of things.

f. By that last statement we do *not* mean that you or the rest of the children or the teacher must be solemn and serious all of the time. We expect the noise level of the class to be high, and laughter is one of the most legitimate of activities. We expect only that the laughter and the activity will not be excessively trivial or get too far out of hand.

7. See Appendix D for a rough and tentative suggested plan for the physical set-up of this kind of a classroom (to be altered as necessity and the teacher's tastes dictate).

B-3: The Director's Expanded Document Subsequently Passed Out to the Teachers (The January Document)

I. Assumptions: Preliminary Platitudes

1. *What American society most requires of its schools in this day and age is that they assist children to become independent, responsible, thinking adults.*

There are, of course, many central assumptions which could and undoubtedly do underlie any educational system. We have selected this one, however, because we believe that this is the one conscious function that a school system can undertake with some chance of success.

In choosing this as our leading assumption, we hope we are facing up to the fact that formal "school" is only one of many modes by which children "learn" or are shaped or become acculturated in a twentieth-century postindustrial society. Indeed, the available evidence—as well as common sense—would indicate that school is, in fact, one of the *minor* shaping forces when compared to the effectiveness of social class, ethnic origin, the family, the peer group, and perhaps even the popular arts such as television, films, the press, popular music, and "teen-age culture."

It is for these reasons that little will be said in this document about the role of the school in the inculcation of "values"—civic virtue, patriotism, moral standards, religious attitudes, and the like. We do not believe that the school is utterly powerless to affect children in these areas—especially since the school by its existence and methods of operation constitutes a set of models and objectives for all children whether we or they like it or not. It is, rather, that we feel that the effect of school in these areas will be minimal at best. A sick society is going to produce a sick educational process (Nazi Germany and its highly effective school system), while a relatively healthy society will have a better chance of producing a process with a healthy amount of diversity and freedom.

We *do* believe, however, that as contemporary society becomes increasingly complex and increasingly dependent upon more abstract symbolic processes, the ability to use one's mind with clarity, power, and delight becomes increasingly crucial to the survival of the individual in society and to the survival of society itself.

2. *It is not possible for any human being in the middle of the twentieth century to comprehend in any meaningful fashion more than a small fraction of the immense body of knowledge and the intellectual and technical skills available to man in the contemporary world.*

The paramount problem that faces the American educational system at this point in time *cannot* be how best to transmit the accumulated knowledge of the race to individuals in succeeding generations. The traditional educational approach that stresses "coverage," that is, the storage and appropriate retrieval of large quantities of specific information, is no longer a workable or useful approach. We do *not* mean here that "knowledge" or "information" or "facts" are useless. What we do mean is that an educational system that devotes much of its energy to insisting that children acquire a certain set body of probably obsolete knowledge, a system which then judges children by how much of that knowledge they can retain and repeat is not using its own brainpower or the brainpower of its students wisely or well.

3. *It is no longer possible for human beings to construct a series
of "correct" answers or interpretations of observed facts that all
thinking people can agree to.*

Although this may or may not have been true in the past, recent
history suggests that large-scale changes in basic knowledge—and in
our ways of looking at what we think we know—are occurring ever
more frequently. This is particularly true in the natural and social
sciences, but it is true in other realms as well. We are beginning to see
that our theories and beliefs are at best little more than approxima-
tions of some elusive set of ultimate "truths," that everything is
"subject to revision" as we gather more and disturbingly new information in every field and develop new, more sophisticated, and increasingly more tentative hypotheses based upon that new information. We are thus forced more and more into seeing the futility and
downright error of attempting to set forth for students a series of
"right answers" or "basic set of fundamental and important concepts"
or the "basic structure" of a field that every child should, after
twelve years of schooling, have indelibly printed on his brain ready
for use.

If we attempt to construct such a series of right answers or basic
structures, we rapidly discover that agreement is difficult if not
impossible to reach (could we all agree, for instance, that men every-
where and at all times have had basically the same "human nature"?).
We also discover that many of our cherished "right" answers turn
out to be based on totally obsolete information or wholly inappropriate and false interpretations. (Columbus discovered America in
1492, every word of which is wrong or subject to substantial if not
total revision.)

There are, of course, many large, important ideas, modes of thinking, or models of reality that are extremely productive and with
which children should become acquainted in some fashion. These
would include many of the hypothetical explanatory constructs upon
which our contemporary intellectual world is based, such as the idea
of biological evolution, the model of the atom as set forth by Bohr,
Rutherford, and Schrodinger, the conceptions of time, space, energy,
and matter of Einstein's general and special theories of relativity or
the model of the mind as proposed by Freud. Nor have we any desire
to suggest that children should not become acquainted with the in-
sight and pleasures afforded by the arts and humanities—by a Shake-
speare, a Bach or Handel, a Michelangelo or Picasso. Indeed, they should.

What we *are* saying is that we are being forced—often against our will—to surrender our cherished idea that an educated human being is a person who has command of a set and necessarily quite limited by them of facts, ideas, and skills at the end of one, two or even sixteen years of schooling. In the first place, it should be apparent to all of us that under the present system of forced storage of information (conventional teaching) and forced retrieval under stress (tests that ask for the recall of facts), most children simply do not retain information. Indeed, they tend to forget it as quickly as they can once the test is over or once the high school or college diploma is obtained. And this is particularly true of the conventional textbook (a series of predigested facts and progably outdated interpretations) as used by teachers in the typical chapter a day, memorization and testing for right answers way.

This, of course, brings into question the whole traditional idea of what a "curriculum" is or should be. Clearly, *something* must be used by the school and its teachers as the basis for getting children involved in the process of learning, even if children are to be given a wide choice concerning what they will get involved in. A school and its teachers have to decide, for instance, that the children *will* study the nature of the physical universe and that they will *not* study how to make a zip gun or how to steal bicycles. Thus, in a real sense, the school and its staff (or the school and parents and the community at large) are inevitably going to make the basic educational decisions.

But we believe that the world of the mind these days, the world of intellectual and aesthetic pleasure, is too large, too exclusive, too exciting to be encompassed within the range of our conventional curriculum guides and conventional educational materials such as textbooks.

The proper job of a "curriculum" therefore is not to decide what facts are going to be "covered" and what the "right" answers are going to be, but to provide a broad array of valuable, intriguing materials that is highly relevant to the lives of the children themselves. The task of the school and the teachers then becomes how best to guide and assist the children to become involved with the materials, how to make the children's *own* explorations and discoveries possible.

4. *It is not how much we know that is important but what we are able to do with what we know.*

Information itself is all too prevalent, and we are already building computerized retrieval systems to provide us with the information we need when we need it. But all of this information gathering is wasted unless individual people are equipped to use it in the performance of tasks that make valid intellectual, aesthetic, or social (or all three) sense. If, when we have called for or accumulated some batch of information, we have not the slightest idea of how to manipulate it, how to make sense of it, how to make it work for us and serve our purposes, then we are simply engaged in a foolish and futile enterprise.

At the most primitive level, we are here talking about what are often called "skills," that is, the "skills" of being able to read the written word, or writing, of performing rudimentary operations with numbers, etc. All of these things are, of course, eminently desirable.

But at some more sophisticated level, we are speaking of far more important things—ways of handling complex masses of information, of generating and manipulating abstract ideas, of sensitizing oneself to and enjoying magnificent works of art, in short, ways of using one's available mental and emotional faculties toward both personal and socially satisfying ends.

It is this kind of "skill"—essentially the ability to make connections between things and to follow logical sequences, in other words the ability to "think"—that is becoming increasingly important to both individuals and to contemporary society. As we all know, the day is long since past when a straightforward command of the 3 R's could enable a person to function adequately in a complicated industrial world. Indeed, much of the furor over education these days stems from a rather sudden and annoying realization that the human products being turned out by the schools have simply not been adequate to the tasks being thrust upon them by that great world out there. Much of this fuss, ironically enough, has been created by the colleges and universities, which in general operate on educational principles far more antediluvian than those of the public schools. But more importantly, fuss has also come from business and industry who clearly recognize that, while the public system can hardly be expected to provide highly specialized training, the schools might well be expected to produce people sufficiently equipped intellectually to be able to adapt well to a wide variety of new situations and experiences.

Indeed, business and industry have of necessity created for themselves a vast educational system at least equaling if not surpassing the public system in size. Most of this education is post-high school training for specific jobs, but much of it is general education as well.

Perhaps one of the most interesting developments here is the recognition by business and industry that, with automation and the constant shifting of needed job skills, training for specific skills and specific jobs is rapidly becoming obsolete. What is really important now is training (or education) that prepares people to handle many different kinds of tasks and to be able to shift easily and quickly to new tasks as the situation may require. Especially important as technology continues to evolve rapidly is the ability to recognize new problems as they arise and to solve those problems imaginatively. In short, what is increasingly needed by higher education, business and industry is *general intellectual skills*—again essentially the ability to put one and one together and to solve problems, many of which have not as yet been discovered or even thought of.

These types of general skills we know considerably less about than the primitive ones of reading, writing, and arithmetic. Academic psychology—from whence all our answers must ultimately come—has only recently found itself in a position to begin to investigate systematically how our cognitive processes work and especially how they develop in children. Cognition (the study of how we "know" anything at all) has, of course, been the subject of philosophical and psychological debate for centuries. But the systematic and scientific study of the *processes* by which our minds—and especially the minds of children—operate is a relatively new field.

Most of these investigations are taking place (as they should) in the laboratory or in laboratory settings. That is, the investigators are interested in discovering and tracing the processes in as raw, uncluttered a form as it is possible to get them. This is what Bruner has called the "random encounter" between a child and the tasks he is to perform in order that the psychologist may grasp what is happening inside the child's head.

This is a very important and very necessary way of finding out some very important and very necessary things about how children think and learn. But it is quite a different thing from the nonrandom, more educationally relevant encounter between a child and some (hopefully) meaningful material that takes place in the instructional process.

What we really need here is a special group of people, made up of psychologists and specially trained school people, to study the very particular set of problems that occur in the process of *assisted* learning—what is going on in the minds of children (and teachers) in the

classroom as they move through the instructional process and especially what happens when that process is altered, for instance, in
some of the ways described in this document. To refer to Bruner
once again the problem is not so much how to apply in schools what
we already think we have learned in the laboratory, but rather how
to *formulate* appropriate questions and hypotheses as they arise in an
instructional context.

Perhaps what we are talking about here in some ultimate sense is a
center or institute for the study of instruction. While waiting for this
miracle to occur, we intend to make our own contributions to the
advancement of this kind of knowledge through our own instructional research group, although we know full well that this can never
be a substitute for the full-scale, fully staffed center devoted solely
to this problem.

We do know a few, tentative things, however, with which we can
begin to re-examine and reformulate what we are doing. We know,
for instance, what some of the rules of logical thinking are. We know,
too, a little about how these rules have been applied in the past and
are currently applied, especially in the sciences. Our situation, therefore, is not hopeless. We can even set a few of these approaches
down, always realizing that when we set these forth as objectives we
are assuming that they are being used on content—although in many
cases that content or subject matter may well be selected by the students themselves. We outline what some of these "higher skills"
might be under the Objectives section of this paper.

5. *Human beings tend to "learn" best those things which they feel
to be relevant to their own lives and to their own interests, those
things which they feel that they themselves have in some measure
chosen to learn.*

If we look at ourselves, we will probably agree that this is certainly true of all adults. We feel that it is equally true of children,
even very young children. This does *not* mean, however, that we
should let children decide in all cases what they are going to study
in school. Children are just as capable as adults of devoting a great
deal of time to the sheerest trivia (what was that about arrogance?).

What we do mean is that within very broad limits the range of
quite justifiable alternatives is so large that one body of content or
one avenue of approach into a subject is most often just as good as
another. Some examples:

In the natural sciences, there are uncountable ideas of major importance—the notion of biological, and especially human, evolution, the structure and operations of the atom, the nature and origins of the solar system and the universe, the nature of chemical bonds, the nature and operations of the human mind and body, the study of the earth and the sea, and so on endlessly. Who is to say that it is "better" to study the nature of the atom than the question of the origins and development of man? Does it in the longest of runs really make that much difference if a child becomes captured by one rather than the other? We would hope that he might become acquainted with both and with all of the others as well. But we are trying to be sensible.

In the social sciences, the case for a rigid, predetermined curriculum is even harder to make than in the natural sciences or in mathematics, where at least attempts have been made to set forth some logical sequence of what must be learned first before something else can be learned (although there are apparently no hard and fast rules about it). Attempts to establish such logical sequences or sets of basic concepts for the social sciences have proved relatively futile. Again, however, this does not disturb us greatly, for the range of available data is enormous and unavoidably fascinating—if it is not denatured by being crammed into a textbook. We are finally beginning to get some first-rate material to work with—everything from a complete ethnographic film record of a single Eskimo group through vast collections of original historical documents on down to the whole world waiting outside the classroom. Again, who is to say that a study of the American Revolution (even if it is done only once rather than five times) is preferable to a study of the origins and structure of human society?

The dangers of rigidly prescribing what should be studied in the arts and humanities, where individual taste is rampant, are too obvious to merit consideration. Except to point out that while we may feel strongly that children should be exposed to "King Lear," to "Messiah," the B Minor Mass, to the ceiling of the Sistine Chapel, to the Symphony of Psalms, and perhaps even in extreme circumstances to "Silas Marner," our ability to destroy any hope of arousing interest in these great human experiences so far outstrips our ability actually to arouse that interest that we had better be quite careful. Perhaps the way into "Romeo and Juliet" is through "West Side Story" or the way into "Messiah" is through the Rolling Stones. Perhaps the best way to encourage children to read is to encourage them to read

"Batman" or books about the National Football League. It might be wise for us to maintain a very open mind in these matters.

Perhaps one of the major clues to success here is the hunch (verified by common sense, at least) that both children and adults will always be attracted to and learn most easily about those things which seem to them to have some honest relevance to their lives, things which appear to them to be important. If we wish children to become intrigued by a "Lear," then it behooves us in some ingenious way to demonstrate its possible relevance to the life the children see about them. If we cannot do this, we have already lost the battle. We are wasting both their time and ours.

What emerges from all this, we feel, is a belief that the problem is not so much *what* we should ask to children to sink their intellectual teeth into—there is plenty of "what"—but rather how best to get children involved. The problem thus comes down to *materials* and *methods* (and to teachers who are willing to throw away the book and pay attention to the students). How, in other words, to so arrange our facilities and our instructional process so that children have an enormous range of valuable and relevant material to engage their minds and energies and a wide range of choice about what, at any given moment, they will devote themselves to.

6. *It is possible as well as desirable to devise an educational process that will encourage children to become increasingly responsible for their own learning.*

If we claim, as we do, that children will learn more eagerly and much better those things which are relevant and self-selected, then clearly we are saying, too, that children will of necessity have to shoulder an increasing share of the responsibility for their own schooling.

By "responsibility" here we mean the opposite side of the venerable coin of "freedom." We do not expect, for instance, that every child will simply do as he or she pleases all day in school. While we are desirous of making the process of learning pleasurable, we still intend that it be a process of learning and in that sense a very serious business. Indeed, we would assume that, to a large extent, the degree of freedom and choice extended to a child will depend upon his exercise of responsibility—in not belting other children or his teachers, in having some minimum respect for school property and the rights of others, and if possible some minimum respect for himself as a human

animal capable of being involved in the process of using his intellectual and aesthetic faculties. True, the basic responsibility for providing a humane and intellectually intriguing environment rests squarely
with the school. But as children grow older and, hopefully, become
increasingly involved in the instructional process, we would hope and
expect that they will demand and be capable of assuming that larger
share of educational responsibility, more capable of wisely and imaginatively exercising their freedom of choice.

This, to us, is a clear necessity, for if we seriously hope to produce
or enable children to become independent, responsible, thinking
adults, then we have to give them the opportunity to think, to be
independent and to be responsible for their own actions and beliefs.
If we claim this as a goal and then do not increasingly turn over this
educative responsibility to children as they grow older, we are simply
being hypocrites operating in a fashion that is going to produce more
rote memorizers and exam takers, that is, human beings who are
much less than they should be.

7. *The profession of the teacher—as it is presently conceived and
practiced—is neither a sensible nor a possible one to expect large
numbers of people to practice successfully.*

For far too many years now, we have been asking teachers to perform an essentially impossible task—or at least a task impossible for
all but the most gifted and inexhaustible of human beings (and such
paragons are rare). We have been asking a lone individual to be totally
responsible for the education of up to thirty-five children in something called a "class," to handle all of the individual idiosyncrasies of
those thirty-five children, all of their differing abilities, levels of
achievement, peculiar talents, all of their various virtues and problems. We have demanded of teachers that they should treat each of
these children as individuals and devise a program that will suit each
child's individual needs and capacities.

In the case of elementary teachers we have not only required all
this of them but we have simultaneously told them that they should
keep all of their children gainfully occupied throughout a full six-
hour day. If they pull a smaller group out of a larger thirty-five, for
reading instructions, we of course assume that all of the remaining
children will not be doing just busy work but that somehow the
teacher will invent all sorts of wonderful learning experiences for
them while she is tending to that small group. In addition we assume

that this teacher is, of course, an expert in every conceivable subject from reading, math, science, social studies on down to music, art, and foreign languages. To assist the teacher in doing all this, we provide her with a few battered books and twenty-five dollars per child for all "materials" for one whole school year.

In the secondary schools, we expect a teacher to remain inventive and full of instructional vigor while a succession of 150 students march in and out of his or her room in strict periods of forty-five minutes. And again we provide twenty-five dollars worth of materials for each of those students to learn with. In general we have given these teachers no time at all to think or plan or talk together or to try new and possibly better ways of getting children involved in the process of learning. And as a crowning achievement, we manage to underpay them as well.

In recent years, it is true, some newer approaches have been in-vented or—reinvented—in an attempt to relieve this poor, harassed creature called a teacher—team or cooperative teaching (or at least the idea that a teacher should not be required to carry all of the burden), the idea of nonprofessional aides, of auxiliary and specialist teachers in particular subject areas, etc. But the basic job has still re-mained in most cases, and the burden is still primarily on the teacher.

No matter how vigorously we innovate, we do not expect that the teacher's burdens will be removed or that the job will suddenly be-come all fun and games. Nor can we think of ways by which the role of the teacher can or should be made any less crucial to the educative process than it is now. Indeed, it is more likely that the job will be-come in many ways even more demanding. But we do want to make the job much more possible and much more professional. Some of the things we hope to do are listed under the Objectives section of this paper, especially the things listed under No. 5.

8. *The institution called "school" as we know it today is rightly and of necessity undergoing vast changes not only in the instructional process that occurs inside its walls but in its relationship to the world outside those walls—to parents, the local community, to other civic and social agencies and forces, and to the community at large.*

It is becoming increasingly clear that the traditional ways of operating a "school" are no longer functioning adequately. We are already extending the school day with after school programs, ex-tending the school year with summer programs, extending the range of legitimate educational interest with additional health and social service programs such as Headstart, and more pupil adjustment and psychiatric counseling.

But these things are only the beginning of changes to come. The twelve-month school year is just around the corner (with optional vacation periods). We are heading quite rapidly toward a twelve or fourteen hour day in which schools are open for voluntary programs (especially art, music, dance, science, drama), for both children and adults. The schools, too, will become more and more "community" schools—more attached and responsive to the local community (even though many of the students in the local school will come from other communities and vice versa). The "school" will also become not only a community center but will begin to serve or at least house cooperatively other civic functions—health and day care services, welfare if needed, housing and urban renewal offices, job centers. It is even possible that a system of local community committees with considerable influence might be set up to help run the schools and coordinate all of the various community agencies.

We do not know exactly what direction history is taking us here or just what the new shape of the "school" institution will be. But we had better be thinking about all of these matters.

II. Objectives

From all of the myriad aims that an educational system could and probably does have, we would select six as the ones we feel have paramount importance at this point in time (subject, as always, to total revision):

1. We feel the single, most important thing we could do for all children is to make it possible for them to discover the *intrinsic satisfaction and delight* that can come from the successful employment of their own intellectual and aesthetic energies at whatever level those energies are or can become capable of operating.

2. If we can succeed in proving to children that such intrinsic delight exists and that they can experience it, then we would like to have those children become increasingly self-motivated and increasingly *responsible* for their own learning and education. If, given a chance to display such responsibility, they do show it, then we would

like to give them an increasing freedom of choice (within broad
limits) to determine what they are going to become most deeply involved in. We would like to make their education as *self-directed* as
possible. We do not know at the moment what the minimum and
maximum limits to that range of choice and self-direction will be.
The range will also, obviously, vary with individual children. But it is
clear to us that none of the children are going to become intellectually responsible adults unless they have considerable experience in
behaving responsibly as students and being free to exercise some
control over their own behavior.

3. As an extension of the above aims, we would very much like
to have children emerge from our schools convinced that they are, to
some large extent, able to cope with the world, that they possess the
necessary intellectual and aesthetic skills and are therefore *competent*
to manage themselves and their lives in such a fashion that they
might have some positive effect on that world if they so choose.

4. Although the list of "necessary intellectual and aesthetic skills"
could probably be endless, we believe strongly that the following
mental skills (perhaps *operational competencies* is more apt) should
rank high, perhaps even highest, in priority among those we assist or
guide children to acquire. These are the "skills" along with and including reading, writing, and figuring mentioned in assumption No.
2 above. Some of them (tentatively and with basic credit to J.S.
Bruner, Piaget and others) are:

OBSERVATIONS

We would like to sharpen the capacity of children simply to see,
hear, touch, smell, and taste, to be open to and aware of themselves
and the world about them. We want them to be aware of small
things—bugs, blades of grass, tiny animals—as well are large things—
clouds, cities, oceans, and elephants. We would like them to be able
to *feel* all these things and be more aware of their own feelings
about them.

COMPARISON

We want children to be able to *compare and differentiate* between
all of the various sights, sounds, tastes, smells, and touches, to separate them out and distinguish between them with some accuracy, to
begin to see differences and similarities.

CLASSIFICATION AND CATEGORIZATION

We would like children to be able to take the evidence, information, and feelings they gather and to *organize* them into some order so that they can be in the first instance simply thought about and manipulated. In short, we want children to be able to perform the fundamental act that George Gaylord Simpson has called "the perceptual reduction of chaos." We would also like to have them begin to discover that all human systems of classification are arbitrary and exclusive rather than God-given and all-inclusive.

THE PERCEPTION OF PROBLEMS

While this may not fit as a strict "operational competency," we would like to help children begin to sense the problems that inevitably arise from any attempt to impose order on what we see all around us—the inconsistencies, gaps, and inadequacies in all ordering systems. We would like children to become disturbed and bothered by and acutely aware of the flimsiness of most theories and explanations offered by the adult world and its books, lectures, films, and the like. We would like them to be suspicious of pat and glib answers, to have their curiosity engaged by what the better answers might be. We would like them, in short, to become intrigued by the whole process of being dissatisfied with existing explanations or beliefs; of sensing that dissatisfaction as presenting a "problem" that they might wish to explore and wrestle with; and of feeling impelled by their own doubt and curiosity to delve into the matter and attempt to come up with a more adequate solution or answers, no matter how tentative.

INTUITION AND HUNCHING

After the children have sensed that a problem exists and is perhaps worth pursuing, we would like them to be able to play with possibilities, to begin to be able to accumulate relevant information and to manipulate it in a relatively free, unrestricted, perhaps quite left-handed way. We would like them to be able to take intuitive leaps, to play their hunches, to bring all of their imaginative faculties to bear, to go beyond the information given, even if for the moment they may not be able to support the leap or the hunch with all of the relevant data. Eventually we would like them to be able to see and understand that the act of thinking and learning, the act of using their minds is not by any means the cold application of icy logic or a dogged and routine use of some mysterious formula called the "scientific method." We would like them to see that nothing of value—no scientific theory or symphony, play or work of art—was ever created by simply following some bleak set of methodological rules. As they discover this, we would like them at the same time to experience the pleasures of employing their own imaginative faculties—the passions of their own hearts and hands—in the pursuit of answers to their own nagging questions and problems.

HYPOTHESIS BUILDING AND TESTING

We would like to have children realize, too, that while intuitive speculation is vital, it is only the beginning of the process, that the hunch or leap becomes important or useful only when it has been turned into an hypothesis that can be persuasively supported either by a reorganization of existing facts or by new facts gathered in the process of building the hypothesis—or both. (The analogous situation in the arts would be that the initial creative impulse is useless or wasted until it is subjected to the rigorous discipline of being wrestled down on paper as a story, novel, or poem, or written down and performed as a play, or written down and performed as a piece of music, or transformed through the medium of paint into a picture, etc.) We would also, therefore, hope to get children involved in the process of putting their hypothesis (and creative impulses) to the test (or going through the pleasurable agonies of producing their creative works). By this we mean exposing them to the test of experiment (in the natural sciences), to the test of either experiment or the exposure to more and wider data (in the social sciences) or exposed to production and critical opinion (in the arts and humanities). This also clearly implies exposure to the cut and thrust of debate, to argument and controversy with one's fellow students and teachers, for it is in heat of this debate and controversy that much of the light and pleasure is generated.

EXTRAPOLATION

In the process of building and testing their ideas, the children will in all probability discover that none of their beautiful theories quite takes care of all of the evidence or covers all of the holes. In the case of gaps in the theories or those vast areas where adequate information is simply not available, we would like to see the children involved in the process of speculative extrapolation, or going beyond the information given in the sense of filling the gaps with a controlled imagination and a respect for what *is* known. For instance, if little is known about the market economy of pre-Sumerian urban complexes in Mesopotamia, then it might be fun for students to see if they could build an input–output model of how it might have worked.

INTERPRETATION

After hypotheses have been constructed and tested, extrapolations made and theories derived, there still remains the never-ending problem of what it all means. This generally appears to be a communal activity. Although everyone always performs his own interpretive acts, especially where his own data are concerned, no one has a sufficiently broad grasp of all the information and ideas in a field to go it completely alone. Much of the pleasure and enlightenment of learning come out of the exchange of ideas and information, out of disagreements and the process of forcing oneself to figure out what one's ideas and hypotheses really mean and how they contribute to a clarification—or perhaps a sudden obscuring—of the problem and the general field.

THE BUILDING OF MODELS

We would also like to engage the children in the practice of constructing intellectual models—models, for instance, of the world-view of existing cultures or of ancient civilizations, or of natural phenomena, such as the atom.

APPRECIATION

Since we hardly expect that all of our children will turn out to be original creators in scholarly pursuits or the sciences or in drama, music, literature and art, we would like them to become very much aware of the pleasures and satisfactions that can be derived from less than skilled participation in or simple appreciation of the world of thinking and of the arts. By this we mean very clearly *not* just what are normally thought of as the "higher" expressions of these pursuits, not just George Eliot, Mahler, Ibsen, Einstein, etc., but the broader and more popular aspects as well. It is difficult and somewhat arrogant for us to be that certain that Bach is somehow ultimately superior to jazz (remember what Hanslick said about Brahms) or folk-rock. What is important here is that young people be open to and curious about all of these things as valuable expressions of the human species. It is equally important that the schools not always find themselves the representatives and purveyors of the dead hand of the past, insensitive to and scornful of those things which evoke an immediate and highly relevant response in the young people themselves. After all, *they* are the future, and we are not.

5. We would like to make the job of teaching more productive and professional by doing the following things:

First, add personnel to the schools and to the classroom, personnel of great variety and differing talents. These would include parents and community people, college and high school students (for the elementary and middle schools), student teachers and volunteers. Some of these people might be doing essentially assistant teaching, others arriving on special occasions for special kinds of instruction (music, art, drama, or as resource people in special topics), still others as aides assisting in routine chores.

Second, transfer as much of the instructional and "motivational" responsibilities as possible from the teacher to the total classroom (or academic space) environment and to the greatly enhanced (both quantitatively and qualitatively) materials with which the rooms should be filled. This kind of environment will be highly structured in the sense that the school and the teachers will have complete control over what kinds of materials go into the room and therefore complete control over what is studied and how. But within the overall structure, we would like the materials to be such that *they* can generate the intrinsic interest of the children and thus relieve the teacher of much of the need to "motivate" children. In addition, we would hope that many of the materials can be self-instructional, that they can be used by students with a minimum amount of guidance from the teachers. Within this kind of a framework, we would hope that the students would be able to have a wide variety of choice about what, at any given moment, they might decide to get involved in. If the teacher has adequate assistance and adequate amounts of high-quality, self-instructional materials, perhaps she will have a great deal more time to spend helping individual students who need her attention while other students can progress at their own speed and largely on their own.

6. We would, finally, like to make schools into instruments that better reflect and better serve their community. This may mean in the first instance much greater communication between school and

community, more powerful and broadly representative parent and community groups, afternoon and evening programs designed by and for the community. But it may also (as under current Title III projects) mean new schools and school-centered complexes devoted to many things other than formal schooling—welfare and psychological services, day care, libraries, employment centers, adult education, etc. These complexes, again, must be designed with and for the community. But even beyond these things, there may well be modes of education that can be best accomplished outside of "school"—within community organizations or business and industry. If so, we would like to encourage their growth and build linkages with the more formal school programs. Education might thus become the result of the total involvement of everyone and thus become as effective as it might and should be.

III. Hypotheses

(not intended to be an exhaustive list, and no operational definitions provided at this time)

A. CONCERNING CHILDREN

1. *The intelligence of children (or adults) is not genetically fixed.*
Without getting too deeply involved in the nature-nurture argument and using "intelligence" here to mean the active and effective employment of one's intellectual and aesthetic energies, we would guess that society (culture) and the instructional process society imposes upon a child have a great deal to do with the level at which that child becomes capable of employing his "intelligence." We would suggest the further possibility that the traditional instructional process as created and used by Western European and American culture has in general done as much to inhibit the growth of intelligence in children as it has to enhance it. We would also like to begin conceiving of intelligence not as something one scores on a paper and pencil test but as something one *does*.

2. *Children's minds operate in ways that are qualitatively different from (but not by that token inferior to) the minds of adults.*
Although this is a question for psychologists and not educators to answer, we suspect that children, especially young children, simply do not operate by the same cognitive rules that adults imagine apply

to adults. Children are not merely inept adults but have ways of looking at the world and handling information that at least appear to be
quite different from adult ways. As these ways of thinking get shaped
by society and its schools, they change and begin more to approxi-
mate adult ways. Perhaps much of value is lost in this process. At any
rate, if we knew more about what these qualitative differences might
be, we would perhaps be able to devise a more effective and certainly
more courteous instructional process.

3. *The development of a child's intellectual and aesthetic energies
appears to be a logical and coherent if still mysterious process.*

Again a problem primarily for psychologists rather than educators,
but if Piaget, Bruner, Vigotsky et al., are correct, then we would like
very much to become clearer on just what the process is, how the
mechanisms involved operate, and how these operations might best
be used to create an instructional process that is more congruent
with children's development and will therefore be more effective.

4. *All normal children are curious.*

Inquisitiveness is a basic human trait, at least as present in children as in adults. Although it would be difficult to find an uninquisi-
tive preschool or out-of-school child, it is not at all difficult to find
one in school. This should give us pause and much food for thought.
Perhaps many of our current practices—scheduling, adults always de-
ciding what children should be doing, schools organized for the convenience of teachers and administrators rather than children—perhaps
these practices are cutting us off from the enormous energies within
the children themselves. It should be possible for us, with all of our
wisdom and ingenuity, to devise ways of maintaining and using the
curiosity of children rather than viewing it as something that must
always be curbed, regulated, and channeled.

5. *Children tend to "learn" at different speeds and in individual
ways and by means of different learning "styles."*

By this we mean simply that all children may not "learn" best or
most effectively through solely verbal means or primarily through
books. Some children may need a great deal more manipulation of
concrete materials, others may rely heavily on visual images. All
children undoubtedly have all styles or modes at their disposal, but
the balance between them appears to vary. It is obviously important
in a society such as this to assist all children to attain a high degree

of proficiency in verbal and symbolic skills, but this should not lead us to ignore less verbal avenues to knowledge, nor should we assume that everyone can or must learn the same thing at the same time or by the same age.

6. *There are (may well be) "learning" differences among children that vary in level according to social class and in pattern according to ethnic group.*

Recent research (Lesser) tends to indicate that different ethnic groups emerge from a series of mental ability tests with different patterns of ability and achievement. These patterns tend to remain constant for such ethnic groups but levels of achievement within these patterns will vary by social class (higher class groups generally do better than lower class groups). If this is so, it raises the spectre of the necessity to tailor the instructional process not only according to individual differences but according to social class and ethnic differences as well.

B. CONCERNING THE INSTRUCTIONAL PROCESS

(Instructional process here defined as assisted learning within a situation designed for that purpose.)

1. *The instructional process can have a significant impact on the lives of children independent of social class and ethnic group.*

Recent research (Coleman) tends to suggest that schools as they are currently operated have little impact on children beyond the passing on of a certain amount of rudimentary knowledge and the skills of reading, writing, and figuring. In general, those schools housing children of high social and economic status and white or oriental ethnic background will produce children who score well on standardized intelligence and achievement tests. Schools housing children with lower socio-economic status and nonwhite or non-oriental ethnic background produce children who score poorly. We can, as a start, assume that there is a suspiciously high correlation between schools containing largely middle-class whites and intelligence and achievement tests largely standardized with white middle-class children, tests in addition that are designed to test what is taught in a typical white middle-class educational system. But what Coleman's research seems to imply is that the instructional process as currently practiced is quite at the mercy of social class and ethnic origin—there is little it can do to overcome, let's say, the possibly deleterious effects of a child's being born poor and Negro. Nor, apparently, is there much school can do to destroy a middle-class white child's ability to do well on tests. We are not willing to accept (nor is Coleman) this conclusion. We tend to believe that a radically different instructional process (and therefore radically different schools) along with tests that measure a much broader range of skills, attitudes, and achievements can at least begin to make a substantial impact on the lives of children, whether the children be white or Negro, poor or rich.

2. *The instructional process will make a substantial impact on children only if, by design or accident, it is able to be congruent with the abilities and interests of children at each stage of their develop-ment, if it is "courteous" toward what is going on inside the heads of children, takes this into account, and makes use of it.*

This means only that what children are asked or expected to do in school must, in some way, be in tune with children—with whatever their individual abilities and interests may be, with what is bothering or delighting them, with what seems relevant to them. If strict atten-tion is not paid to this, as is too often the case, then children will simply turn school off as trivial, boring, and a waste of time. "Moti-vating" them will suddenly become a major problem where no prob-lem need basically exist. This does *not* mean that therefore the cur-riculum should be invented by children as they go along. Adults (teachers, administrators, parents) have to make some basic deci-sions—it is better to study science through balance beams, live ani-mals, mystery powders, etc.) than to study how to steal bicycles. Indeed, adults in some form are going to determine what the basic environment of school and classroom is going to be, what essentially is going to be there to be used and what is *not* going to be there and not be used. What we are suggesting here is an instructional process in which both children and teachers are not so constrained that if children do become grabbed by a topic or a gadget or an animal they are allowed to pursue that engagement and are not cut off by some (to them) arbitrary and irrelevant external demand that "it is now time to . . . ." We would guess that this kind of process would be more effective if only because it might have a chance of turning children on about learning, of convincing them that school is worthwhile.

3. *Children will "learn" better if the environment in which they are asked to operate is "responsive," if it includes both structure and*

freedom, if it is full of intriguing material that asks questions, and if it provides ways of finding answers to those questions.

"Learn" here means to become involved in the process of employing their intellectual and aesthetic energies upon productive (as defined largely but not solely by the school) tasks. A "responsive environment" (with apologies to O.K. Moore) then would essentially be one that a child can manipulate and do things to and which, when the child does this, answers the child back. This means it must be filled with things—books, films, kits, animals, games, easels, paints, clay and adults—which are not only intrinsically interesting but which are structured in such a way that with a minimum of assistance a child can get answers to the questions that arise in his mind. As children grow older (high school), they may not need such a profusion of materials but may rather need more ability to get out of the school altogether and investigate the outside world and its operations (a different kind of responsive environment).

4. *Children will learn better if, as much as possible, they are allowed to find answers to questions.*

"Discovery" can easily be carried to ridiculous extremes, and certainly there are many times when straight factual information is best simply given. But, in general, minds are not stirred by the predigested conclusions contained in textbooks and other people's formulae. The problem is how to get children involved in the whole process of sensing problems, finding data, etc., and building answers, and the heart of this problem then lies in the development of materials that makes this possible.

5. *Children will learn better if teachers, while being responsible for structuring the environment, act within that structure more as guides and assistants to the learners rather than instructors in the traditional sense.*

This suggests that teachers should not act as the fountain of all knowledge and right answers but as people who are there primarily to assist children in getting involved in a process that may end up being largely self-instructional.

6. *Children will learn better if they are not kept in a state of constant anxiety and worry caused by the fear of constant judgment by adults and "school."*

Constant tests, grades, assessments, etc., can easily lead to the destruction of the very qualities of involvement and intrinsic delight that should be the primary rewards of learning. These practices of never-ending tests also lead teachers into the trap of teaching to achieve high scores on tests. A little tension may be a good thing, but repeated failure to succeed in passing tests can also lead children to conceive of themselves as stupid when they are only bad test-takers and as intelligent when they are only good test-takers.

7. *Children will learn better if they have a chance to assist other children to learn.*

One never learns anything quite so thoroughly as when one has to help someone else learn it (back to the Lancastrian School).

8. *The errors children make are one of the best sources of information we have as to what is going on inside the child's mind.*

Errors, far from being treated as crimes and punished, should be looked upon as opportunities to discover the state of a child's mental operations, what he is really thinking. A correct operation or a "right" answer can be arrived at for quite wrong reasons. An error is *probably* always made for the wrong reasons and usually indicates that some kind of inadequate or inefficient processing is going on inside the child's head. As every good teacher knows (if only he or she had the time), this is *not* the moment to give the child a bad mark and write him off as stupid but the cue for action, the moment for an adult to move in and begin to help the child work his way through the problem until the source of the error can be discovered and corrected, preferably by the child himself.

C. CONCERNING SCHOOLS

1. *School can be a pleasurable and satisfying experience not only for children but for teachers and parents as well.*

Although an equally good hypothesis might be that there are inevitable tensions between teacher and pupil, teacher and parent, school and parent, school and community, we would hold that these tensions are to a large extent artifacts of the way schools have traditionally been organized, operated, and staffed. This does not mean that a tensionless, perfectly smooth, and therefore perfectly dull situation can be created in this best and worst of all possible worlds. What it does mean is that it is possible to create an institution in which these potentially antagonistic forces can be so shaped that they are essentially heading in the same general direction, a situation in which each force is contributing to and receiving support from the others.

2. *Children will respond more positively toward school and the instructional process and will "learn" better if school is not rigidly organized by grades, if teachers are guides rather than purveyors of knowledge and punitive judges, if each child is not fed into a blind machine but a process tailored to his specific talents and liabilities.*

This is an argument for an ungraded school with an extremely flexible curriculum and for a quite different (and much harder and more important) role for the teacher. It also argues for a much larger ratio of adults to children with not all of the adults being conventional teachers. Additional personnel might include subject area specialists, assistant teachers, neighborhood aides, special teachers for the arts, community instructors for after-school and evening programs, school volunteers, pupil personnel service people, community liaison workers, teacher interns, etc. Only by radically reducing the child-adult ratio can a school begin to provide the individual attention required for a flexible curriculum, even though much of the learning may be done by students working on their own.

3. *Under the kind of program described above, "discipline" and "control" problems will tend to disappear or be minimized.*

Many of the problems usually listed under the general rubric of "control" may in fact be created by an instructional process which appears to children to be dull, insipid, trivial, and boring and by "schools" which too often give the appearance of and act like prisons. Bored, uninspired children will, of course, act up and seek vengeance upon the innocent (in many cases) teacher. Control is always a problem in highly regimented institutions such as the armed forces and schools. If, on the other hand, children have a wide variety of interesting and engaging things to do, if they are not ordered about according to strict and arbitrary (to them) schedules, if teachers are not continually cast in the role of punitive judge, then perhaps children will lose some of their strong motivations toward rebellion.

4. *Teachers will lead more satisfying and more professional lives if they are not confined to prescribed patterns of content and method, if they are free to develop their individual styles and competencies, and if they are supplied with adequate amounts of assistance so that they are relieved of petty details and annoyances.*

It could be added that if teaching becomes this kind of profession, it will perhaps attract an even higher calibre of person than it does now.

5. *Parents and the community will be happier with the institution called school if they become convinced that the school in some very real sense belongs to them, if it serves not only the purpose of schooling children but also acts as a major community resource and service center, and if they feel that as the community they can have some real impact on what happens in that school.*

It must be clear to everyone that in this day and age schools and school systems can no longer operate as empires apart from the world around them. A school can no longer be that grim institution down the street that children long to escape from and adults learn to ignore as largely irrelevant. This requires some rethinking of the way schools operate—perhaps even some changes in the laws by which school systems are constituted. Whatever the eventual result of this rethinking, it seems clear that schools will have to be a great deal more responsive to the particular communities in which they find themselves— responsive not only in terms of providing a greater variety of services and more of them but in giving parents and the local community a greater share in the responsibility of operating the school and its programs. For now, this must be an advisory role, but there are other models of schools and school-community relations that should be tried also.

6. *The physical facility within which a school program operates has significant effects—both positive and negative—on the effectiveness of that program.*

All practicing educational people are aware of how destructively an inadequate and inflexible facility can operate to restrict an instructional program. What we are not so often aware of is the enormous positive benefits an appropriate and adequately flexible facility could bring to an educational operation. We tend to be far too resigned to bestial conditions for children, teachers, and the community. We have only begun to use our imagination to design the educational environments we need.

D. CONCERNING DISADVANTAGED, ESPECIALLY NEGRO, CHILDREN

1. *No child is genetically inferior simply because he is born to poor parents or is born both poor and Negro.*

2. *However, being born poor and especially being born both poor and black constitutes—in this society—being born "disadvantaged" to some degree if typical white middle-class advantages are used as the standard of comparison.*

This may well be a dubious proposition in that typical white middle-class standards may themselves be dubious standards of measurement. It could just as easily be argued that white middle-class suburban children are "disadvantaged" because they live in homogenized, white, and excessively comfortable ghettos and are thus deprived of the knowledge of what the larger world and life are all about.

3. *Poor children, and especially poor Negro children, may have linguistic and cognitive deficiencies—again if the standard of comparison is typical white middle-class patterns of linguistic and cognitive behavior.*

By all available evidence, poor children and especially poor Negro children do not score as well on standard achievement tests as middle-class whites. Whether this difference is due to the way the tests themselves are constructed and standardized or to differences in the cultural patterns of poor and middle-class children or a combination of both remains to be unraveled by social scientists. However, it is interesting to note that, if Coleman is correct, poor children (even Negro children) do *not* receive an "inferior" education in American schools, by the somewhat narrow standards used in that study. They are no more discriminated against than middle-class white children in terms of facilities, money spent, materials, special programs, etc. Assuming for a moment that these linguistic and cognitive differences *do* exist (and putting aside the problem of tests), several possible alternatives arise, to wit:

4. *Poor, and especially Negro, children have different but possibly quite valuable linguistic and cognitive patterns that are well worth in some fashion preserving.*

It is possible that these children view the world, people and human institutions in ways that are much closer to "reality" than do middle-class white. Children who have experienced violence, poverty, broken homes, inadequate housing, hunger etc., are not liable to be easily convinced by glib answers and pat solutions to social—and perhaps intellectual—problems. They are perhaps tougher, less sentimental, less amenable to cant and hypocrisy, less easily fooled, perhaps even more honest with themselves and others. Their language, too, while it may have certain deficiencies, may also be in some ways much more colorful and poetic as well as considerably more lurid than white middle-class language. Perhaps much of this should not be stamped out by school but rather used and essentially shaped up so that it becomes not less but more powerful and expressive.

5. *The culture of poverty, especially Negro poverty, may contain within it forces that make it difficult for poor children to accept the typical American school and its educational practices.*

Since the American educational system has traditionally been a system for whites (although by no means only for rich whites, since it has been the primary means by which the country has assimilated waves of poor immigrants), it is possible that most schools and school programs are not adequately designed to deal with the children of contemporary poverty.

6. *Poor, especially Negro, children need a radically different and much more powerful educational process than do white, middle-class children.*

It is possible that poor, especially Negro, children need to start school at a younger age, that they need an even broader and richer educational experience including many more services ranging from health, psychological counseling, afternoon and evening programs, day care services, etc. We would hesitate to say at this point that these children need an instructional process different from or better than the one outlined above, at least until that one has been tried and proved insufficient. It may have to be slightly different for Negro children—providing more special material on Negro history (although why this would not also apply to white children we are not quite sure).

7. *The central problem for poor, especially Negro, children is not "self-image" as conventionally thought but rather the problem of believing that they can cope with the world and have an effect upon it.*

This, which appears to us to be one of the most interesting of Coleman's findings, is a real surprise. It would indicate that, in so far as school can have an effect independent of class and ethnic origin, one of the main things an instructional process could and should do for these children is to give them a taste of success, a chance really to exercise their intellectual and aesthetic powers and to prove to themselves that as individuals they can exert a considerable influence on the course of their own lives and upon the condition of the world around them.

E. CONCERNING SCHOOLS FOR DISADVANTAGED CHILDREN

1. *"School"—assuming a markedly more effective instructional process—can be of more assistance to disadvantaged children than to white middle-class children.*

This is a tricky one, but it is based upon Coleman's belief that existing school programs do not assist disadvantaged children in overcoming the effects of their social and ethnic origins. Since, in this society, white middle-class children presumably do not need to overcome the effects of their social and ethnic origins, the hypothesis has to be that a radically more effective educational process is not only needed for disadvantaged children but—if successful—will actually help them overcome such effects and will therefore be of greater assistance. (Actually, we do not accept the notion that white middle-class children do not also need to overcome the effects of *their* social and ethnic origins—but let that pass for the moment.) If we accept Coleman's interpretation that the present educational system is not capable of closing the gap between the longitudinal performance of disadvantaged and nondisadvantaged children but actually causes the gap to increase, then clearly something quite different is needed for disadvantaged children. We propose that the instructional process suggested above, plus afternoon and evening programs plus close relationships with the parents and the community, will be a start toward an educational system that can close that gap—and perhaps even begin to create a gap in the other direction.

2. *The creation of such a radically more effective educational process for disadvantaged children may require special materials and special approaches.*

If it is true that the basic problem for disadvantaged children is convincing them that they can have an effect on their world, then we may have to introduce some peculiar and spectacular experiences into the "curriculum." We do not mean here simply introducing Negro history into predominantly Negro classes (if the recent experience of some curriculum revision group can be relied upon white suburban children need this more than Negro children). It may be necessary, for instance, for disadvantaged children to get out of the classroom

with great frequency and *do* things in the great world out there—
actually *see* what is going on, make their presence felt, observe and
work with models of success and competence and prove to themselves that they can do it too.

3. *Integration—not just racial but social integration as well—may
be one of the most powerful ways of improving education for both
advantaged and disadvantaged children.*

One of the most fascinating of Coleman's results is the indication
that both lower-class *white and Negro* children appear to benefit
from attendance at either white or Negro middle-class schools. In
other words, the factor that was most significant was not race but
social class—lower-class white children would presumably benefit
more from attending a predominantly Negro but middle-class school
than would lower-class Negroes if they attended an all-white but still
lower-class school. One problem being that there are so few middle-
class Negro children, especially since *40 per cent* of them are sent by
their parents to private schools. Apparently middle-class children are
not injured by going to school with lower-class children. What all this
may imply for the education of the disadvantaged is not too clear, except to suggest that the best kind of school for all children—but especially for the disadvantaged—would be a school that was a careful
mixture of all classes and all ethnic groups *if* one could be quite
certain that there would be no ability grouping or tracking that
might result in ethnic or class (or both) segregation within the school.

4. *It may be necessary in the long run—before the educational
problems of disadvantaged (and advantaged) children can be worked
out—to rethink the entire idea of what a "school" is and what "education" should be.*

We suggest this long range possibility because we are not at all
sure that "schools" as they are presently institutionalized in this
society are or can be adequate to the enormous task that is being
thrust upon them. It is not easy to be all things to every man and
his first cousin.

But it is clear to us that school systems must begin to pay close
attention to all of these problems. And if it wishes to "pay attention," a school system must develop within itself the capability for
doing it. This means a staff of people equipped by experience and
desire to think creatively and with freshness, a group equipped with
freedom, funds, and facilities to do honest and continuous research

and development and provided with ways of moving developed ideas into the school system at large. Unless such a capability exists as a permanent part of the system, the schools will always be in danger of falling behind, of not being able to take advantage of or making a contribution to the creation of new and better ways of educating children.

B-4: **The Announcement to the Teachers at the End of January Requesting that They Begin to Make Efforts to Implement the Innovation and a "Suggested Daily Program Schedule"**

Announcement

As discussed at our last teacher's meeting, we are now planning to direct our energies toward implementing the philosophy of the innovation. (Refer to Preliminary Draft "Some Reasons and Suggested Ways of Organizing the Classroom")

We shall institute the following reorganization:

1. We shall no longer attempt at departmentalization or specialization. Every teacher will come familiar with all aspects of the activities and experiences planned for the *whole* classroom.

2. Teachers will want to work in *all* subject areas. Wherever possible *two* teachers will work in the *same* room—giving individual attention to the students. Planning should permit:

   1) Where possible—a variety of activities from which children may elect
   2) A free but safe and industrious attitude manifested by high activity
   3) Self-learning
   4) An emphasis on self-discovery and the process goals (tool skills are not to be neglected)
   5) Teachers will guide children by suggestions
   6) Purposeful behavior—our aim—self discipline
   7) Creative modes of individual learning through*

---

*The page ended with this incomplete sentence.

Suggested Daily Program Schedule

8:30-8:45	Student arrival
8:45-9:00	Daily announcements
9:00-9:15	A.M. orientation
9:15-10:30	A.M. activities—emphasis on language and arithmetic tool skills
10:30-10:50	Recess
10:50-12:00 Noon	Prenoon activities
10:50-11:00	Orientation
11:00-11:30	Activity period—emphasis on science and social studies
11:30-12:00 Noon	Alternate a practice teacher
	Written skills
	Teacher (2nd) at lunch
12:00-12:30	(Suggested game learning) Teacher (2nd) at lunch
12:30-1:20	Reading phases
1:20-1:30	Orientation for P.M. activities
1:30-2:20	P.M. activities
2:20	Dismissal

1. Practice teachers will be here only until noon each day.

2. Teacher need attempt only those directions leading toward the innovation as he or she desires and can handle with confidence.

3. Watch control. Plan for purposeful behavior. If at anytime activities are not purposeful learning experiences revert to traditional class situation so that you can rethink your plan and discuss your organization with the subject specialists or at a staff meeting.

C

Summary Tables of Selected Background and Personality Characteristics of the Teaching Staff

Table C-1.   *Percentages and Frequency Distributions of Selected*
Social Characteristics of the Teaching Staff (N = 11)

Social Variables	Categories	N	%
1. Sex	Male	4	36.3
	Female	7	63.7
2. Age	20-29	6	54.4
	30-40	2	18.2
	41+	3	27.4
3. Race	Caucasian	10	90.9
	Negro	1	9.1
4. Marital status	Single	4	36.3
	Married	6	54.6
	Other	1	9.1
5. Present income	-4,999	1	9.1
	5,000-7,499	6	54.6
	7,500-9,999	3	27.2
	10,000+	1	9.1
6. Father's occupational level[a]	White collar	8	72.8
	Blue collar	3	27.2
7. Father's educational level	College	5	45.5
	Graduate from high school	1	9.1
	Some high school	3	27.2
	Less than high school	2	18.2
8. Mother's educational level	College	3	27.2
	Graduate from high school	4	36.4
	Some high school	2	18.2
	Less than high school	2	27.2
9. Where major part of youth spent	Farm	1	9.1
	Town	1	9.1
	Small city	2	18.1
	City	7	63.7

[a]White collar = education; other professional or scientific; managerial, executive, or proprietor of large business; small business owner or manager; farm owner or renter; clerical or sales. Blue collar = skilled worker or foreman; semiskilled worker, unskilled worker or farm laborer.

Table C-2.   *Percentages and Frequency Distributions of*
Educational Background Characteristics of the
Teaching Staff (N = 11)

Characteristics	Categories	N	%
1. Kind of elementary education	Public	7	63.8
	Parochial	2	18.1
	Private	2	18.1
2. Kind of secondary education	Public	8	72.8
	Parochial	1	9.1
	Private	2	18.2
3. Undergraduate work	Public college (university)	4	36.3
	Private college (university)	7	63.7
4. Graduate work	State teacher's college	6	54.4
	Private college (university)	2	18.2
	Not yet begun	3	27.4
5. Highest degree	—Bachelor	0	—
	Bachelor	7	63.7
	Master	2	18.1
	Master +	1	9.1
	Doctorate	0	—
	Professional	1	9.1
6. Self-estimate of college work	Honors	0	—
	Above average	5	45.5
	Average	6	54.5
	Somewhat below average	0	—
7. Future education plans	No plans	1	9.1
	Take courses but not towards a degree	2	18.2
	Study for a master's	5	45.5
	Study for a doctorate	3	27.2

Table C-3. *Percentages and Frequency Distributions of Professional Experience Characteristics of the Teaching Staff (N = 11)*

Characteristics	Categories	N	%
1. Years as a teacher	1-2 years	3	27.3
	3-4 years	4	36.3
	5-10 years	1	9.1
	11 or more	3	27.3
2. Years in this school system	1-2 years	5	45.5
	3-4 years	4	36.3
	5-10 years	1	9.1
	11 or more	1	9.1
3. Number of schools in this system taught in	1 school	4	36.4
	2 schools	4	36.4
	3 schools	1	9.1
	4 or more	2	18.1
4. Years in this school	1 year	8	72.8
	2 years	2	18.1
	3 years	1	9.1
	4 or more	0	—

Table C-4. *Frequency Distributions of the Teaching Staff on Fourteen Personality Dimensions (N = 11)[a]*

	Percentile											
	1	10	20	25	30	40	50	60	70	75	80	90	99

Achievement

Deference

Order

Endurance

Change

Exhibition

Affiliation

Dominance

Autonomy

Intraception

Succorance

Abasement

Nurturance

Aggression

Consistency of responses

[a]As measured by the Edwards Personal Preference Schedule, which used college graduates as the norm group. Each dot represents a teacher's score on a particular need dimension.

APPENDIX

D

Classroom Schemata

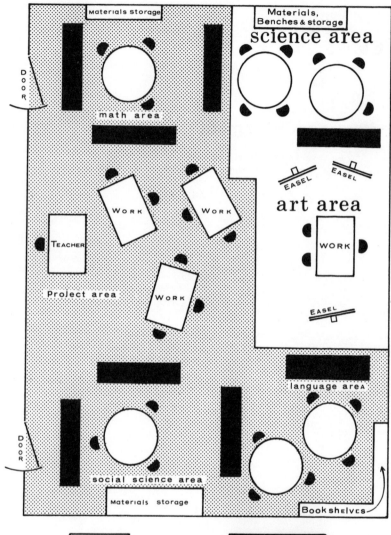

Materials storage

science area
Materials, Benches & storage

math area

Door

EASEL   EASEL

art area

WORK   WORK

WORK   TEACHER

WORK

Project area

EASEL

language area

Door

WORK

social science area

Materials storage

Bookshelves

• CARPETING

• VISUAL DIVIDERS AND
STORAGE AREAS (Each
faced with chalk and/or
tack board).

References

Abbott, Max. G. "Hierarchical Impediments to Innovation in Educational Organizations." In Max Abbott and John T. Lovell, eds., *Change Perspectives in Educational Administration*. Auburn, Ala.: The School of Education, Auburn University, 1965, pp. 40-53.

Agnew, Paul C. and Hsu, Francis L.K. "Introducing Change in a Mental Hospital." *Human Organization*. 19, no. 4 (Winter 1960): 195-198.

Anderson, Robert H. "The Organization and Administration of Team Teaching. In J.T. Shaplin and H.P. Olds. *Team Teaching*. New York: Harper and Row, 1964, Ch. 6.

Argyle, Michael. "The Social Psychology of Social Change." In T. Burns and S.B. Saul, eds. *Social Theory and Economic Change*. London: Tavistock Publications, 1967, pp. 87-101.

Argyris, Chris. *Interpersonal Competence and Organizational Effectiveness*. Homewood, Ill.: The Dorsey Press, 1962. *a*.

Argyris, Chris. "The Integration of the Individual and the Organization." In C. Argyris et al., eds. *Social Science Approaches to Business Behavior*. Homewood, Ill.: The Dorsey Press and Richard D. Irwin, 1962, pp. 57-98. *b*

Atkin, J. Myron. "Basing Curriculum Change on Research and Demonstration." *The Educational Forum* 31, no. 1 (November 1966): 27-33.

Barnes, Louis B. "Organizational Change and Field Experimental Methods." In Victor H. Vroom, ed. *Methods of Organizational Research*. Pittsburgh: University of Pittsburgh Press, 1967, pp. 57-112.

293

Barnett, H.G. *Innovation.* New York: McGraw-Hill, 1953.

Barton, A. and Anderson, B. "Change in an Organizational System: Formalization of a Qualitative Study." In A. Etzioni, ed. *Complex Organizations: A Sociological Reader.* New York: Holt, Rinehart, and Winston, 1964, pp. 400-419.

Becker, Howard S. "Personal Change in Adult Life." *Sociometry* 27, no. 1 (March 1964): 40-53.

Benne, Kenneth D. and Birnbaum, Max. "Change Does Not Have To Be Haphazard." *School Review* 68, no. 3 (Autumn 1960): 283-293.

Bennis, Warren G. *Changing Organizations.* New York: McGraw-Hill, 1966.

Bennis, Warren G.; Benne, Kenneth D.; and Chin, Robert, eds. *The Planning of Change.* New York: Holt, Rinehart, and Winston, 1961. Revised edition, 1968.

Bishop, David W. "The Role of the Local Administrator in Reorganizing Elementary Schools to Test a Semi-departmentalized Plan." *Journal of Educational Sociology* 34 (April 1961): 344-348.

Blau, Peter M. and Scott, W. Richard. *Formal Organizations.* San Francisco: Chandler Publishing Company, 1962.

Bradford, L.P.; Gibb, J.R.; and Benne, K.D. *T-Group Theory and Laboratory Method.* New York: John Wiley and Sons, 1964.

Brickell, H.M. *Organizing New York State for Educational Change.* Albany, N.Y.: State Education Department, 1961.

Brim, Orville G. and Wheeler, Stanton. *Socialization after Childhood.* New York: John Wiley and Sons, 1966.

Brown, George I. *Operational Creativity: A Strategy for Teacher Change.* Santa Barbara, California: University of California, 1966. Presented at the meeting of the American Educational Research Association, at Chicago, Illinois, February 1966.

Buchanan, Paul C. "Crucial Issues in Organizational Development." In G. Watson, ed. *Change in School Systems.* Washington, D.C.: National Training Laboratories, NEA, 1967, pp. 51-67.

Buchanan, Paul C. "Innovative Organizations: A Study in Organization Development." In *Applying Behavioral Science Research in Industry.* Monograph No. 23. New York: Industrial Relations Counselors, 1964.

Burns, T.B. and Stalker, G.M. *The Management of Innovation.* London: Tavistock Publications, 1961.

Buros, Oscar K., ed. *The Sixth Mental Measurements Yearbook.* Highland Park, N.J.: The Gryphon Press, 1965, pp. 190-207.

Byerly, Carl L. and Rankin, Stuart C. "The Detroit Nongraded Program. In Richard I. Miller, ed. *The Nongraded School.* New York: Harper and Row, 1967, pp. 29-46.

Carlson, Richard O. *Adoption of Educational Innovations.* Eugene, Ore.: The Center for the Advanced Study of Educational Administration, University of Oregon, 1965. *a*

Carlson, Richard O. "Barriers to Change in Public Schools," In R.O. Carlson, ed. *Change Processes in the Public Schools.* Eugene, Ore.: Center for the Advanced Study of Educational Administration, University of Oregon, 1965, pp. 3-8. *b*

Chauncey, Henry. *Educational Testing Service Annual Report: 1965-66.* Princeton, N.J.: Educational Testing Service, 1967.

Childs, J.W. *Study of Belief Systems of Administrators and Teachers in Innovative and Non-innovative School Districts.* Detroit: Wayne State University, 1966.

Clark, David and Guba, Egon. *An Examination of Potential Change Roles in Education.* Columbus: Ohio State University, 1965.

Coch, Lester and French, John, Jr. "Overcoming Resistance to Change." *Human Relations* 1, no. 4 (1948): 512-532.

Cronbach, Lee J. "The Role of the University in Improving Education." *Phi Delta Kappan* 47, no. 10 (June 1966): 539-545.

Cumming, Elaine; Clancey, I.L.W.; and Cumming, John. "Improving Patient Care Through Organizational Changes in the Mental Hospital," *Psychiatry* 19, no. 3 (August 1956): 249-263.

Dentler, R.A. *Strategies for Innovation in Education: A View from the Top.* New York: Public Policy Institute, Second Workshop, Institute of Urban Studies, Columbia University Teachers College, 1964.

Dufay, Frank R. *Ungrading the Elementary School.* West Nyack, N.Y.: Parker Publishing Company, 1966.

Eicholz, G.C. "Development of a Rejection Classification for Newer Educational Media." Doctoral dissertation, Ohio State University, 1961.

Eicholz, G. and Rogers, E.M. "Resistance to the Adoption of Audio-Visual Aids by Elementary School Teachers: Contrasts and Similarities to Agriculture Innovation." In M. Miles, ed. *Innovation in Education.* New York: Teachers College, Columbia, 1964, pp. 299-316.

Fallon, Berlie, J., ed. *Educational Innovation in the United States.* Bloomington, Ind.: Phi Delta Kappa, 1966.

Fantini, M. and Weinstein, G. *The Disadvantaged Challenge to Education.* New York: Harper and Row, 1968.

Fantini, M. and Weinstein, G. "Strategies for Initiating Educational Change in Large Bureaucratic School Systems." Paper presented to Public Policy Institute, at Columbia University, Teachers College, April 1963.

Featherstone, Joseph. "Schools for Children." *The New Republic,* August 19, 1967, 17-21; "How Children Learn," September 2, 1967, 17-21; "Teaching Children to Think," September 9, 1967, 15-19.

Fliegel, F.C. and Kivlin, J.E. "Attributes of Innovations as Factors in Diffusion." *American Journal of Sociology* 72, no. 3 (November 1966): 235-248.

Fowler, Burton P. *The Yale-Fairfield Study of Elementary Teaching.* Report Prepared for the Board of Education, New Haven, Conn. 1956.

French, J.R.P.; Israel, J.; and Dagfinn, D. "An Experiment on Participation in a Norwegian Factory." *Human Relations* 13 (1960): 3-19.

Gale, Richard D. "The Administrative Role in Initiating a Nongraded School. In Richard I. Miller, ed. *The Nongraded School.* New York: Harper and Row, 1967, pp. 16-28.

Gellerman, S.W. "Motivation and Productivity." Paper read at the American Management Association, New York, 1963.

Ginzberg, E. and Reilly, E. *Effective Change in Large Organizations.* New York: Columbia University Press, 1957.

Glogau, Lillian and Fessel, Murray. *The Nongraded Primary School.* West Nyack, N.Y.: Parker Publishing Company, 1967.

Goode, William J. and Hatt, Paul K. *Methods in Social Research.* New York: McGraw-Hill, 1952.

Goodlad, John I. and Anderson, Robert H. *The Nongraded Elementary School.* New York: Harcourt, Brace and World, 1963.

Gordon, Edmund W. and Wilkerson, Doxey A. *Compensatory Education for the Disadvantaged.* New York: College Entrance Examination Board, 1966.

Greenblatt, Milton; Levinson, D.J.; and Williams, Richard H. *The Patient and the Mental Hospital.* Glencoe: The Free Press, 1957.

Greiner, Larry E. "Antecedents of Planned Organizational Change." *Journal of Applied Behavioral Science* 3, no. 1 (1967): 51-85. *a*

Greiner, Larry E. "Patterns of Organizational Change." *Harvard Business Review* 45 (May-June 1967): 119-128. *b*

Greiner, Larry E. "Organization Change and Development: A Study of Changing Values, Behavior." Doctoral dissertation, Harvard Business School, 1965.

Gross, Neal; Mason, Ward S.; and McEachern, Alexander W. *Explorations in Role Analysis.* New York: John Wiley and Sons, 1958.

Guba, Egon G. A letter about the purposes of the National Institute for the Study of Educational Change, to the Director of the Center for Research and Development on Educational Differences, Harvard Graduate School of Education, September 14, 1966, p. 1.

Hand, Harold C. "Integrity and Instructional Innovation." *The Educational Forum* 30, no. 1 (November 1965): 7-16.

Havelock, Ronald G. and Benne, Kenneth D. "An Exploratory Study of Knowledge Utilization." In G. Watson, ed. *Concepts For Social Change.* Washington, D.C.: National Training Laboratories, NEA, 1967, pp. 47-70.

Heathers, Glen. *Organizing Schools Through the Dual Progress Plan.* Danville, Ill.: The Interstate Printers and Publishers, 1967. *a*

Heathers, Glen. "Influencing Change at the Elementary Level." In Richard I. Miller, ed. *Perspectives on Educational Change.* New York: Appleton-Century-Crofts, 1967, pp. 21-53. *b*

Heathers, Glen. "Research on Implementing and Evaluating Cooperative Teaching." *The National Elementary Principal,* 44, no. 3 (January 1965): 27-33.

Heathers, Glen. "The Role of Innovation in Education." *The National Elementary Principal* 43 (September 1963): 9-14.

Herzberg, F.; Mausner, B.; and Synderman, B. *The Motivation to Work.* New York: John Wiley and Sons, 1959.

Hillson, Maurie, ed. *Change and Innovation in Elementary School Organization.* New York: Holt, Rinehart, and Winston, 1965.

Homans, George C. "Strategy of Industrial Sociology, *American Journal of Sociology* 50 (1949): 330.

Hovland, C.I. and Weiss, W. "The Influence of Source Credibility on Communication Effectiveness." *Public Opinion Quarterly* 15 (1951): 635-650.

Hymen, Herbert H.; Wright, Charles R.; and Hopkins, Terence K. *Applications of Methods of Evaluation: Four Studies of the Encampment for Citizenship.* Berkeley and Los Angeles, Calif.: University of California Press, 1962.

Jacques, E. *The Changing Culture of a Factory.* London: Tavistock Publications, 1951.

Jennings, Frank G. "Education Reform 1957-1967: It Didn't Start With Sputnik." *Saturday Review,* September 16, 1967, pp. 77-79, 95-97.

Jung, Charles C. "The Trainer Change-Agent Role Within A School System." In G. Watson, ed. *Change in School Systems.* Washington, D.C.: National Training Laboratories, NEA, 1967, pp. 89-105.

Katz, Daniel and Kahn, Robert L. *The Social Psychology of Organizations.* New York: John Wiley and Sons, 1966.

Katz, Daniel and Festinger, Leon, eds. *Research Methods in the Behavioral Sciences.* New York: Dryden Press, 1953.

Katz, Elihu; Levin, Martin L.; and Hamilton, Herbert. "Traditions of Research on the Diffusion of Innovation." *American Sociological Review* 28, no. 2 (April 1963): 237-252.

Kelly, James A. "Priorities in Urban Education." Address presented at the Conference on a National Agenda for American Education, Washington, D.C., July 17, 1969.

Kline, E.E. "Leader Behavior, Curricular Implementation and Curricular Change." Paper presented at American Educational Research Association, Chicago, Illinois, February 1966.

Kravetz, Nathan. *Evaluation of New York City Title I Educational Projects: 1966-67.* New York: The Center for Urban Education, 1967.

Lawrence, Paul R. "How to Deal with Resistance to Change." *Harvard Business Review* 32, no. 3 (May-June 1954): 49-57.

Leavitt, Harold J. "Applied Organizational Change in Industry: Structural, Technological, and Humanistic Approaches." In J.G. March, ed. *Handbook of Organizations.* Chicago: Rand McNally, 1965, pp. 1143-1170.

Lewin, Kurt. "Group Decision and Social Change." In Macoby et al., eds. *Readings in Social Psychology.* New York: Holt, Rinehart and Winston, 1958, pp. 197-211.

Lewin, Kurt. "Frontiers in Group Dynamics." *Human Relations* 1, no. 1 (1947): 5-41.

Liddle, G.P.; Rockwell, Robert E.; and Sacadat, Evelyn. *Education Improvement For The Disadvantaged In An Elementary Setting.* Springfield, Ill.: Charles C Thomas, 1967.

Lionberger, R.F. *Adoption of New Ideas and Practices.* Ames, Iowa: Center for International Affairs, 1964.

Lippitt, Ronald; Benne, Kenneth; and Havelock, Ronald. "A Comparative Analysis of the Research Utilization Process." Paper presented at American Educational Research Association, Chicago, Ill. 1966.

Lippitt, Ronald et al. "The Teacher as Innovator, Seeker, and Sharer of New Practices." In R.X. Miller, ed. *Perspectives on Educational Change.* New York: Appleton-Century-Crofts, 1967, pp. 307-324.

Lippitt, Ronald; Watson, Jeanne; and Westley, Bruce. *The Dynamics of Planned Change.* New York: Harcourt, Brace and World, 1958.

Lipset, Seymour Martin; Trow, Martin; and Coleman, James. *Union Democracy.* Garden City, N.Y.: Doubleday Anchor Books, 1962.

Mann, F.C. and Neff, F.W. *Managing Major Change in Organizations.* Ann Arbor, Mich.: Foundation for Research on Human Behavior, 1961.

Mann, F.C. and Hoffman, L.R. *Automation and The Worker.* New York: Henry Holt, 1960.

Marland, Sidney P. *Winnetka: The History and Significance of an Educational Experiment.* Part II. Englewood Cliffs, N.J.: Prentice-Hall, 1963.

Merton, Robert K. *Social Theory and Social Structure.* Revised edition, Glencoe: The Free Press, 1957, pp. 85-117.

Miles, Matthew B. *Innovation in Education.* New York: Bureau of Publication, Teachers College, Columbia University, 1964. *a*

Miles, Matthew B. "Educational Innovation: The Nature of the Problem." In M.B. Miles, ed. *Innovation in Education.* New York: Teachers College, Columbia University, 1964, pp. 19-22. *b*

Miles, Matthew B. "Innovation in Education: Some Generalizations." In M.B. Miles, ed. *Innovation in Education.* New York: Teachers College, Columbia, 1964, pp. 651-653. *c*

Miles, Matthew B. *Learning How to Work in Groups.* New York: Teachers College, 1959.

Miles, R.E. "Human Relations or Human Resources?" *Harvard Business Review* 43, no. 4 (July-August 1965): 148-157.

Miller, Richard I., ed. *Perspectives on Educational Change.* New York: Appleton-Century-Crofts, 1967. *a*

Miller, Richard I. "An Overview of Educational Change." in Richard I. Miller, ed. *Perspectives on Educational Change.* New York: Appleton-Century-Crofts, 1967, pp. 1-20. *b*

Miner, Horace. "Culture Change Under Pressure: A Hausa Case." *Human Organization* 19, no. 3 (fall 1960): 164-167.

Moore, Wilbert E. *Social Change.* Englewood Cliffs, N.J.: Prentice-Hall, 1963.

Morris, Robert and Binstock, Robert H. *Feasible Planning for Social Change.* New York: Columbia University Press, 1966.

Morse, N. and Reimer, E. "The Experimental Change of a Major Organizational Variable." *Journal of Abnormal and Social Psychology* 52 (1956): 120-129.

Morse, N.C.; Reiner, E.; and Tannenbaum, A.S. "Regulation and Control in Hierarchical Organizations." *Journal of Social Issues* 7, no. 3 (1951): 41-45.

National Elementary Principal. "A Point of View About School Organization, and School Organization and Leadership." *The National Elementary Principal* 41, no. 3 (December 1961): Chap. 1, 2.

New York State Education Department. *To Facilitate Educational Innovation.* New York: Basic Systems, August 1965.

Ogburn, W.F. *Social Change.* New York: The Viking Press, 1938.

Oliver, Albert I. *Curriculum Improvement.* New York: Dodd, Mead, 1965.

Owens, Robert G. *Organizational Behavior in Schools.* Englewood Cliffs, N.J.: Prentice-Hall, 1970, pp. 148-151.

Parloff, Morris B. "The Impact of Ward-Milieu Philosophies on Nursing Role Concepts." *Psychiatry* 23, no. 2 (May 1960): 141-152.

Peterson, Carl H. *Effective Team Teaching.* West Nyack, N.Y.: Parker Publishing Company, 1966.

Plowden, Bridget (Chr.). *Children and Their Primary Schools.* Vol. 1. London: Her Majesty's Stationery Office, 1967, pp. 189-201. Report of the Central Advisory Council for Education.

Radcliffe, Ruth W. "Introducing New Mathematics in Northside Elementary School." In Richard I. Miller, ed. *Perspectives on Educational Change.* New York: Appleton-Century-Crofts, 1967, pp. 213-227.

The Rockefeller Foundation. *The President's Five Year Review and Annual Report, 1968.* New York, 1968, p. 127.

Rocky Mountain Study Council. "Procedures and Guidelines for Initiation of an Ungraded Primary Unit." In R.I. Miller, ed. *The Nongraded School.* New York: Harper and Row, 1967, pp. 224-242.

Rogers, Everett M. *Diffusion of Innovations.* New York: The Free Press of Glencoe, 1962.

Schein, E.H. and Bennis, W.G. *Personal and Organizational Change through Group Methods.* New York: John Wiley and Sons, 1965.

Schwartz, Charlotte Green. "Problems for Psychiatric Nurses in Playing a New Role on a Mental Hospital Ward," In Milton Greenblatt, Daniel J. Levinson, and Richard H. Williams. eds. *The Patient and the Mental Hospital.* Glencoe, Ill: The Free Press, 1957, pp. 402-426.

Scott, W. Richard. "Field Methods in the Study of Organizations." In James G. March, ed. *Handbook of Organizations.* Chicago: Rand McNally, 1965, pp. 261-304.

Shaplin, Judson T. "Cooperative Teaching: Definition and Organizational Analysis." *The National Elementary Principal* 44, no. 3 (January 1965): 14-20.

Sorokin, Pitirim. *Social and Cultural Dynamics.* New York: American Book Company, 1937.

Stufflebeam, Daniel L., ed. *Ohio Educational Innovations Survey: Catalog of Educational Changes in Ohio Public Schools.* Columbus, Ohio: College of Education, Ohio State University, 1966.

Talmon, Yonina. "Comparative Analysis of Adult Socialization." First draft of a working paper prepared for the Social Science Research Council Conference on Socialization Through the Life Cycle, May 17, 1963.

Tannenbaum, P.H. "Initial Attitude Toward Source and Concept as Factors in Attitude Change Through Communication." *Public Opinion Quarterly* 20 (1956): 413-425.

Trump, J. Lloyd. "Influencing Change at the Secondary Level." In Richard I. Miller, ed. *Perspectives on Educational Change.* New York: Appleton-Century-Crofts, 1967, pp. 54-75.

U.S. Commission on Civil Rights. *Racial Isolation in the Public Schools.* Vol. I. Washington, D.C.: U.S. Government Printing Office, 1967.

Washburne, Norman F. *Interpreting Social Change in America.* New York: Random House, 1954.

Watson, Goodwin, ed. *Change in School Systems.* Washington, D.C.: National Training Laboratories, NEA, 1967. *a*

Watson, Goodwin, ed. *Concepts for Social Change.* Washington, D.C.: National Training Laboratories, NEA, 1967. *b*

Webb, Eugene; Campbell, Donald T.; Schwartz, Richard D.; and Sechrest, Lee. *Unobtrusive Measures.* Chicago: Rand McNally, 1966.

Westinghouse Learning Corporation. *An Evaluation of the Effects of Head Start Experience on Children's Cognitive and Affective Development.* Athens: Ohio University, April 1969. Preliminary draft.

Wigren, Harold E. "The Process of Change in Educational Television." In Richard I. Miller, ed. *Perspectives on Educational Change.* New York: Appleton-Century-Crofts, 1967, pp. 148-184.

Wilkie, Raymond A. "Garden Springs Elementary School: A Case Study of Educational Innovation." In Richard I. Miller, ed. *Perspectives on Educational Change.* New York: Appleton-Century-Crofts, 1967, pp. 253-277.

Wrightstone, J. Wayne, Forlano, G., Frankel, E., et al. *Evaluation of The Higher Horizons Program for Underprivileged Children.* New York: Bureau of Educational Research, Board of Education of the City of New York, 1964.

York, Richard H. "Motivating Patients on Chronic Wards at Metropolitan State Hospital," in Milton Greenblatt, Richard H. York and Esther Lucile Brown, eds. *From Custodial to Therapeutic Patient Care in Mental Hospitals.* New York: Russell Sage Foundation, 1955, 2: 349-406.

Zander, Alvin. "Resistance to Change: Its Analysis and Prevention," In W.G. Bennis, et al., eds. *The Planning of Change.* New York: Holt, Rinehart, and Winston, 1961, pp. 543-548.

Index

Abbott, Max G., 30
academic performance, upgrading of, 2, 4, 10
academic psychology, 259
achievement tests, 10
adoption studies, 20-22, 39
aesthetic skills, development of, 11, 266
after-school programs, community instructors for, 277
age grouping, 139, 140, 142, 169, 171
Agnew, Paul C., 26
agricultural innovations, adoption and diffusion of, 20
Anderson, Robert H., vi, 3, 25, 26
anthropological studies, 20
appreciation, development of, 11, 269-270
Argyle, Michael, 26, 36, 37
Argyris, Chris, 26, 27, 33, 38n.
Atkin, J. Myron, 2
attempted implementation, period of, 17, 202-203, 206
authority structure, 12n., 15
automation, 259

Barnes, Louis B., vi, 33, 34, 47n.
"Barriers to Change in Public Schools," 31
barriers to implementation, 1-2, 7-10, 31-32, 37-39, 57, 122-148, 210-212; capability to perform new role model, lack of, 129-135, 159-167, 197, 199; clarity about innovation, lack of, 123-129, 150-159, 196, 199-200, 202; commitment, lack of, 211; feedback mechanisms, lack of, 193, 194, 201, 210, 212; incompatible organizational arrangements, 139-142, 169-171, 174, 197-200; resistance (see resistance to change); teacher motivation, lack of, 142-147; 171-190, 200, 209-210; unavailability of necessary materials, 135-139, 168-169, 173-174, 197, 199, 200
basic skills, importance of, 13
"Bearing of Empirical Research on Social Theory, The," 195
behavioral changes, 15; studies on, 34-35
Benne, Kenneth D., 24, 25, 28, 30, 31, 33, 36n., 38n.
Bennis, Warren G., 8, 24, 28, 38n. 39
biological evolution, 256
Birnbaum, Max, 25
Bishop, David W., 25
Blau, Peter M., 50
Bohr, Niels, 256
Bradford, L. P., 38n

Brickell, H. M., 2, 25, 30
Brown, George I., 30
Bruner, J. S., 259, 260, 266, 272
Buchanan, Paul C., 24
Bundy Report, 6
Bureau of Educational Change, 44, 45, 52-53, 55, 62, 68-70, 78, 168, 175, 180, 216
Burns, T. B., 23
Buros, Oscar K., 61*n*., 217
busing, 66
Byerly, Carl L., 25, 32

Cambire Elementary School, 14; age grouping, 139, 140, 142, 169, 171; barriers to implementation (*see* barriers to implementation); Bureau of Educational Change and, 68-70; classroom observations, 51, 52, 61, 62, 86-87, 92-121; climate for educational change at, 64-89; commitment of top school officials to change in, 66-68; community attitudes to change in, 65-66; curricular reforms, 76-77, 82, 85-87; degree of implementation in (*see* degree of implementation); departmental organization, 85, 140, 142; director's implementation strategy, 190-193, 201, 214; double staffing, introduction of, 179-180; as an experimental school, 75-79; external conditions, 65-71; internal conditions, 71-88; normative climate for change in, 72-84; physical characteristics, 53-55; practical implications of study, 207-216; report card system, 139, 141, 169, 171, 174; research for study of (*see* research procedures); research implications of study, 204-207; school time, scheduling of, 139, 171, 198; self-contained classrooms, 85, 141, 170, 176; spot checks in, 94; teacher performance to introduction of innovation, 84-88; teaching partners, interpersonal tensions between, 163, 172, 174, 177-180, 203; theoretical implications of study, 196-203; timing of decision to introduce innovation, 175-176; up-

heaval and transition, period of, 74-75. *See also* educational innovations; teachers
career anxieties, teacher, 181-184
Carlson, Richard O., 21
case study method, rationale for use of, 42-43
catalytic role model, 10-16, 56, 65, 71, 79, 82, 85. *See also* Cambire Elementary School
categorization, acquisition of skill, 11, 267
change(s), behavioral, 15, 34-35; evolutionary, 20*n*., industrial, resistance to, 36; prison, resistance to, 36. *See also* organizational change; organizational innovations
change agents, 23-25, 27-29, 31-32, 36, 212
change effort(s), 31, 33
change program, 31
Changing Organizations, 31
chaos, perceptual reduction of, 267
Chauncey, Henry, 2
Childs, J. W., 34
Chin, Robert, 24, 28
Civil Rights Commission, 4, 5, 7
civil rights movement, 2, 66
clarity, implementation and, 25-27, 29-31, 123-129, 150-159, 196, 199-200, 202
classification, acquisition of skill of, 11, 267
classroom environment, enrichment of, 12-13
classroom observations, 35, 51, 52, 61, 62, 86-87, 100-121; data-collection procedures, 92-98; schedule for, 236-239
client system, 29, 31
closed-circuit television, 90
Coch, Lester, 27, 36*n*.
cognitive processes, 259
Coleman, 273, 279, 281, 282
commitment, lack of, implementation and, 211; subordinate participation and, 25, 29
community action groups, pressures of, 2
community control of schools, plans to increase, 3
community instructors, 277

community liaison workers, 277
comparison, acquisition of skill in, 11, 266
Compensatory Education, Department of, 68
compensatory education programs, 3-7, 21
control problems, school, 277
Coulson, John, vi
Cronbach, Lee J., 2
Crowley, Marion L., vi
Cuisenaire Rod approach (mathematics), 82, 87, 137, 253
culture of poverty, 280
curricular reforms, 2, 76-77, 82, 85-87, 281

Dagfinn, D., 27
data-collection procedures, for assessment of degree of implementation, 92-98; documents, collection and examination of, 245-284; research, 51-63, 217-284. *See also* specimen research instruments
de facto segregation, 66
decentralization, 3
decision-making, Managerial Grid training and, 22-23; role of management in, 213-215; subordinate participation and, 24*n.*, 25, 27-29, 215
degree of implementation, 27, 34-36, 39, 90-121; classroom observations for measurement of, 92-121; data-collection procedures for assessment of, 92-98; data-reduction procedures, 98-107; evaluation rationale, 90-92; findings, 107-121; use of term, 16
Dentler, R. A., 25
desegregation, 6
Detroit Great Cities Project, 2-3
Detroit School District, 32, 33
diffusion studies, 20-22, 39
disadvantaged children, educational reforms for, 3, 278-283
discipline problems, school, 277
disruptive children, 13
division of labor, 15, 52
documents, collection and examination of, 245-284
Dreeben, Robert, vi

Dufay, Frank R., 25, 34
Dynamics of Planned Change, The, 29

EDC curriculum (science), 82
education, federal aid to, 2, 3, 67; innovations in (*see* educational innovations); progressive, criticisms of, 2; revolutionary changes in, 2; self-directed, 11, 13
educational ferment, 2
educational innovations, 2-7; awareness about, lack of, 31-32; catalytic role model, 10-16, 56, 65, 71, 79, 82, 85; change agents and, 31-32; compensatory programs, 3-7, 21; curricular reforms, 2, 82, 85-87, 281; decentralization, 3; disadvantaged students and, 3, 278-283; effectiveness of, evaluation of, 22; implementation of (*see* implementation); in New York State, 2; nongrading, 2-3, 34, 35; in Ohio, 2; studies on, 20-22, 31-35; team-teaching, 2-3, 34, 35; *See also* Cambire Elementary School; organizational innovations
Edwards, Allen, 83*n.*
Edwards Personal Preference Schedule, 61, 62, 83-84, 217
Eicholz, G., 21
Einstein, Albert, 256, 269
Elementary and Secondary Education Act, 67
Eliot, George, 269
evening school programs, community instructors for, 277
evolution, biological, 256
evolutionary change, 20*n.*
explosive growth, 2
extrapolation, 11, 268-269

Fallon, Berlie J., 2
Fantini, M., 6, 26*n.*, 30
Featherstone, Joseph, 141
federal government, aid to education, 2, 3, 67
feedback mechanisms, importance of, 193, 194, 201, 210, 212, 213
Fessel, Murray, 34
Festinger, Leon, 43*n.*
fieldworkers, role of, 45, 47-48
Forlano, G., 7*n.*

formal organizations, concept of, 15
Fowler, Burton P., 30
Frankel, E., 7*n*.
freedom, responsibility and, 262-263, 265-266
French, John, Jr., 27, 36*n*.
Freud, Sigmund, 256

Gale, Richard D., 26, 34
Gellerman, S. W., 23
general intellectual skills, 259
ghetto schools, Rockefeller Foundation Report on, 4
Giaquinita, Joseph, 247
Gibb, J. R., 38*n*.
Ginzberg, E., 30
Glogau, Lillian, 34
Goode, William J., 43
Goodlad, John I., 3, 25
Gordon, Edmund W., 3-5, 7
Great Cities Project (Detroit), 2-3
Greiner, Larry E., 22-23, 31, 38*n*.
Gross, Neal, 15, 246
group discussions, 24
Guba, Egon G., 8, 39

Hamilton, Herbert, 20
Hand, Harold C., 2
Harvard Graduate School of Education, vi, 246
Hatt, Paul K., 43
Haughey, Charles F., vi
Havelock, Ronald, 30
Heathers, Glen, 8, 25, 30, 39
Herriott, Robert E., vi
Herzberg, F., 28
higher skills, 260
Hodgkins, Benjamin L., vi
Hoffman, L. R., 25
Homans, George C., 41
Hopkins, Terence K., 7
Hovland, C. I., 23
Howe, Harold, 5
Hsu, Francis L. K., 26
human relations training, 38
hunching, 11, 267-268
Hymen, Herbert H., 7
hypothesis building, 11, 141, 268
hypothesis testing, 11, 268

implementation, 1, 19-20; attempted, period of, 17, 202-203, 206; barriers to (*see* barriers to implementation); change agents and, 25, 29, 31-32, 212; clarity and, 25-27, 29-31, 123-129, 150-159, 196, 199-200, 202; commitment and, 25, 29; complexity of process, 208-210, 212, 214; conditional inquiries, need for, 205-206; degree of (*see* degree of implementation); facilitators of, 30, 31; leadership and, 211, 215; literature on, 29-40; management, role of in, 36, 199-203, 212-216; maximal, 91-92; minimal, 92; quality of, measurement of, 95, 115-119; replication studies, need for, 205; staff morale and, 25; subordinate participation and, 25-26, 29, 214; theoretical assumptions, 202-203
industrial changes, resistance to, 36
initial resistance, 1, 8, 26, 36, 39, 195, 198, 204-205, 210. *See also* resistance to change
innovations, adoption and diffusion of, 20-22. *See also* educational innovations; organizational innovations
instructional process, 273-276
integration, 282
intellectual skills, acquisition of, 11, 266; general, 259
interpretive skills, acquisition of, 11, 269
interviews, teacher, 34-35, 51, 52, 57-61, 85, 143-147, 152-157, 159-166, 170-171; schedule for, 217-235
intuition, 11, 267-268
Israel, J., 27

Jacques, E., 38*n*.
Jennings, Frank G., 2
job skills, training for, 259
Jung, Charles C., 30

Kahn, Robert L., 15, 38*n*.
Katz, Daniel, 15, 38*n*., 43

Katz, Elihu, 20
Kelly, James A., 3
Kline, E. E., 34-35
knowledge explosion, 2
knowledge utilization, lack of awareness about, 31-32
Kovich, Theresa, vi
Kravetz, Nathan, 7n.

labor, division of, 15, 52
Lawrence, Paul R., 36n.
leadership, implementation and, 211, 215
leadership behavior, study on, 34-35
learning process, new theoretical insights into, 2
Leavitt, Harold J., 24, 28, 37, 38n.
Lengel, Lawrence M., vi
Lesser, 273
Levin, Martin L., 20
Lewin, Kurt, 17, 38n.
Lewis, Ralph G., vi
Liddle, G. P., 7n.
Lionberger, R. F., 20
Lippitt, Ronald, 24, 29-30
Lipset, Seymour Martin, 43n.

McEachern, Alexander W., 15
management, role of in implementation, 36, 199-203, 212-216
Managerial Grid training, 22-23
Mann, F. C., 23, 25, 33
Marland, Sidney P., 34
Mason, Ward S., 15
mathematics, Cuisenaire Rod approach, 82, 87. 137, 253
Mausner, B., 28
medical innovations, adoption and diffusion of, 20
mental skills, acquisition of, 11, 266
Merrill Series, 82
Merton, Robert K., 195
Miles, Matthew B., 21, 22 38n.
Miles, R. E., 38n.
Miller, Richard I., 30
Miner, Horace, 17n.
models, building of, 11, 269
Moore, Wilbert E., 20n.
More Effective Schools Program (New York), 2-3

Morse, N., 27
motivation, self-, 11; teacher, lack of, implementation and, 142-147, 171-190, 200, 209-210

National Elementary Principal, 25
National Institute for the Study of Educational Change, 8
Neff, F. W., 23
Negro children, 62, 65-66, 278-283
neighborhood aides, 277
"new school," basic purpose of, 12
New York State, educational innovations in, 2
New York State Education Department, 30
nongrading, 2-3, 34, 35

observational skills, acquisition of, 11, 266
observer involvement, 33
Ogburn, W. F., 20n.
Ohio, educational innovations in, 2
Oliver, Albert I., 25, 26
operational competencies, acquisition of, 11, 141, 266, 267
opinion leaders, influence of, 20
organizational change, concept of, 15-16; planned (*see* planned organizational change); power-equalization approaches, 37-38, 199; proposed, use of term, 16; resistance to (*see* resistance to change); unplanned, 19n.
organizational innovation, use of term, 16
organizational innovations, 1-10; antecedents of, 22-24; educational perspective, 2-7; evaluative studies, 206-207; implementation of (*see* implementation); incorporation of, 17; initiation of, 17, 24-29, 39, 208; key concepts, 15-17; social science perspective, 7-10. *See also* educational innovations
Owens, Robert G., 21

Parloff, Morris B., 30, 35
participation, subordinate (*see* subordinate participation)

perceptual reduction of chaos, 267
Peterson, Carl H., 26, 34
Piaget, J., 266, 272
planned organizational change, 1; lit-
    erature on, 1, 19-40; use of term,
    16-17. *See also* organizational
    change; organizational innovations
Planning of Change, The, 28
poverty, culture of, 280
power equalization, 37-38, 199
prisons, resistance to changes in, 36
problems, perception of, 11, 267
programmed instruction, 21
progressive education, criticisms of, 2
proposed organizational change, use
    of term, 16
pupil personnel service people, 277

Radcliffe, Ruth W., 30
random encounter, 259
Rankin, Stuart C., 25, 32
rapport, establishment of, 48-52, 58
reading, linguistics approach to, 76,
    82
reappointment, teacher, uncertainty
    about, 181-184
Reilley, E., 30
Reimer, E., 27
report cards, 139, 141, 169, 171, 174
reports, teacher, 55, 85, 86
research procedures, 41-63; adminis-
    trative permission, securing of, 44-
    45; case study method, rationale
    for use of, 42-43; data collection,
    51-63, 217-284; documents, col-
    lection and examination of, 245-
    284; fieldworkers, role of, 45, 47-
    48; gaining entry into school, 45-
    46; rapport, establishment of, 48-
    52, 58; selection of school, 43-44.
    See also specimen research instru-
    ments
resistance to change, 29, 196, 202;
    basic, 26; change agents and, 31,
    36; industrial, 36; initial, 1, 8, 26,
    36, 39, 195, 198, 204-205, 210;
    management and, 36, 203; possi-
    bility of development of, 198-199;
    prison, 36; schemes for overcoming

of, 36-38; subordinate participation
    and, 26
resocialization of teachers, need for,
    200, 211
responsibility, freedom and, 262-263,
    265-266
Rockefeller Report on ghetto schools,
    4
Rockwell, Robert E., 7n.
Rocky Mountain Study Council, 25
Rogers, Everett M., 20-22
role, concept of, 15
role overload, teacher, strain and
    fatigue from, 174, 180-181, 203
Rutherford, Ernest, 256

Sacadat, Evelyn, 7n.
Schein, E. H., 38n.
school boards, demands from, 3
school systems, decentralization of, 3
schools, community control of, plans
    to increase, 3; control problems,
    277; de facto segregation in, 66;
    for disadvantaged children, 281-
    283; discipline problems, 277;
    domestication of, 32; ghetto,
    Rockefeller Foundation Report
    on, 4; improvement of, recom-
    mendations for, 276-278; inte-
    grated, 282; urban, problems of,
    3-7
Schrodinger, Erwin, 256
Schwartz, Charlotte Green, 14n.
science, EDC curriculum for, 82
Scott, W. Richard, 43n., 48, 50
segregation, de facto, 66
self-administered teacher question-
    naires, 51, 61-62, 83-84; specimen,
    240-244
self-contained classrooms, 85, 141,
    170, 176
self-directed education, 11, 13
self-motivation, 11
Senish Plan, 82
sensitivity training, 38
Shaplin, Judson T., 3
Simpson, George Gaylord, 267
Snyderman, B., 28
social organization, change and, 36

social studies, Senish Plan in, 82
sociocultural drift, 19n.
Sorokin, Pitirim, 20n.
specimen research instruments, 217-244; classroom observation schedule, 236-239; self-administered teacher questionnaire, 240-244; teacher interview schedule, 217-235
Sputnik, 2
SRA Program, 137
staff morale, subordinate participation and, 25, 29
Stalker, G. M., 23
Stinchcomb, James A., vi
Stufflebeam, Daniel A., 2, 8, 39
subject matter specialists, 79-80, 277
subordinate participation, 24-29; clarity and, 25-26; commitment and, 25, 29; decision-making and, 24n., 25, 27-29, 215; implementation and, 25-26, 29, 214; resistance and, 26; staff morale and, 25, 29

T-groups, 24, 38, 215
Tannenbaum, P. H., 23
Taylor, Ray, vi
teacher interns, 277
teacher professionalism, 215
teacher questionnaires, self-administered, 51, 61-62, 83-84; specimen, 240-244
teachers, catalytic role model, 10-16, 56, 65, 71, 79, 82, 85; interviews with, 34-35, 51, 52, 57-61, 85, 143-147, 152-157, 159-166, 170-171; lack of capability to perform new role, 129-135, 159-167, 197, 199; lack of motivation, 142-147, 171-190, 200; obstacles encountered by, 149-194, 196-200, 209 (see also barriers to implementation); reappointment, uncertainty about, 181-184; reports prepared

by, 55, 85, 86; resocialization of, need for, 200, 211; role overload, strain and fatigue from, 174, 180-181, 203; summary tables of selected background and personality characteristics of, 285-289. See also Cambire Elementary School
teaching job, improvement of productivity of, 11, 270
teaching partners, interpersonal tensions between, 163, 172, 174, 177-180, 203
team-teaching, 2-3, 34, 35
technical innovations, adoption and diffusion of, 20
technological revolution, 2
Thornton, Russell G., vi
Trow, Martin, 43n.
Trump, J. Lloyd, 25

unplanned change, 19n.
Urban Coalition, 3
urban schools, problems of, 3-7

Van Egmond, Elmer, vi
Vigotsky, 272

wage incentive schemes, 36
Washburn, Norman F., 19n.
Watson, Jeanne, 24, 29-30
Weinstein, G., 26n., 30
Weiss, W., 23
Westley, Bruce, 24, 29-30
Wigren, Harold E., 30, 34
Wilkerson, Doxey A., 3-5, 7
Wilkie, Raymond A., 35
Wright, Charles R., 7
Wrightstone, J. Wayne, 7n.

York, Richard H., 30

Zander, Alvin, 36n.